Augustus Welby Northmore Pugin, Augustus Pugin, Edward James Willson

Examples of Gothic Architecture

Vol. III

Augustus Welby Northmore Pugin, Augustus Pugin, Edward James Willson

Examples of Gothic Architecture
Vol. III

ISBN/EAN: 9783337177287

Printed in Europe, USA, Canada, Australia, Japan

Cover: Foto ©ninafisch / pixelio.de

More available books at **www.hansebooks.com**

EXAMPLES

OF

𝕲𝖔𝖙𝖍𝖎𝖈 𝕬𝖗𝖈𝖍𝖎𝖙𝖊𝖈𝖙𝖚𝖗𝖊;

SELECTED FROM VARIOUS

ANCIENT EDIFICES IN ENGLAND:

CONSISTING OF

PLANS, ELEVATIONS, SECTIONS, AND PARTS AT LARGE;

CALCULATED TO EXEMPLIFY

THE VARIOUS STYLES,

AND

THE PRACTICAL CONSTRUCTION

OF THIS

ADMIRED CLASS OF ARCHITECTURE;

ACCOMPANIED BY

𝕳𝖎𝖘𝖙𝖔𝖗𝖎𝖈𝖆𝖑 𝖆𝖓𝖉 𝕯𝖊𝖘𝖈𝖗𝖎𝖕𝖙𝖎𝖛𝖊 𝕬𝖈𝖈𝖔𝖚𝖓𝖙𝖘.

VOL. III.

By AUGUSTUS PUGIN, AND AUGUSTUS WELBY PUGIN.

THE LITERARY PART BY E. J. WILLSON, F.S.A.

𝕰𝖉𝖎𝖓𝖇𝖚𝖗𝖌𝖍
JOHN GRANT
31 GEORGE IV. BRIDGE
1895

THE

HISTORY AND ANTIQUITIES

OF

The Vicars' Close, Wells,

SOMERSETSHIRE:

CONSISTING OF

PLANS, ELEVATIONS, SECTIONS, AND PARTS AT LARGE;

FROM SKETCHES AND ADMEASUREMENTS, TAKEN IN 1832.

By AUGUSTUS WELBY PUGIN, Architect,

UNDER THE DIRECTION OF

THE LATE AUGUSTUS PUGIN, Architect;

FORMING PART I. OF

"Pugin's Examples of Gothic Architecture,"

THIRD SERIES:

ACCOMPANIED BY

Historical and Descriptive Accounts,

By THOMAS LARKINS WALKER, Architect,

HONORARY TREASURER OF THE ARCHITECTURAL SOCIETY OF LONDON.

———

WITH

AN APPENDIX,

CONTAINING TRANSLATIONS OF THE ORIGINAL LETTERS PATENT OF KING EDWARD III.,
BISHOP RADULPHUS DE SALOPIA'S DEED OF GIFT, AND A TABLE
OF THE STATUTES AND INJUNCTIONS.

TO

WILLIAM BARNARD CLARKE, Esq. F.R.A.S. President,

THOMAS HENRY WYATT, Esq. Vice-President,

GEORGE MAIR, Esq. Vice-President,

E. H. BROWNE, Esq. Secretary,

THE COMMITTEE AND THE MEMBERS

OF THE

Architectural Society of London,

THIS VOLUME

Is Inscribed,

WITH EVERY SENTIMENT OF RESPECT, GRATITUDE, AND ESTEEM,
BY THEIR MOST OBEDIENT HUMBLE SERVANT,

THE AUTHOR.

PREFACE.

WHEN the lamented death of the late AUGUSTUS PUGIN took place, two Parts only of the "*Second Series*" of his Work, entitled "*Examples of Gothic Architecture,*" were published; but in his last Will, of which he appointed me an executor, in conjunction with Mr. JAMES MORGAN (an honour which, as his pupil, I trust ever duly to appreciate), he requested that the Volume might be completed by his Son, who had accompanied him in his last professional tour, for the purpose of making sketches in Somersetshire, during the Autumn of 1832. By the indefatigable exertions of the latter, accurate Sketches, geometrically drawn and measured, were taken of *the Deanery* and *the Bishop's Palace*, at Wells, *the Abbot's Kitchen, the Tribunal House, the George Inn,* and *the Abbot's Barn*, Glastonbury; which buildings were delineated in the *Third* and *Fourth Parts*, completing the "*Second Series;*" but it was found expedient to omit *the Vicar's Close, Wells,* of which also Sketches and Admeasurements had been taken, as the limits of that Volume would not admit of so great an addition of Plates as were necessary to elucidate that highly interesting building. Mr. PUGIN intended giving it as an Appendix to that Work; but was prevented from undertaking so desirable an addition, by various professional engagements, and other business, accumulating on his hands. Had the late Mr. PUGIN been spared, a Third Volume would, ere this, have been before the Public; and, actuated by a desire to carry the intentions of the Author into execution, I was induced to communicate my wishes to his Son, who immediately allowed me to become the purchaser of his Sketches, which form the subjects delineated in the following Plates. I was anxious, also, to enlist the services of Mr. WILLSON, whose original design these valuable Works were, and whose Descriptive and Historical Notices of the several buildings contained in the two former Volumes, render them so much more interesting; but, at that time, from several severe family afflictions and illness, together with professional engagements, he had been prevented finishing the Second Volume, which he has only very lately been enabled to complete; and he found himself precluded from granting me his able assistance, without laying aside the letterpress description of the "Gothic Ornaments." To this I could not conscientiously assent, well knowing how anxious the Subscribers were for that portion of the Work, and how serious an injury it had already sustained by remaining in an incomplete state; and, accordingly, have been presumptuous enough to lay my own shoulder to the wheel, in order that so valuable an addition, as I knew these Plates would form to the library of the Architect and Amateur, should be made with as little delay as possible.

How far my boldness may have conduced to success, must be left for a liberal public opinion to determine; but should it be deemed that any additional interest has been given by the short Historical Account of the building and the Description of the Plates, I claim no credit for originality, having contented myself with carefully collecting all the information possible, and condensing it into the following pages; and, to give additional interest, have added a Biographical Sketch of each Benefactor in the Notes.

I have also been induced to give an Appendix, containing a table of the Statutes and Ordinances by which the body of the *Vicars'-Choral* were governed, laid down by the founder, Bishop Ralph of Shrewsbury, and confirmed and enlarged by Bishop Beckington, which are partially in force to this day: also, translations of the *Letters Patent*, granted by King Edward III., and of the original Deed of Gift, as confirmed by the two Chapters of the united sees of Bath and Wells; but regret my limits would not allow me to transcribe the Statutes themselves and the New Charter granted by Queen Elizabeth. For these valuable documents, I am indebted to the present venerable Bishop, the Right Reverend GEORGE HENRY LAW, LL.D., whose promptness in affording facilities to research by antiquarian authors, has already formed the subject of several eulogies in works of a similar nature, and which, I trust, will be duly appreciated by the curious who may peruse the present Volume.

I am greatly indebted to Mr. THOMAS T. BURY, who has engraved the Plates, for the care and attention he has bestowed upon them; and have little doubt but that these specimens of an art he has only lately been induced to follow, will bring him ostensibly before the notice of lovers of illustrated literature. I was induced to engage his services, on account of the intimate knowledge he possessed of Gothic forms, acquired by a long series of study under the late Mr. PUGIN. To Mr. G. B. WOLLASTON, who was lately my pupil, I feel myself also called upon to tender thanks for his exertions, and trust they may be the means of leading him on to the higher walks of Architectural Study.

From my Subscribers and the Public I must crave the usual indulgence, so much and so often needed by authors for their first attempts in literary labours; and take a respectful leave; hoping soon again to address them in the two following portions of this Volume: but, that I might not be guilty of undue intrusion, in case of my success not being so complete as vanity might prompt me to imagine, and also for the convenience of such as, from old associations alone, would wish to possess Illustrations of so "faire a place," I have made this, the first of three Parts, a complete Work in itself.

THOMAS LARKINS WALKER.

Examples
of
Gothic Architecture,

THIRD SERIES.

LIST OF PLATES CONTAINED IN PART I.

THE VICARS' CLOSE, WELLS, SOMERSETSHIRE.

1. GENERAL Ground Plan of the CLOSE, as completed by Bishop Beckington's executors.

THE VICARS' DWELLINGS.

2. Elevation and Transverse Section of each House.
3. Plan and Longitudinal Section of ditto.
4. Chimney-shaft and Window at large of ditto.
5. Elevation and Section of a small Oriel Window towards the Road.
6. Plan and Details of ditto, and end Elevation of the East Row of Houses.
6.* Plan, Elevation, Section, and Details of a Porch; Rebuses, Coat of Arms, &c.

THE CHAPEL AND LIBRARY.

7. South Elevation and Transverse Section, looking East.
8. Plans and Details.
9. Elevation and Section of the Door-case and Door, with Details.
10. Plans, Sections, and Elevations of the Windows, and Details.
11. Bell Turret, Niche at the Corner of the Parapet, &c. at large.

THE COMMON HALL AND THE CHAIN-GATE.

12. Ground Plan of THE ENTRANCE-GATEWAY to the Close, and THE CHAIN-GATE.
13. First-Floor Plan of THE HALL, BUTTERY, KITCHEN, and GALLERY over the CHAIN-GATE.
14. Elevation of THE HALL towards the Road, and Transverse Section of THE CHAIN-GATE.
15. Elevation, Section, and Details of the South Oriel Window.
16. Plan, Interior Elevation, Section of Soffit, and Details of ditto.
17–18. Transverse Section of THE HALL through the Entrance-Gateway of the Close, East Elevation of the CHAIN-GATE and GALLERY over, and of the TOWER and STAIRCASE.
19. One of the Centre Compartments of the GALLERY over the CHAIN-GATE, and Details.
20. Elevation of THE HALL towards the Close, and Transverse Section of the STAIRCASE.
21. Exterior and Interior Elevations, Section, and Details of one of the Windows of the Hall.
22. Longitudinal Section of THE HALL from E. to W. looking S.
23. Plan, Section, Elevation, and Details of the Fireplace and Fire-dogs in the Hall.
24. Transverse Section of THE HALL through the Door-ways, Staircase, and small Lobby.
25. Plan of the Groining of the PORCH leading to the Staircase, Coats of Arms, and top of Oak Panelling at large.

A

HISTORICAL ACCOUNT

OF THE

Vicars' Close at Wells,

SOMERSETSHIRE.

THE *Chantry Priests* attached to the *Choir* of the Cathedral Church of St. Andrew at Wells, were first ordained by Bishop *Joceline de Welles*, or *Trotman*,* A.D. 1237,† who created many new prebends or canonries, and appointed a *chanter* to each benefice, three excepted.‡ These chantry priests he styled *Vicars-Choral*, and intended they should supply the places of the canons in chanting and performing divine service; but they do not seem to have had any regular establishment until *Walter de Hulle*, subdean of this cathedral in 1334, and archdeacon of Bath in 1342,§ gave two messuages and lands in Wells, that the thirteen chantry priests who officiated in the choir might live in common together. For their better government,

---

* Vicarios chorales primus ordinavit, qui Canonicorum vices in canendo et sacris operando peragerent.—GODWYN *De Præsulibus Angliæ Commentarius*, in Vitâ Jocelini de Wells, p. 371. Richardson's edition, Canterbury, 1743.

† Joceline de Wells, called, in the *Annales Marganenses*, Joceline Trotman, elected by the joint suffrages of the canons of Bath and Wells, was consecrated at Reading in the Chapel of St. Mary, May 28th, 1206.—DUGDALE's *Monasticon*, vol. ii. p. 277. During his episcopacy, the monks of Glastonbury obtained a dissolution of their enforced union with this see; agreeing to surrender some valuable manors and the advowsons of several churches; and Joceline afterwards resumed the title of Bath and Wells, which has continued to be used by the bishops to this day. He was forced into exile by King John, for having interdicted the nation, pursuant to the Pope's command, in 1208; but on his return, five years afterwards, he applied himself particularly to the improvement of the Church of Wells. He obtained from Hugh, bishop of Lincoln, the valuable manors of Congresbury, Chedder, and Axbridge, and annexed them to his see. He rebuilt and dedicated anew the cathedral on the 23d of October, 1239; added a chapel to the Bishop's Palace at Wells, and built many other edifices. He died on the 19th of November, 1242, and was buried in the middle of the choir in Wells Cathedral, under a marble tomb inlaid with his figure in brass; but the latter had been torn away in Godwyn's time, and the tomb was "shamefully defaced."— *History and Antiquities of the Cathedral Church of Wells*, by J. BRITTON, F.S.A., pp. 33, 34, and 106.

‡ Vicarios in Ecclesiâ singulis Præbendariis ordinavit; tribus exceptis, quibus non provisit morte præventus. —WHARTON's *Anglia Sacra*, pars i. p. 564. See also COLLINSON's *History of Somersetshire*, vol. iii. p. 381. GODWYN *De Præsulibus*, p. 370. Harl. MSS. 6968, PL. XLV. G.

§ LE NEVE's *Fasti*, pp. 42 and 45. DUGDALE's *Monasticon*, vol. vi. Pt. III. p. 1466. London, 1830.

B

Bishop *Radulphus de Salopia*, or *Ralph of Shrewsbury*,* made certain statutes and ordinances, dated 7 Id. April, A.D. 1347,† a table of which is given in the Appendix; and in the following year began to erect a new college for their residence, obtained the king's letters patent confirming his gift, ‡ and had the same ratified by the prior and chapter of Bath, and the dean and chapter of Wells, appointing "a certain place of the soil of the church" " of St. Andrew at Wells, and the houses in the same place, built and to be" " built by the said Ralph, to have and to hold to them and their successors," " vicars of the church aforesaid, for their common and perpetual cohabitation." Also, allowing him to charge his "lands and tenements in Congresbury," " parcel of his bishopric aforesaid, with an hundred shillings annuity," and " certain other lands and tenements with the appurtenances in Wookey," " with another hundred shillings annuity," and " to give and assign the same " " ten pounds annuity to the said vicars, celebrating and which shall celebrate " " divine service in the said church, in augmentation of their sustenance, to be " " perceived and had yearly out of the said lands and tenements to the same " " vicars and their successors for ever." It appears that this college consisted of " the hall, kitching, bakehouse, and other houses in the same place, built " " and to be built."§ He endowed their body with other lands which he had obtained from the Feoffees of Walter de Hulle, in Wellsleigh, Eston, and Dulcot,‖ together with a yearly charge of £6. 13s. 4d. upon the vicarage of Chew.

* Radulphus de Salopia, multum hic à Wellensibus nostris celebratur, quod Collegii Vicariorum primus extiterit fundator. *De Praesulibus*, p. 376, in *Vitâ Radulphi de Salopia*. He was Keeper of the King's Wardrobe, Chancellor of the University of Oxford (in 1328), and was elected Bishop of this diocese by the two chapters of Bath and Wells on the 2d of June, 1329; he was consecrated, prior to obtaining the Pope's approval, on the 3d of December following; and Walsingham says, it cost him "a huge sum of money" before he could procure a full confirmation from the Court of Rome. He was a munificent benefactor to his Cathedral and diocese, rebuilt the Church at Winscombe from the foundations, constructed the court-house at Claverton, and a great chamber at Evercreech, with many other edifices upon the episcopal estates. He erected a house for the choristers and their master on the west side of the cloisters, and surrounded the episcopal palace at Wells with a strong stone wall and a moat. He also procured, " with great cost," the disafforestation of Mendip forest, and gave some rich ecclesiastical vestments, with many other things, to his churches at Bath and Wells, of which Godwyn says that he believed, in his time, nothing remained but a great chest bound with iron, in which the chapter seal was kept. He died at Wivelliscombe on the 14th of August, 1363, and was buried before the high altar in the presbytery at Wells, but his tomb was removed to its present situation in the north aisle, close to the second column from the east, at the back of the choir: because, says Leland, in his *Itinerary*, vol. iii. p. 108, it obstructed the priests in their ministration. BRITTON'S *Wells Cathedral*, pp. 38, 39, and 109. See also *Anglia Sacra*, pars i. in *Vitâ Radulphi de Salopia*, p. 568. DUGDALE'S *Monasticon*, vol. ii. pp. 278, 279.

† *Monasticon*, vol. vi. p. 1466, and notes. See, also, the Appendix.

‡ Pat. 22. Edward III. p. 3. m. 16. Pro mansio vicariorum et terris in Congresbury et Woky.

§ See this deed of gift in the Appendix.

‖ Pat. 26. Edward III. p. 2. m. 6. Pro ten. in Wellesie, Eston, et Dulcot, ex dono feoffatorum Walteri de Hulle, archdiacon. Bathon.

Godwyn says, that a picture of inferior workmanship, expressive of the memory of this benefit, was placed on the wall over the porch leading to the hall stairs, in which the vicars, kneeling in the choir, seemed to address the bishop, seated on his throne, in the following words:—

"Per Vicos positi villa, pater alme rogamus,
"Ut simul uniti, te dante domos maneamus:"

to whom he thus seemed to reply:—

"Vestra potunt merita, quod sint concessa petita:
"Ut maneatis ita, loca fecimus hic stabilita,"

and mentions that, this picture being nearly worn out, another of excellent workmanship was placed in the hall commemorative of this and other donations, of which more will be said hereafter.* Time must have made sad havoc of the buildings erected by this prelate, as few traces now remain of the original design; it will be seen, however, by referring to Plate XXII., which shews a longitudinal section of the hall, kitchen, &c. &c., that the room under, and the two-light windows in, the hall, which latter are given on a larger scale in Plate XXI., are much older than the other portions, being beautiful examples of the *Early Pointed Style*. It may safely be presumed that there were more of these windows, and that a symmetrical arrangement existed, as, in plan, there are two exactly opposite each other in the north and south walls east of the present doors. Three only remain, one towards the road shewn in Plate XIV., and two towards the Close, Plate XX.; the others must have been destroyed by alterations and additions made by subsequent benefactors. The windows of the chapel on the ground floor, see Plates VII. and X., seem also of the same period, the door having been inserted under the tracery-head of one of them; which, on examining the masonry, will be found to be the case, there being a straight joint on the right-hand jamb, from the spring to the ground, and the basement moulding has been cut away, as shewn in Plate VII.; also, in the west wall, there is an appearance outwardly of a counter-arch, where, probably, a door existed, but which must have been stopped up when the gardens were added in front of the houses.

There are letters patent referred to by Tanner in the time of Richard II.

---

* GODWYN *De Præsulibus*, in Vitâ Radulphi de Salopia, p. 376.

and Henry V. which are grants to this college.* The former may have been in the time of Bishop *Ralph Erghum*, who was a great benefactor to the Cathedral Church of Wells, having, in his will, requested his executors to build a *College* in the street then called *La Mountery*, but, afterwards, *College Lane*, for fourteen *priests*† or *chaplains*,‡ daily ministering in the Cathedral, that they might live in common together; this has been by some confounded with the *Vicars' Close*; and in notes taken by S. and N. Buck,§ at Wells, this prelate is made the "founder" of "a neat college for the vicars and singing men, on the north side of the Cathedral;" evidently referring to the *Vicar's College*; but *Mountery College*, or *Mounterox College*, was destroyed, its revenues were confiscated at the time of the suppression of the monasteries,‖ and, in the reign of Elizabeth, a mansion was built on its site which went by the name of *Mountroy House*. This mansion was pulled down about five years ago, and the site thrown into a pleasure-ground. These worthies have also made him the builder of the embattled wall round the Bishop's Palace: and in pages 50 and 51 of the Lansd. MS. 905, interlined but erased, is the name of *Ralph de Shrewsbury*, as if the writer had received contradictory information.¶

The grant in Henry the Fifth's time may have been bestowed by Bishop

* TANNER, *Notit. Monast. XLII. Somersetshire.*—Pat. i. Richard II. p. 5, m. 19, pro eccl. de Meriet approprianda.—Pat. i. Henry V. p. 3, m. 8.

† *Sacerdotibus* porro *quatuordecim* Collegium fundavit Wellim, ad exitum vici qui inde *College Lane* appellatur.— GODWIN *De Præsulibus*, p. 378.

‡ Fecit etiam construi per Executores suos in vico vocato *La Mounterye*, mansiones pro XIV. *Capellanis* in dictâ Ecclesia Wellensi indies celebrantibus. *Anglia Sacra*, pars. i. p. 570. See, also, Harl. MSS. 6968, under the head of *Nomina Epôrum in Somers*. In which the above quotation, in the notice of Ralph Erghum, occurs verbatim, and is extracted from the register of Wells.

§ MCS. BRIT. BIBL. *Lansd.* 1233, LXXIX. G. "Ralph Erghum built a neat college for vicars and singing men, adjoining to the N. part of the church: and also enclosed the B^{ps} palace with a wall. [but certainly Ralph Erghum did it.] Qui ob 10 April die Sabbi, & vallavit muris et fossis Palatm Epi. apd. Wolls, et jacet ibm A.D. M.CCCC. ī:a dnical C. *i.e.* on the Sabbath day."—Ibid. 905. Pl. LXXIX. F. pp. 49 and 50. "The palace on the south side of the cathedral is neatly built, and, on that side, appears like a castle, being fortified with an embattled wall and a ditch by Ralph de Erghum, who came to the chair A.D. 1388. He also made the college for the vicars and singing men on the north side of the church.

‖ WILLIS's *Mitred Abbeys*, vol. ii. p. 200.

¶ *Lansdowne, MS.* 905, LXXIX. F. p. 50. "The B^{ps} Palace on the So. side the cathedral is a fabrick to be admired for its grandeur, looking towards the South like a Castle, being fortified with an embattled wall " by Ralph de Erghum : by Ralph de Shrewsbury, B^p of Wellens here." and a ditch, and the prebendarys houses are handsomely built on the other side. This B^p also built a neat college for the vicars and singing men on the North side of the Church." And, in p. 51, "The Bishop's Palace is a handsome structure, standing on the south side of the cathedral, and appears like a Castle, being fortified with an embattled wall and a ditch, by Ralph de Erghum, elected bishop A.D. 1388. He also built a neat college for the vicars and singing men on the North side of the Cathedral."

In CAMDEN's *Britannia*, Bishop Erghum is also said to have built the "*College of Vicars*, first founded by R. de Salopia," and "enlarged by Bekington," see vol. i. p. 77, London, 1789. See, also, p. 187 of the edition, London, 1772. See PUGIN's *Examples*, 2d series, p. 43.

Nicholas Bubwith, as his arms occur on the door of the Chapel, and also on the painted glass of the windows.

The next and principal addition made to this building was by Bishop *Thomas Beckington,** who built the *Close-Hall-Gate,* or *Chain-Gate,* which connects the Vicars' Close with the Cathedral; it extends from the Hall to the staircase leading (from the North Transept) to the Chapter House; of which the flight is continued to the floor of the gallery over this gateway. This eminent and distinguished person, who, by Godwyn, is characterised as "a good statesman, a good churchman, a good townsman, a good subject, a good kinsman, a good master, and a good man," was a munificent benefactor to the church and city of Wells. Soon after his promotion to this see, he built a row of houses on the north side of the market-place, which he called his *Nova Opera;* and granted a supply of water from St. Andrew's Well, in the grounds of the Episcopal Palace, to a conduit in the market-place, flowing night and day, which he vested in the master, brethren, and burgesses of the City of Wells for ever;† in commemoration of which benefit, they bound themselves to visit yearly the spot in the cathedral where he should be interred, there to pray for his soul, and the souls of all the faithful deceased: and he granted an indulgence of forty days to all such as

---

* Thomas de Beckington, LL.D., succeeded to the see of Bath and Wells on the 13th of October, 1443, in the peaceable enjoyment of which he remained till his death, which took place on the 14th of January, 1464-5. He seems to have been of obscure origin, as he took his name from the small town of Beckington, near Frome, Somersetshire: and in a Journal of Beckington, published in 1828 by Nicholas Harris Nicolas, Esq., Barrister-at-Law, it is conjectured that his birth took place about 1395, which would make him 80 years of age at his death; this is by no means improbable, as he was obliged to apply for permission to absent himself from parliament on account of his advanced age. He was educated at William de Wykeham's College, at Winchester; and, whilst there, seems to have attracted the attention of that prelate for his abilities and comeliness of person; having distinguished himself, he was removed to Wykeham's New College, at Oxford, of which he became a fellow in 1408; he took the degree of Doctor of Laws, and obtained various ecclesiastical dignities. He was afterwards appointed tutor to the young King Henry VI., was made Dean of the Arches, Chancellor to Humphrey, duke of Gloucester, Archdeacon of Buckingham, Prebendary of Lichfield, York, and Wells, Rector of St. Leonards, near Hastings, and of Sutton, in the diocess of Salisbury. He seems to have acquired great fame by writing a refutation of the Salique Law, which proved the right of the Kings of England to the crown of France. This called forth additional favours from the court, and he was made principal Secretary of State and Keeper of the Privy Seal. In 1442, he was entrusted, with Robert Roos, knt., and Edward Hull, esq., with an embassy to negociate a marriage between the king, Henry VI., and a daughter of the Count of Armagnac. Henry at length got him elected to this see, to which he was consecrated in Eton College Chapel, October 13th, A.D. 1443.—See a Life of this bishop affixed to a *Journal of one of the Suite of Beckington,* by NICHOLAS HARRIS NICOLAS, Esq., Barrister-at-Law. GODWYN *De Præsulibus.* BRITTON's *Wells Cathedral,* pp. 43-48, and 111. *Anglia Sacra.* WILLIS's *Survey of Cathedrals, &c.* CASSAN's *Lives of the Bishops of Bath and Wells.*

By many, Beckington is styled the *Founder of the Vicars' Close;* but he himself did not presume to such distinction; as, in the statutes and injunctions revised by him, is one which enjoins, "That every vicar going out or going in att the Close Gate shall say a Pater Noster and an Ave Maria for the soul of the Bishop *Ralph of Shrewsbury, founder of the said Close,* and for the souls of his predecessors, fathers, and mothers, and their benefactors, and for all Christian souls."—*The Statutes and Charter of Close Hall,* p. 12, MS. in the possession of the Bishop of Bath and Wells.

† GODWYN *De Præsulibus,* p. 380.

should duly perform this solemn service. He built three gate-houses, one leading from the market-place into the palace, one from the same into the Cathedral Close to the south, and a third, the Chain-gate referred to, extending from the Vicars' Close to the cathedral on the north, which seems to have been the principal addition made to this building by him in his lifetime; see Plate XVII.—XVIII., which shews a transverse section through the hall looking west, with an elevation of this gate-house on the left or south side, and the tower and staircase, on the right or north side, ascending from the close to the hall. This gateway, which formed the entrance into the Cathedral Close from the north-west, consists of a vaulted carriage-way and a passage on each side for pedestrians; over these, and leading from the hall into the chapter-house staircase, is a gallery of communication for the vicars-choral when required to perform service in the choir.* This building is chaste and elegant in design, and is ornamented with mouldings beautifully executed in freestone; over the centre arch are two compartments or bays, divided by enriched pinnacles terminating in crockets and finials above a panelled parapet; each bay contains a window of two lights, divided by a transom, with a canopied niche and statue in the centre, under one arch and label; one of these compartments is shewn on a larger scale in Plate XIX. Over each passage is a window of two lights with similar tracery, and the same design is carried through, by windows of three lights, till it abuts against the north wall of the chapter-house staircase, except that the pinnacles are stopped under the parapet by a sculptured head or foliated boss. On this building Beckington's arms and rebus occur three times, viz. on the key-stone of the vaulting, and under each of the two windows of the small ante-room which communicates from the hall to the passage or withdrawing-room. See Plates XII., XVII.-XVIII., and XIV.

In his will, after various bequests to the churches of Bath and Wells,

* *Itinerarium Willelmi de Worcestre*, ed. J. NASMITH, 1778, p. 286. Under the works by Beckington, at Wells, he has the following referring to this gateway: "Item fecit aliam portam apud le close, extendendo de le close usque le cathedrall chyrch per vias et voltam sicco pede cooperto ad mat—— et constabat in edificiis ultra 1) marcas." See COLLINSON, vol. iii. p. 403. In BRITTON's *Wells Cathedral*, Pl. III. shews the commencement of the staircase, from the north transept to the chapter-house on the left of the picture; Pl. I., ground-plan, shews, in the plan of the chapter-house, the stairs continued beyond the entrance, up to the Vicar's gallery; Pl. IV. shews the west elevation of this gateway, but the two centre windows ought not to be shewn glazed in the middle, as statues occupy niches there; Pl. XX. shews a view of the Entrance Gateway of the Close, and the Chain-gate and gallery, from the east; Pl. XVIII. shews an interior of the staircase to the chapter-house, which leads up to the *Vicar's Gallery*, the steps winding to the right into the chapter-house. In BRITTON's *Picturesque Antiquities of English Cities* are two perspective views of the *Vicar's Close, Wells;* one shewing *The Chapel;* on the left, part of the *Chaplain's House,* and on the right, part of the *Vicar's Dwellings,* and one of the small *Porches,* which has a good effect. The other is a view through the *Entrance Gateway,* shewing the *Vicar's Dwellings,* and the *Chapel* in the distance.—See p. 72 of the Descriptions.

and others in his diocess, as also to his servants and dependants, he left twenty pounds to each of his three executors, who were *Richard Swan,** Precentor of Wells and Rector of Yevelton; *Hugh Sugar, alias Norris, LL.D.*,† Treasurer of Wells; and *John Pope,** alias *Talbot, D.D.*, Prebendary of St. Decumans, and Rector of Shyre; with a request that they would bestow the residue of his property, "*in pios usus,*" a trust which they conscientiously fulfilled by adding to the *Close* or *College of the Vicars-choral*, which they rendered the most beautiful of the kind in England.‡ It is to be presumed that they restored or rebuilt entirely the *Vicars' Dwellings*, which consist of forty-two houses, twenty-one on each side of the area, with gardens attached, divided by dwarf walls, and having each a porch at the entrance; as on the chimney-shafts of these houses, under the arms of the see and those of Beckington alternately, their several rebuses are introduced successively; see Plates II. and IV.

* "John Pope & Ric. Swan, clici dederunt manerium de Schepham & advocaceõem ecclīe ejusd., quæ habuerunt ex dono et feoffamento Tho. de Bekynton epī, Willo Witham, decano Well. et capitulo, ac alrum totum jus suum in manerio de Ceddre eisdem decano et capitulo, in usum et sustentacõem vicariorum choralium eccl. cath. Well. 9. E. IV."—Harl. MSS., 6968. p. 65.

† *Hugh Sugar, alias Norris, LL.D.*, was collated Archdeacon of Bath, Feb. 26, 1459, and Treasurer of Wells, May 1, 1460; he died in the latter end of April, or beginning of May, 1489 (Le Neve's *Fasti*), as on the 29th of May, 1489, Oliver Benham was installed, by procuration, Prebendary of Lutton, vacant by *his death*. Harl. MSS. 6968. By the same MS. it appears, that he was at continual variance with the dean and chapter, as, in vigil Pasch. Richard Worthington, of Wells, was unjustly and privily installed Precentor of Wells, and Prebendary of Combe 12 annexed, by Hugh Sugar, the treasurer, against the statutes and ordinances of the church. The dean and chapter wrote two admonitory letters, but he refused to give up the three keys of the common seal which were in his keeping; and, on the 19th May, 1487, it was ordained by the dean and chapter, that in the suit pending between the dean and chapter of the one part, and Richard Worthington, the rejected precentor, of the other part, that the three keys which were in the custody of Hugh Sugar, as senior residentiary, should remain in the hands of the precentor or the next senior residentiary, and that the said Hugh Sugar, in the absence of the dean and sub-dean, should not occupy the place of president of the chapter, but the precentor, or the next senior residentiary. Richard Worthington was fined twenty pounds for disobedience and contempt; he submitted to the dean and chapter, and was forthwith admitted Precentor of Wells, and installed Prebendary of Combe 12, annexed to that office, vacant by the death of *Richard Swan*. On the 19th Oct. 1487, there was a dispute between him and the dean and chapter, for felling and injuring trees growing in the cemetery, and for letting out graves, also for neglecting to supply lights for divine service, settled by compromise. On the 2d of April, 1488, an ecclesiastical suit was instituted against Hugh Sugar, for diminishing the number of lights, and for other serious injuries. Hugh Sugar is said by Godwyn, *De Præsulibus*, p. 381, to have built *the beautiful Chauntry Chapel*, opposite to that of Bishop Dubwith *in the Nave*, but by this MS. it appears that it was built by *his, Sugar's, executor, William Bocat*, in lieu of a wooden one, which originally stood there: "22 Jun. 1489, Magʳ Will. Bocat, canon resident, nomine ac vice executor Magʳi Hug. Sugar, nup. Thesauri licentiam petiit a dec. et capꝉo, ad prosternend. & abstrahend. capellam ligneam in navi ecclie & ne novo erigend. & rædificand. cande ibidem." Mr. Britton has cited Godwyn, see p. 112 *Hist. of Wells Cathedral*. He built a stone lantern, which was removed by the order of the dean and chapter. "7 Sep. 1489, decrett est qᵈ duo cerei ardere deberent in pulpito juxta antiquam consuetudinem dīe eccl. ac prout juxta ordinale ejusd. ecclie ordinatur: decrotum etiam est qᵈ *laterna lapidea nup ꝑ Mag. Hug. Sugar facta et constructa* distruatur et amoveatur." This, probably, may have led to the mistake.

‡ "Opes ab Episcopo relictas impenderunt istī universas, in *Collegio augendo Vicariorum Choralium*; quod omnium totius Angliæ ejus generis speciosissimum reddiderunt."—Godwyn *De Præsulibus*, p. 381. "Under three Gravestones, parallel to each other, lie *Sugar*, *Swan*, and *Talbot*, executors of Bishop *Beckington*, who finished the *Vicars' Choral Close*; of whom see an Account in *Godwyn de Præsulibus*."—Willis's *Mitred Abbeys*, vol. ii. p. 375.

On the side of the south oriel window of the hall is a shield bearing a cross of St. Andrew, with the name of **Ricūs Pomeroy**; see Plates XV. and XVI., but to whom this refers it is difficult to say; these two windows and the fire-place bear marks of later date than any other portion of the building, and seem inserted after it was finished, as the manner in which the oriel, shewn in Plate XV., cuts into the buttress, indicates. On the chimney-piece of the hall this benefactor's name again occurs in a flowing scroll, which runs thus:

In vestris preci habeat^s comedatū dom Ricardū Pomeroy quem salvet Ihs. Amen.

On this scroll, at intervals, are five shields emblazoned; the first very nearly resembles the arms borne by Sir John Trevellyan, of Nettlecombe Hall, Wiveliscombe,* in this county, at which place Ralph of Shrewsbury died; the next those of Beckington; the centre are the royal arms of England and France; the next those of Bath and Wells impaled in one; and the last resembles those which Edmonstone gives for the name of Pomeroy,† the blazoning only being different, which may easily be accounted for, as they are painted, and in renewing them they may have been varied. Ralph Pomeroy, the first of that name in this country, accompanied William the Conqueror from Normandy; he was a Norman by birth, and for his valuable assistance in the Conquest by that prince had fifty-eight lordships granted to him in Devon, and others in *Somerset*. The first of the name of *Richard*, which occurs in this family, was *Sir Richard Pomerai, Knt.*, eldest son of Henry Pomerai and Alice, daughter of Walter Raleigh of Fardell, his first wife; whose son, Sir Edward Pomerai, was a knight of the Bath at the creation of Henry Prince of Wales, afterwards King Henry VIII.;‡ whether this was the person remains doubtful, but seems more than probable from the connexion of the family with this county. From this family Lord Harberton, of Carbery, in the county of Kildare, Ireland, is descended, and the arms borne by that nobleman very nearly resemble those before-mentioned.§

* The *Trevillian* arms, according to Edmonstone, are "*gu*. ten bars wavy *ar*. and *az*., a demi-horse, issuant rampant, *ar*.:" and these are the only arms charged with a *demi-horse issuant rampant*.—*Heraldry*, vol. ii. p. 34 of the *Ordinary of Arms*.

† The *Pomery*, or *Pommeroy* arms, given by the same author, are "*or*, a lion rampant *gu*., within a bordure engrailed *sable*."—*Ibid.* p. 18, *ibid.*

‡ LODGE's *Peerage of Ireland*, vol. vii. p. 216. The name was first written *de Pomerio*, afterwards *de Pomery*, and now *Pomeroy*.—*Ibid.* p. 214.

§ They are, *or*, within a bordure engrailed *sable*, a lion rampant *gules*, holding in the dexter fore paw an apple slipped.—DEBRETT's *Complete Peerage*, 1836, p. 521. This family were possessed for centuries of Berry-Pomeroy Castle, Co. Devon.

On a building adjoining the west wall of this chapel, which may be considered as part of the chaplain's dwelling, under a large window (now nearly destroyed) are four shields; the first bears the arms of Beckington; the second, those of the see of Wells; the third, those of Bath and Wells conjointly; and the fourth, quarterly; first and fourth, *argent*, three blackmoors' heads proper, two and one; second and third, *gules*, on a fesse, between three leopards' heads, *or*, as many fleurs-de-lis, *sable*; the last quarterings are the arms of *Stillington*, as given by Edmonstone; and Bishop Stillington succeeded Beckington in this see, A.D. 1466.*

At the Reformation this establishment did not share the fate of other religious houses, although "some sacrilegious people had hoped to spoil it," but Elizabeth, thinking that such a villainous deed would not be borne, granted a charter, which is dated from Westminster in the twenty-fourth year of her reign, constituting them a body corporate and politic, with the title of Principals, Seniors, and Vicars' Choral of the Choir in the Cathedral Church of St. Andrew at Wells, and allowed them a common seal. It restricts their number to not less than fourteen, nor more than twenty.

In the Hall is a painting which represents the vicars kneeling before the Bishop Ralph de Salopia, who is seated on his throne on the left side of the picture, holding in his right hand a petition of the former, which runs thus:—

> Per bicos positi billæ,
> pater almæ rogamus,
> Ut simul uniti, te
> dante domos maneamus:

and in his left hand is his answer, to which the episcopal seal is attached, and runs thus:

> Vestra petunt merita,
> quod sint concessa petita:
> Ut maneatis ita,
> loca fecimus hic stabilita.

and on the painting are the arms of the see of Bath and Wells; this picture must be the one alluded to by Godwyn,† and, after the confirmation of their charter by Queen Elizabeth, must have been added to, as the seventeen figures to the right of those kneeling are entirely in a different costume, with ruffles

---

* Collinson gives these the same as above, but, erroneously, *fusils* instead of *fleurs-de-lis*; he does not say whose they are.—Vol. iii. p. 376.
† *De Præsulibus in Vitâ Radulphi de Salopia.*

such as were worn in Elizabeth's time; between is a portion of a curtain as if the original had extended no further, the figures, also, are larger, and do not at all harmonise with the others; immediately under the bishop is the following inscription, which must also have been added at the same time :—

> Quas primus struxit
> summa pietate Radulphus
> Dispersis nobis hospitioque debit
> Aedes, consimili studio
> pia facta secutus,
> Beckingtonus eas
> auxit honore, bonis.
> Regali tandem firmabit
> singula nobis
> Assensu, princeps Elizabetha suo.
> Elizabetha bonis nunquam
> contraria cœptis,
> Aspirans studiis Elizabetha bonis.
> His nos ornati donis,
> regina, precamur
> Sceptra tenens bibas
> Elizabetha diu.

There is no account of any further benefaction to this body since the last-named charter of incorporation granted by Queen Elizabeth, nor of any addition having been made to the buildings; and, in concluding the history of this unique and interesting college, which Godwyn says "the executors of Beckington had rendered the most beautiful of the kind in all England,"* it were, indeed, to be wished that a more agreeable task were allotted to the author, than a faithful description of the manner in which the whole Close has been maintained in repair since that period. It would naturally enough be supposed, after so munificent a gift by the founder, and so many valuable additions to the temporalities and comforts of the inhabitants by subsequent benefactors, that a true spirit of gratitude would have been manifested among the successors of those immediately receiving so sumptuous an asylum with many other benefits, and that their first care would have been to retain, as much as possible, the pristine beauty of the several buildings composing their

---

* Opes ab Episcopo relictas impenderunt isti universas, in Collegio augendo Vicariorum Choralium, quod omnium totius Angliæ ejus generis speciosissimum reddiderunt.—GODWYN *De Præsulibus in Vitâ Tomæ de Beckington.*

college and delineated in the following Plates. But, alas, how lamentably the reverse of this has been the case! for no one, who was not intimately acquainted with the peculiarities of the various styles of Gothic architecture, and able to discover from the present ruinous condition of the exquisitely carved work what it originally has been, would persuade himself that these were faithful representations of the *Vicars' Close*. The chapel he would find in disuse and filled with lumber; the ceiling of the Hall hanging down in large patches; the rooms under converted into a malting-house; the houses modernised with common sash windows, bastard Italian doors, and plain parapets; and a common shop front within a few short weeks inserted under the beautiful little oriel window shewn in Plates V. and VI., at the very entrance to the Close from the street, *and this by one of their own body*, as if in positive defiance of the advocates of good taste and a proper feeling of reverence. The elegant pinnacles and panelled parapet of the gallery over the Chain-Gate, are so completely decayed and ruinous, that the loose stones threaten danger to the passers by, and the profiles of the mouldings are hardly discernible. On a visit to Wells, in May last, the author could not but congratulate himself, that his lamented friend, Mr. Pugin had so opportunely snatched, as it were, the beauties of this example of Gothic art from utter oblivion, and that he should have been the means of thus handing them down to posterity. He knows it will be advanced by the participators in this reckless spoliation, that in catholic times, when celibacy was enjoined, their predecessors, not having to provide for families, could better afford repairs; but when some of the founder's statutes and injunctions are acknowledged, all should be equally in force, and one of them provides for the repairs of each house by its respective inhabitant vicar. It is under the head of " *The Office and Power of the Principals,*" and runs thus: "Moreover they shall yearly see and oversee the defaults of every man's house situate within the said Close, and shall judge and esteem the reparation thereof, and shall admonish the said vicars, that, within a certain time by them appointed, they shall sufficiently repair and amend all such faults in and upon their houses under certain pains, to be moderated by the arbitrement of the said principals." The original number of thirteen was augmented greatly before Beckington's time, and we may presume kept pace with the augmentation of the prebends, as his executors provided forty-two houses; which number corresponds with the number of prebendaries at present attached to the cathedral who are not residentiary. By Elizabeth's charter, as before stated, their number was restricted to twenty; consequently, many of the houses have been thrown into one and modernised, retaining only the mouldering remains of the elegant chimney shafts represented in Plate IV. Surely, an uniform retention of the original design could be insisted upon by the bishop as visitor, and, also, an enforcement of the statutes and ordinances by the principals, who seem sadly to have neglected their duty, in thus allowing "so faire a place" to hasten to decay.

DESCRIPTION OF THE PLATES.

PLATE I. GENERAL GROUND PLAN OF THE VICARS' CLOSE AND THE CHAIN-GATE.

THIS is a *Ground Plan* of the whole range of buildings, as completed by Bishop Beckington and his executors, forming the *Vicars' College*, or *Close;* and, also of the *Chain-Gate*, by which it is connected, across the road, with the Cathedral at AA. B is a *room under the Common Hall*, used, probably, as a beer-cellar. C is a *vaulted room under the Kitchen*, communicating with other offices to the left, or west. D, *vaulting under the Great Stair-Case* leading from the Close to the Hall, and which is entered at F by a richly groined *Porch** under the *Tower*.† E is the *Entrance-Gateway* leading from the road or street to the Close.‡ GG are two rows of houses forming the *Vicars' Dwellings*, each containing, on the ground floor, one living-room, a staircase, and a privy, with a small garden in front, walled round, and entered by a porch, with a yard behind; on the first floor, one sleeping-room: each room has a fire-place, one window and a loop-hole in front, and one window in the rear.§ H is a beautiful little *Chapel* at the north end of the area, connected to the first house, on the left hand, by a small building which is supposed to have formed part of the chaplain's dwelling, which is ornamented by four panels under the window, containing shields; the first to the left hand bears the arms of the see of Wells; the second, those of the united see of Bath and Wells; the third, those of Beckington; and the fourth, what are supposed to be those of Stillington; these last are delineated in Plate VI*. Over the chapel is a *Library*, approached by a small circular staircase in the north-west corner.∥ I is the situation, on the first floor, of the elegant little *Oriel Window* represented in Plates V. and VI. This house, we may safely presume, was the dwelling, originally, of one of the principals; it communicates with the entrance-gateway by a lobby and door. KK are two *Wells*, which have, to this day, a plentiful

---

* A plan of the groining is given in Plate XXV. † See Plates XVII.-XVIII.
‡ This portion of the plan will be better understood by referring to Plates XII. and XIII., and the descriptions of the same.
§ These houses are more fully delineated in Plates II., III., IV., V., and VI.
∥ See Plates VII., VIII., IX., X., and XI.

14   DESCRIPTION OF THE PLATES.

supply of water. The area within the buildings is, from N. to S., 436 feet long, and from E. to W., at the north end, 56 feet broad, and at the south end, 65 feet broad. This difference in the breadth may be accounted for by a wish on the part of the architect to command as good a view as possible from the street under the entrance-gateway,* and thereby to assist the perspective in giving an idea of great length. The width, within the garden walls in the centre of the area, is, at the north end, 19 feet, and at the south end, 21 feet; references are engraved on the plate for convenience.

THE VICARS' DWELLINGS.

PLATE II. shews an *elevation* of each house, as originally completed, on the left-hand side of the Plate. A *chimney-shaft* rises from the ground, between the *door* and the *windows*,—it is octagonal at top, and is perforated like a lantern by two openings on each side; immediately above the cornice, under the eaves of the roof, is a panel containing a quatrefoil and a shield with the arms of the united see of Bath and Wells impaled in one, which occurs along the whole range of buildings on either side, with those of the see of Wells and those of Beckington. Below the cornice is another panel which also contains a shield, bearing the *rebus*, or *device*, *of Richard Swan*, one of Beckington's executors; this occurs consecutively with those of his coadjutors, *Hugh Sugar* and *John Pope*,—see Plate VI*. On the right-hand side of the plate is a *transverse section* of each house cut through the doorways, and shews a profile of the chimney-shaft; it will be better understood by referring to

PLATE III. which gives a *ground plan* of each house; the rooms are 19 ft. 11 in. by 12 ft. 10 in. in the clear inside. The *staircase* lies at the back, and is 6 ft. 2 in. square. From centre to centre of party wall is 21 ft. This plate also shews a *longitudinal section* of each house; the room on the ground floor is 8 ft. 7 in. high; that on the first floor is 8 ft. 9 in. high to the top of the wall plate, and 13 ft. to the point of the arched rib. This section shews the *door*, the *windows*, and the *fireplaces*; also the *oak roof*, which is open to the point of the rafters, and ornamented with moulded ribs and cross braces, the purlins being canted off on the inside angles; above the wall plate, the ends of the rafters are concealed by a neat battlemented cornice.†

* See Plate in page 72 of BRITTON's *Picturesque Antiquities of English Cities*, where this very view is given, but shewing the modern additions to the houses.
† One only of these houses remained in its original state, but sadly dilapidated, when Mr. Pugin visited Wells; and that one is now altered and modernised ! ! !

PLATE IV. gives, at No. 1., the *chimney-shaft* to a larger scale, with plans taken at different heights, and sections of the mouldings still larger, which are explained by letters of reference on the Plate; and, at No. 2, *the window* of the first floor: those of the ground floor are similar, but are longer, and divided by a transom,—see Plate II.

PLATE V. This Plate shews an elevation and section of the *Oriel Window*, which looks into the street; it is terminated at the top by mouldings, in three divisions, or stages, surmounted by a *fleur-de-lis*; below the sill are two quatrefoils with plain shields in front, and one in each angular return. It is ornamented below by tracery-headed panels, terminating in a point at the bottom and resting on a stone corbel sculptured into a head. This window, no doubt, originally had tracery-headed lights, the centre divided into two by a mullion as shewn in dotted lines, which, for the sake of modern convenience, have been destroyed and cut square. A plan of the *soffit*, or *corbelling*, is shewn under the elevation. The section shews its projection from the wall, which is 1 ft. 1 in.

PLATE VI. No. 2 is a plan of this *Oriel Window*, half shews the soffit inside, the supposed mullion is dotted in: to the left are different details and sections of the mouldings referred to the section on Plate V. by letters. No. 1 shews the end elevation of the east row of houses towards the street,* in the centre of which the Oriel Window is situated.† The apex of the gable terminates in a finial, and is surmounted by a chimney-shaft similar to that shewn in Plate IV.‡

PLATE VI*. gives one of the *Porches* at the entrance of each garden, with details at No. 1 ; these were originally surmounted by a Lion, similar to that shewn on the Conduit in the Bishop's Garden, which was built by Beckington.§ These porches, however, seem to be of a later date, and so little did they appear

---

* See Letter I, Plate I.

† In late repairs, a small window was discovered to the left of this, but was immediately stopped up again and plastered over; under this unique examp'e of refined taste, *a modern shop front* has been inserted by one of the seniors of the Vicars' Choral, who, being a baker in the town, I presume will carry on his trade here. At the same time, the window itself was threatened with destruction, and, I believe, was partly removed, but restored in consequence of a general outcry against such wilful spoliation !

‡ The chimney-shaft in this gable was the only one existing from which the lantern top could be sketched and measured ; it still exists, but the work is hardly discernible.

§ See Plate LVIII., and page 47, PUGIN's *Examples of Gothic Architecture*, Second Series.

to present that was interesting, that it was not intended at first to give them in this work; but, on a visit to Wells, the author was so much pleased with their effect,* that this, an additional plate, was provided to include them and the following *coats of arms*. No. 3 are supposed to be the arms of Bishop *Stillington*, who succeeded Beckington in the episcopal chair, and in whose time these buildings were completed by the executors of the latter; they are, quarterly, first and fourth, *argent*, three blackmoors' heads proper; second and third, *gules*, on a fesse, between three leopards' heads *or*, three fleurs-de-lis *sable*.† The *rebuses*, or *devices*, shewn at No. 2, viz. a fesse between three *swans* for *Richard Swan*; the letter *H* and three *sugar loaves* for *Hugh Sugar*; and a chevron between two roses in chief, and a *talbot* in base, for *John Pope* or *Talbot*; are those of Beckington's three executors. See description of Plate II.

The Chapel and Library.

PLATE VII. On the right hand is the *south elevation* towards the Close, and, on the left, a *transverse section* looking east. The lower windows, it will be seen, are of an earlier date than those above, and this portion of the building, probably, formed part of the original design by Bishop Ralph de Salopia; the *Library* was added, probably, by Bishop Beckington, as, on the bell turret, shewn in Plate XI., is a shield impaling the arms of the united See of Bath and Wells, with those of Beckington; the windows being square-headed, and the parapet adorned with three elegant niches, both of a later date in style than the chapel or lower windows, seems to favour this supposition; and it corresponds with others of his works in this city, especially the Entrance-Gateway from the Market-place to the Bishop's Palace. This Chapel, originally, was entered from the west, as before mentioned, page 3 of the Historical Account, and when the gardens were added in front of the houses, the door was, most likely, stopped up, as in the west wall a counter-arch is discernible in the masonry, and another inserted under the spring of one of the windows. In the *Section* to the left of the Plate is shewn the Altar with two niches, one on either side, raised on panelled bases. The east window, here shewn, is now blocked up; there is, also, a window to the east in the *Library* over; the roof of this room is open to the point of the rafters, the ribs being slightly moulded and resting on brackets.

* See Britton's *Picturesque Antiquities*, Plate in page 72, where is a view of the Chapel in the Vicars' Close, and shews one of these Porches in perspective.

† Collinson gives the same arms as these as being on the chapel, with the exception of the *fleurs-de-lis*, which he has erroneously written *fusils*; he does not mention to whom they belong.—*History of Somersetshire* vol. iii. p. 403.

DESCRIPTION OF THE PLATES.   17

PLATE VIII. shews at the bottom, a *plan of the Chapel*, one half of the ceiling is dotted in, which is of oak, divided into four compartments by richly moulded girders, each divided again into four, which are again subdivided into four panels; on the intersections are pateras or bosses, one of which is drawn at large at A. Above is the *plan of the Library*, which communicates with the Chapel by a small circular staircase; one of the quarrels of the windows is given one-third full size.

PLATE IX. gives the *Door-case* and *Oak Door* at large; on the tracery are placed four shields, which are so mutilated as to be hardly made out: the first, to the left, arms unknown; on the second are those of the united see of Bath and Wells, on the sinister side of the saltier ought to be shewn two Keys indorsed; the third unknown; on the fourth are those of Nicholas Bubwith, who was bishop of this see in 1407; they are a *fesse* engrailed *gules*, between three groups of conjoined *holly leaves*, four in each, and correspond with those on his monumental chapel in the nave of the cathedral:* these arms occur, also, in the stained glass of the chapel windows. In the jamb-mouldings are pateras to correspond in design with the windows, under one of which this door-case is inserted.

PLATE X. contains the *Windows* of the Chapel and Library to a larger scale; one of the lights of the latter is shewn glazed, the quarrels are like that given, one-third the full size, in Plate VIII.; it also contains details of the same.

PLATE XI. The *Bell-Turret* at large in elevation and profile; the shield impales the arms of the united see of Bath and Wells; which are, *azure* a saltier per saltier, quarterly quartered, *or* and *argent*, [or the cross of St. Andrew, who is the patron saint of the church of Wells]: on the dexter side of the saltier are two keys indorsed, the upper *or*, the lower *argent*, and on the sinister side, a sword *or*; charged with a crozier erect *or*; [these are the arms of Bath Abbey]: with those of Beckington, viz. *argent* on a fesse

---

* Nicholas Bubwith, Bishop of Sarum, and Treasurer of England, was advanced to this See by the Pope, 7th October, 1407. He contributed considerably to the N.W. tower of the Cathedral at Wells, built the Library over the eastern Cloisters, and a small Chapel leading from the cloisters themselves, which last, however, was soon afterwards destroyed; whether this door originally belonged to it may form matter of conjecture, but does not seem unlikely. He also constructed a small Chantry Chapel in the nave, wherein, after his decease, on the 27th October, 1424, he was buried, having appointed three priests to celebrate a daily mass there for the good of his soul. He also founded an Almshouse, near the north side of St. Cuthbert's Church in this City, and erected a small Chapel in Bath Abbey.—BRITTON's *Wells Cathedral*, pp. 42 and 110.

D

azure, between, in chief, three stags' heads caboshed, *gules*, attired *or*, and in base three pheons 2 and 1 *sable*, a mitre labelled of the *fourth*.* No. 2 shews one of the *niches* at the corner of the parapet, which is very elegantly designed, with buttresses, pinnacles, and crockets; the *parapet-mouldings* are drawn one-sixth the full size.

The Common Hall, Entrance-Gateway, and the Chain-Gate.

PLATE XII. is a *Ground Plan* of the Entrance-Gateway to the Close, on the right, which is groined; from the street are two entrances, a carriage-way and a foot-way, see A B, and one arch leads into the Close. From this gateway a door opens to the left into a room E F, which, probably, served as a *beer-cellar*; it communicates with the Hall above, by a circular staircase out of one of the four arched recesses in the north wall, and with the Close, by two doors, one on either side of the building projecting to the north, which contains the *Great Staircase*. I is vaulting under the stairs. G H is vaulting under the kitchen which communicates with other offices to the west, where we may presume the *Bakehouse* was situated. Out of the Entrance-Gateway, another door opens to the east, into what we may safely presume to have been one of the principals' dwellings, which is the first house of the east row, and fronts the street; the small oriel is situated in the south gable of this house, see Plate VI. At C D, under the *Tower*, is the *Porch* leading to the Great Staircase, which is richly groined; the details are given in Plate XXV. to a larger scale. To the south is the *Chain-Gate* or the *Close-Hall-Gate*, built by Beckington over the road, before described. The centre archway is an oblong parallelogram, and is groined similarly to the Entrance-Gateway, except that in the centre is a panel containing the *Arms of Beckington* on a shield, with his *rebus* on each side, which is given at large in Plate XXV. Details of the Piers are given one-eighth the full size, and are referred by letters. References to the various rooms &c., are also engraved on the Plate for convenience.

PLATE XIII. is the *first-floor plan* of the same portion: it shews the *Common Hall*; to the west of which is the Kitchen &c.; to the north is the *Grand Staircase* before referred to, it leads from the Close to the Hall, the ceiling of which is here shewn. In the Tower, and immediately over the Porch, is the *Muniment Room*, the only entrance to which, is from the Hall by a small circular staircase E, into a room over the Great Staircase, and out of the other

---

* A Journal of one of the suite of Beckington, by Nicholas Harris Nicolas, Esq., Barrister at Law, 1828, p. lxvii.

extremity of this room is another small circular staircase F, leading down to this room of safety. A better mode for concealing treasure or documents, and at the same time, for lodging them in safety, could hardly be imagined. The dimensions of this room are 8 ft. square, and it is fitted up with strong presses. Immediately opposite the door from the Grand Staircase is one leading to A the *Small Lobby*, which communicates into the *Vicars' Gallery* B, over the Chain-Gate: at the south end of this Gallery a door opens into a small irregular ante-room, out of which a staircase leads direct south, into that by which the Chapter-House is ascended from the north transept of the Cathedral; thereby always ensuring a dry walk for the Vicars-Choral when required to perform divine service. Various details of this Plan are given one-eighth the full size, some one-fourth the full size, and are referred by letter. References to the various rooms are engraved on the Plate, for convenience.

PLATE XIV. shews the *south elevation* of the Hall and Entrance-Gateway, together with a *section taken transversely* across the Chain-Gate and the Vicars' Gallery. It will be seen that part of the original design by Ralph of Shrewsbury can still be discovered in the lancet-headed window of two lights, divided by a heavy mullion and transom. The style is quite at variance with the Oriel Window and the Entrance-Gateway, the former being quite of a late period of the Tudor, and the latter not much older.

PLATE XV. gives an Elevation Section and details of the *South Oriel Window* in the Hall over the Entrance-Gateway, shewn in the preceding Plate. There are two of these windows, situated opposite each other at the east end of the Hall, and must have been inserted after the buildings were completed, as may be seen by the manner in which this one cuts into the buttress to the right. On the wall inside, is a shield in stone, bearing the arms of the see of Wells, and the name of Ricus Pomcrop, by whom, probably, these windows and the fireplace, together with the napkin or scroll panelling round the Hall, were added.

PLATE XVI. gives a *Plan* of this window, one half of the *Interior Elevation*, and one half of the *Soffit* in section, together with different details referred by letter to Plate XV. and this.

PLATE XVII.–XVIII. A double Plate; shews, in the centre, a *Transverse Section* of the Hall through the Oriel Windows and Entrance-Gateway, looking west. To the left is the *east elevation* of the Chain-Gate and Vicars' Gallery, which is a beautiful and unique specimen of good taste; it is thought by some, that Beckington, by whose munificence this valuable addition was made to the Vicars' Close, was his own architect, and that he acquired his knowledge from William of Wickham; which is not improbable, he having been patronised by that distinguished prelate, and of whose College at Oxford he was a fellow. It is of the *Perpendicular* or *Tudor Style*, before it acquired that excess of ornament observable in many buildings of the subsequent periods. On the west side, the elevation is regular, and one of the niches contains a statue of St. Andrew: whom the two shewn in this elevation represent is not known, as they are so much decayed. To the right of the Hall is an elevation of the Tower and Great Staircase; the details of the lower square-headed windows are given at N in Plate XIII.

PLATE XIX. shews one of the compartments of the Vicars' Gallery over the centre archway of the Chain-Gate. The two lights of this window, which are divided by a canopied niche, form two distinct windows inside. A plan of the jamb is given in Plate XIII., one-eighth the full size, at K: other details are shewn on this plate, and are referred by letters. In the string-course under the window are, alternately, parts of Beckington's arms, viz. a pheon in the centre and two stags' heads, one on each side; and an angel displaying a scroll. The two angels bearing a mitre with the labels displayed, complete his armorial bearings; they support a pinnacle which is exactly over the centre of the arch below.

PLATE XX. is the *north elevation* of the Hall towards the Close, and a *transverse section* of the Great Staircase, with the *passage-room* to the muniment room over. At the top of the stairs is the door into the hall.

PLATE XXI. One of the *Windows* before alluded to, as being of an earlier date than the rest of the hall, is given in this Plate. To the right is the interior elevation, as seen in Plate XXII., and to the left the exterior elevation, as seen in Plates XIV. and XX.; details are given to a larger scale.

PLATE XXII. shews a *longitudinal section* of the Hall and Kitchen, the rooms under, and the Entrance-Gateway. In the Hall, the south Oriel Window, the fireplace, and the entrance into the small lobby, are seen. To the right of the fireplace, is one of the windows shewn in Plate XXI., out of the jamb of which, a pulpit for grace at meal-time opens to the Hall by a small square opening over the fireplace: a strict observance of grace was enjoined in one of the injunctions laid down by the king, to the effect "That every Vicar dining in the Common Hall shall tarry Grace;" it is as follows: "Item, That none of the Vicars of the said new Close sitting in the Common Hall of the same att the time of Dinner or Supper shall not by any manner of means from henceforth depart from Dinner or Supper before Grace be said after Dinner and Supper without Licence first desired and obteined of the Principalls of the same new Close, if they bee att Dinner and Supper, and in their absence of them which shall supply their Room under paine of iiijd. to be paid and applyed to the use of the aforesaid Close as often as he shall be found negligent, and faulty in this behalfe."*

PLATE XXIII. shews the *Fireplace* and the Iron *Fire-dogs* to a larger scale, with details of the same referred by letter. These are of a late style, but the fireplace has good mouldings in the jamb and mantle-shelf; on which latter is the scroll described in page 8, bearing an inscription which solicits the prayers of the vicars in favour of *Sir Richard Pomroy*, and expresses solicitude for the safety of his soul. The five shields are thus emblazoned: the first, to the left, five bars *or* and *azure*, three escalop shells in chief *gules*, charged with a demi-horse issuant rampant *argent*: the second are Bishop Beckington's arms, which are, *argent* on a fesse *azure*, between, in chief, three stags' heads caboshed *gules*, attired *or*, and in base three pheons, two and one *sable*, a mitre labelled of the *fourth*: the third are the royal arms as borne by Henry V. and the subsequent sovereigns of England down to Queen Elizabeth, which are quarterly quartered, first and fourth *azure*, three *fleurs-de-lis*, two and one *or*, second and third *gules*, three lions gardant, passant, in pale *or*: the fourth are the arms of the united see of Bath and Wells, which are, *azure*, a saltier per saltier, quarterly quartered, *or* and *argent*, with two keys endorsed, the upper *or*, the lower *argent*, on the dexter side of the saltier; and a sword *or*, on the sinister side, both erect, charged with a crozier, erect, *or*: the fifth are those of Pomroy, which are *argent*, a lion rampant *or*, within a bordure engrailed *azure*.

* *The Statutes and Charter of Close Hall,* p. 28, MS.

PLATE XXIV. is a *transverse section* from S. to N. of the Hall, looking W. cut through the *Small Lobby* (which leads into the Vicars' Gallery over the Chain-Gate) and the doors. To the north of the Hall is the *Great Staircase*, over which is the *Passage-room* to the Muniment-room, and the *Porch* over which is the *Muniment-room*. Even with the floor of the passage-room, and communicating with it by a doorway on one side, which, in this section, is shewn dotted, is a small room 8 ft. square, in the tower; these two rooms may have served as bed-room and living-room for the Receiver, who was an officer chosen by the principals, annually, upon the feast of St. Matthew the Apostle. The roof over the living-room, which is of oak, is very elegant, being divided by five richly moulded ribs, into four compartments; the ribs rest on a bracketed cornice, above which is a panelled parapet; there are cross braces in each compartment, and the purlins are canted on the inside angles; a transverse section of this roof, shewing its construction, is seen in Plate XX.

PLATE XXV. contains various details before referred to: at the top of the Plate are two panels; that to the left, which contains Bishop Beckington's arms supported by two angels, and a large scroll underneath, is under the east window of the small lobby, or anti-room, shewn in Plate XVII.-XVIII.; and that to the right is in the centre of the groining of the Chain-Gate, and is seen in Plate XIII.; it also contains his arms, supported, on each side, by his rebus, a flaming *beacon* on a cask, or *ton*, making *beacon-ton*.* At the bottom of the Plate is the plan of the groining of the Porch which leads from the Close into the great staircase under the tower, with the curve of the arch, a section of the ribs, and five of the bosses at large. The rest are different specimens of the top of the panelling round the Hall, one-fourth the full size.

* "A *Beacon* (we know) is so called from *beconing*, that is, making signs, or giving notice to the next *Beacon*. This bright *Beacon* doth nod, and give hints of bounty to future ages; but, it is to be feared, it will be long before his signs will be observed, understood, imitated."—FULLER's *Worthies of Somersetshire*, p. 282.

APPENDIX.

No. 1. *Letters Patent of King Edward III., confirmatory of the Gift of Bishop Ralph, of Shrewsbury, to the Vicars-Choral of Wells.*

Edward, by the Grace of God, King of England and of Ffrance, and Lord of Ireland, To all to whom these present Letters shall come, Greeting, because We have received by an Inquisition which Wee caused to be made by our beloved Thomas Carey our Escheator in the County of Somersett That it is not our hurt or prejudice, or of others if Wee Grant to the Reverend Ffather Ralph Bishop of Bath and Wells, That he may give and Assign to the Vicars of the Church aforesaid (not having a common Habitation), a certain place of the Soil of the Church of St Andrew in Wells, and of the Bishop in the same Place, which was lately collated by the Bishop of the same Place upon Mr. Alane of Hotham Canon of that Church, for his Habitation, and the Houses in the same Place by the said Ralph now built and to be built. To have and to Hold to them, and their Successors Vicars of the Church aforesaid for their Common and perpetual Cohabitation, and that the said Bishop may Charge his Lands and Tenements in Congresbury parcell of his Bishoprick aforesaid with an Hundred Shillings Annuity, and certain other Lands and Tenements with the Appurtenances in Wookey which William of Camell, and John his Brother held for term of the Life of either of them the said William and John of the said Bishop and which after the Death of them the said William and John ought to remain to the said Bishop and his Successors with another Hundred Shillings Annuity, and that he may give and Assign the same Tenn Pounds Annuity to the said Vicars celebrating and which shall celebrate Divine Service in the said Church in Augmentation of their Sustenance to be perceived, and had Yearly out of the said Lands and Tenements to the same Vicars and their Successors for ever. Wee commending the godly and wholesome Purpose of the said Bishop in this behalfe which so much respecteth the Praise of God's Name, the Comlinesse of the said Church (which is of the foundation of our Progenitors, and of our Patronage) the increase of Divine Worship, and the security honesty and Quietness of the Colledge of the said Vicars, And considering allso that the said Lands and Tenem^{ts}. in Congresbury to be charged with an Hundred Shillings annuity as afore is said, are come to the Hands of the said now Bishop by the Death of St John Randolffe Knight & Joan his Wife Tennants thereof from the said Bishop by the service of a certain Yearly Rent. And that the said Ralph now Bishop hath purchased, by himselfe and to his Successors the said Lands and Tenements in Wookey which are to be charged with another Hundred Shillings Annuity (our License for that purpose first obtained) and willing to deale favourably with the said Bishop in Regard of the p̄misses, for Twenty Pounds which the said Bishop hath paid unto Us, have granted and given License to the same Bishop for Us and our Heirs (as much as in Us is) that he may give and Assign to the same Vicars the place aforesaid with their Appurtenances together with the Houses so by him thereupon built, and to be built; To have and to hold to them and their Successors Vicars of the same Church for their Habitation, And that the sam Bishop may Charge his said Lands and Tenements in Congresbury and Wookey aforesaid with the said Tenn Pounds Annuity, and likewise give and Assigne the said Tenn Pounds Annuity to the said Vicars. To be perceived and had yearely out of the said lands and Tenements to them and their Successors aforesaid in Augmentation of the Sustenance of the said Vicars and of Divine Service as afore is said, And as the said Bishop as well of the Houses for such Habitation for the said Vicars, as of the said Tenn Pounds between the said Vicars to be distributed shall thinke fitt to be Ordained for ever. And Wee doe likewise by virtue of these presents, give speciall License to the said Vicars that they may receive from the said Bishop and hold to them, and their successors as aforesaid; as before is said the said Place with the Appurtenances together with the Houses, and Tenn Pounds Annuity out of the Lands and Tenements aforesaid. The Statute of Mortmain in any wise notwithstanding. And wee will not that the said Bishop or his Successors or the said Vicars or their Successors by reason of the p̄misses or Statute aforesaid should be sued or molested, or in any sort grieved by Us, or Our Heirs, our Justices, Escheators, Sherriffs, or other our Bayliffs, or Ministers whatsoever. Saving notwithstanding to us and our Heirs, and to other chief Lords of the ffee thereof the services (that may bee due) of the place, Lands, and Tenements aforesaid. 𝕴𝖓 𝖂𝖎𝖙𝖓𝖊𝖘𝖘 Whereof Wee have caused these our Letters to be made Patent.

𝖂𝖎𝖙𝖓𝖊𝖘𝖘 our Selfe att Sandwich the Third Day of December in the Two and Twentieth Year of our Reign of England and Ninth Year of our Reign of Ffrance.

𝕿𝖍𝖊 𝕯𝖚𝖕𝖑𝖎𝖈𝖆𝖙𝖊 *Confirmacon of the Chapter of Bath and Wells of the Houses of the Vicars of Wells, and of Tenn Pounds Rent due to them granted by the Lord Ralph Bishop of Bath and Wells.*

𝕿𝖔 𝖆𝖑𝖑 𝖆𝖓𝖉 𝕾𝖎𝖓𝖌𝖚𝖑𝖆𝖗 to whose notice these present Letters shall come Ralph by God's Providence Bishop of Bath and Wells Greeting in our Lord God everlasting. Know Yee that Wee with the unanimous consent of the Prior and Chapter of our Church of Bath, and Dean and Chapter of our Church of Wells (solemn discourse before had which in this behalfe is required, and other things concurring, which of Right are requisite) have Given Ordained and Assigned for Us and our Successors the Speciall Licence of the most Excellent Prince and our Illustrious Lord 𝕰𝖉𝖜𝖆𝖗𝖉 by the Grace of God King of England and of Ffrance for that purpose had all that place of the Soil of St. Andrew in Wells, which Mr. Alane of Hotham Canon of the same Church did obtain for his Habitation of the Collation of JOHN of good memory late Bishop of Bath and Wells our immediate Predecessor together with the Houses in the same Place, now of new by Us built and to be built, to those of the Vicars of our Church aforesaid for the time being, under this manner and form that is to say, That Wee and our Successors Bishops of Bath and Wells may be holden to conferr the Chambers with th' appurtenances in the said Place built and to be built to every Vicar of the same Church, that is to say every Chamber with his Appurtenances to be had and Enjoyed so long as they shall be Vicars of the same Church, and make their personall abode in the same, Soe that it shall be we and our Successors to conferr and assign the said Chambers when they shall bee void to such Vicars of the said Church as shall please us, att the free will of Us and our Successors, And wee doe further ordain that the Vicars of our Church aforesaid when they shall have gotten Habitations by the Collation of us or our Successors, if they shall leave the said Chambers, and not dwell in them by the space of six months (without a reasonable cause by Us or our Successors to bee allowed) shall be *ipso facto* deprived from the said Chambers so that without a new collation it shall not be lawfull for them to returne to the same Chambers. Moreover Wee doe ordain that the Vicars of the said Church inhabiting the said Chambers as aforesaid, living together att meat and drinke att the Common Costs and Expenses, may have to their Common Use the Hall, Kitching, Bakehouse, and all other Houses in the said Place built and to be built. And that Wee the better Excite the said Vicars so to live together in Common att Meat and Drinke, att the Common Costs and Charges, Wee doe grant for us and our Successors to the Vicars of the said Church for the time being (the speciall Licence of our said Sovereigne Lord the King for that purpose first being had) Tenn Pounds Sterling Money of yearly Rent, that is to say, an Hundred Shillings, to be perceived out of all the Lands, and Tenements which John Randolfe, and Joan his Wife whilst they lived held in the Mannor of Congresbury. And other Hundred Shillings out of all the Lands, and Tenements which William Cammell and John his Brother hold of Us, and our Successors in our Mannor of Wookey for Term of either of their Lives, to be perceived yearly in the Ffeast of St. Michaell, To have and to hold to the same Vicars, and to their Successors, Vicars Inhabiting the same Chambers, and living together in Common as afore is said to whose hands soever the said Lands and Tenements shall come for ever. And if it shall happen the payment of the said Rent to be deferred in Part or in the whole after the said Term (which God forbid) that then and from thenceforth it shall be lawfull to and for the said Vicars the said Lands and Tenements to distreyn and the Distress to deteyn untill they shall be fully satisfied of the said Rent, Ours our Successors or any other Licence whatsoever for that purpose not required, saving it is not, nor was not our Intention that the Vicars dwelling out of the said Chambers, may although they dwell in the said Chambers (Except they live att the Common Charge and Expenses for Meat and Drink with other Vicars living in such Chambers) should perceive any Profitt of the Rent aforesaid, but upon the Receipt of any such Proffitt after the Rate of the time should bee utterly excluded, Moreover, wee doe Ordain that all and every Vicar of the said Church inhabiting the said Chambers, soe often as they shall pass from the said Chambers to the said Church of St. Andrew, or from the said Church to the said Chambers, in recompense of this Benefitt be bound to say the

E

Lords Prayer, and the Salutation of the Angell for Us and our Successors. **In Witness, Wee** Ralph by Gods Permission Bishop of Bath and Wells have caused our Seal to be put to these presents. Dated att Wyvelscombe the last Day saving one of December in the Year of our Lord God One Thousand Three Hundred Fforty and Eight, and of our Consecration the Twentieth.

  And Wee John Prior of the Cathedrall Church of Bath, and the Chapter of the same Place, with one Accord giving our Consent to all and singular the Premisses, and holding them ratifyed and firme (as much as in Us is), confirme them, and have put our Common Seal to these presents, Dated as concerning Us in our Chapter House att Bath the first of January in the Year of our Lord God abovesaid.

  And Wee Walter Dean of the Church of Wells, and the Chapter of the same place with one accord giving our Consent to all and singular the Premises, and holding them ratifyed and firme do (as much as in Us is) confirme the same, and have put our Comon Seal to these presents, Dated as concerning. Us in our Chapter House of Wells the Third Day of the Month of January in the Year of our Lord God abovesaid.

No. 2. Copy of the Table of the Statutes and Injunctions laid down by Bishop Ralph de Salopia, and Confirmed by Bishop Beckington.

Close Hall.

A Table of the Statutes and Injunctions.

1. That the Statutes and Injunctions shall be read once every Year.
2. The Office and Power of the Principals.
6. How the Office of the Stewardship shall run from House to House.
8. How the Steward shall behave himself in his office.
7. What the Steward shall do in the Common Hall, his Office ended.
9. How the Steward shall pay for his Victualls.
10. How the Vicars ought to abstain from Oaths.
12. How that the Vicars ought to pay for their Commons att the Weeks end.
11. What Communication the Vicars ought to have att the Table.
14. That neither Horses nor Doggs ought to be Kept within the Close.
15. How the Vicars ought to behave themselves within the Close att Night time.
16. Against Slanderers and Stirrers up of Strife.
18. How every Man ought to pray for the founder.
17. When the Close Gate ought to be shutt.
19. How the Secretts of the Hall ought to be kept Close.
20. How all suspected Persons ought to be removed.
21. That two shall not dwell in one House together.

23. That none shall strike the Common Servants.
25. Ther shall be soft Commuuication att the Table in the hall.
That no Vicar shall receive any Stranger to continue within the Close.

CONFIRMATION of these STATUTES by
THOMAS BECKINGTON Bishop of Bath
and Wells.

Statut's and Ordinances of
BISHOP BECKINGTON.

28. **Ffor** Reformation of Abuse in the Vicars Apparrell.
29. Ffor like Rounding and Crownes and convenient Apparrell.
30. Ffor Reverence to be given to the Principals and Seniors.
31. That none of the Vicars shall make suit for any Chamber, &c.
32. That none shall sue his fellow at the temporal Law.
33. That no Lay Vicar presume to come to any Hall or Counsell except he be called.
34. How the Principalls ought to punish Offenders.

Hereafter doe follow the King's Injunctions.
1. **That** there shall be one only Receiver.
2. The Election of the said Receiver.
3. What Rents the Receiver shall Receive.
4. How new admitted Vicars shall be taken to the Hall.
5. That none of the Vicars shall wear Weapon.
6. That every Vicar dining in the Comon Hall shall tarry Grace.
7. That every Vicar att his first Admission ought to take a Corporall Oath.
8. That the Principalls may continue in Office three or ffoure Yeares.
9. How the Principalls ought straightly to punish the Offendors against the Statutes.
10. That every Vicar and especially the five Seniors ought to assist the Principalls in executing the Statutes.
11. That the Penalties of the Offendors ought to bee paid out of Hand.
12. That these Injunctions shall be Registered and read openly.
41. Of Perdisons in the Church for Prime Mass and Evensong.

A Statute or Injunction
made by John Still, Bishop of Bath
and Wells, the Seaventh Day of June,
in the Year of our Lord God 1599.

Now that every Vicar being employed about the House Busines, shall within six Days yield an Account into the Exchequer of the said House.

FFINIS TABULÆ.

APPENDIX.

𝔗𝔥𝔢 𝔒𝔞𝔱𝔥 of a Vicar Chorall of Wells.

5. I: N: late admitted unto a Vicar Chorall of the Cathedral Church of Wells make my Oath upon this Holy Book that I from henceforth shall be alway obedient unto the Principalls of this Place for the time being and to all other having their Power, and exercising their Office in their Absence and likewise to all my Seniors in all things that be lawfull and honest, And further I shall with the best of my Power from this day forward keep fullfill and observe, and endeavour my selfe as much as in me shall lye hereafter to cause others in like manner to keep fullfill and observe all Statutes and laudable Customs of this Place. And moreover I shall (not) at any time utter nor yett disclose outwardly any of the Secretts or Counsell of this Place whereby Hurt Loss Prejudice Dislaunder or Grievances might fortune to follow and ensue to this Place, or any of my fellowship. And if it shall happen to hear of any Displeasure Loss Prejudice Dislaunder or Grievance towards this Place, or any of my fellowship I shall as farr for that I cann or may stay and lett it. And if may not I shall, with all speed convenient, open and disclose it unto the Principalls: also I shall to the uttermost of my Power help and Defend maintain and cause others as farr forth as I may to help maintain and Defend all manner of Livelyhoods Rents and Service to this place of Right appertaining and belonging. And to be a diligent helper to defend and recover the same if need shall require from all Enemy's and never consent to deliver it to other Use. And if it fortune me hereafter to be promoted from this Worshipfull Place I shall wherever I come or abide be ever in Word Deed and Will well willed true friend, and in all things to this place apperteyning bee a behoofull and diligent Helper; so God me help and by this Book.

𝔓𝔢𝔯𝔠𝔞𝔣𝔱𝔢𝔯 doe follow the Ordinances of the same Place which ought to be read openly every year in the Hall there.

Then follow the Injunctions, of which the Table is given above, and the new Charter granted by Queen Elizabeth, which is dated at Westminster on the 25th November, in the 34th year of her reign.

END OF PART I.

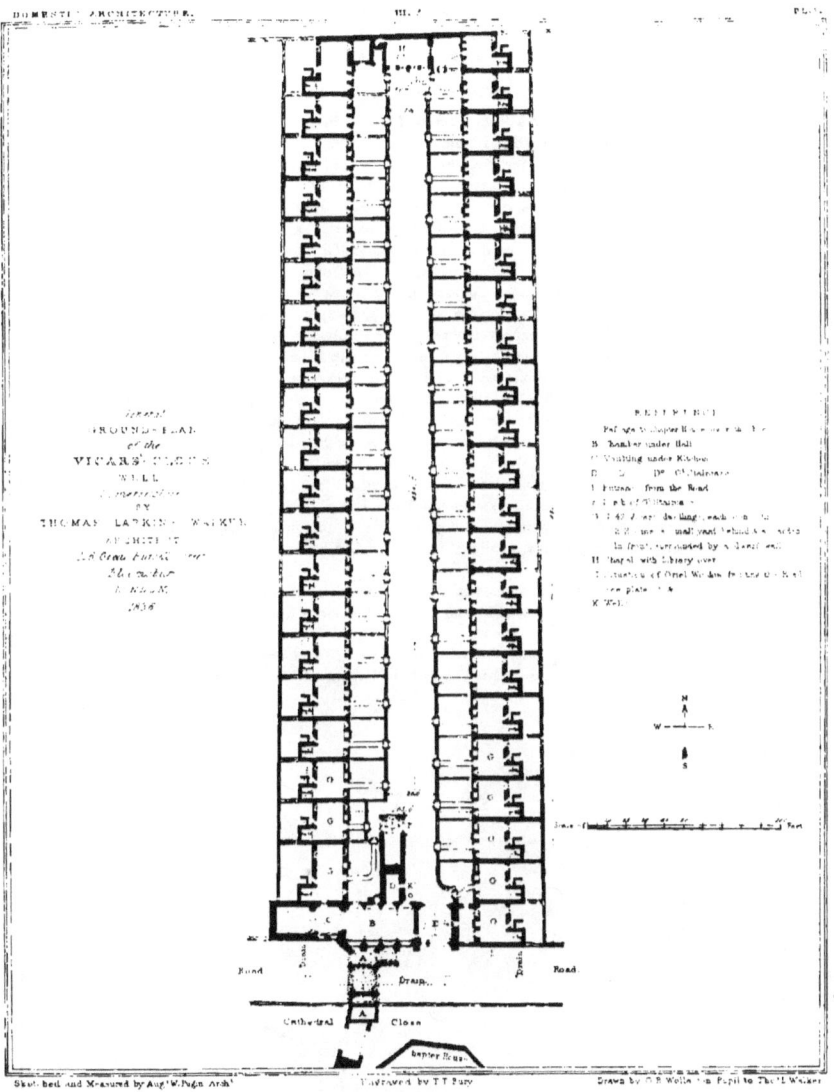

𝕮𝖍𝖊 𝕺𝖆𝖙𝖍 of a Vicar Chorall of Wells.

5. I: N: late admitted unto a Vicar Chorall of the Cathedral Church of Wells make my Oath upon this Holy Book that I from henceforth shall be alway obedient unto the Principalls of this Place for the time being and to all other having their Power, and exercising their Office in their Absence and likewise to all my Seniors in all things that be lawfull and honest, And further I shall with the best of my Power from this day forward keep fullfill and observe, and endeavour my selfe as much as in me shall lye hereafter to cause others in like manner to keep fullfill and observe all Statutes and laudable Customs of this Place. And moreover I shall (*not*) at any time utter nor yett disclose outwardly any of the Secretts or Counsell of this Place whereby Hurt Loss Prejudice Dislaunder or Grievances might fortune to follow and ensue to this Place, or any of my fellowship. And if it shall happen to hear of any Displeasure Loss Prejudice Dislaunder or Grievance towards this Place, or any of my fellowship I shall as farr for that I cann or may stay and lett it. And if may not I shall, with all speed convenient, open and disclose it unto the Principalls: also I shall to the uttermost of my Power help and Defend maintain and cause others as farr forth as I may to help maintain and Defend all manner of Livelyhoods Rents and Service to this place of Right appertaining and belonging. And to be a diligent helper to defend and recover the same if need shall require from all Enemy's and never consent to deliver it to other Use. And if it fortune me hereafter to be promoted from this Worshipfull Place I shall wherever I come or abide be over in Word Deed and Will well willed true friend, and in all things to this place apperteyning bee a behoofull and diligent Helper; so God me help and by this Book.

𝕳𝖊𝖗𝖊𝖆𝖋𝖙𝖊𝖗 doe follow the Ordinances of the same Place which ought to be read openly every year in the Hall there.

Then follow the *Injunctions, of which the Table is given above, and the new Charter granted by Queen Elizabeth, which is dated at Westminster on the 25th November, in the 34th year of her reign.*

END OF PART I.

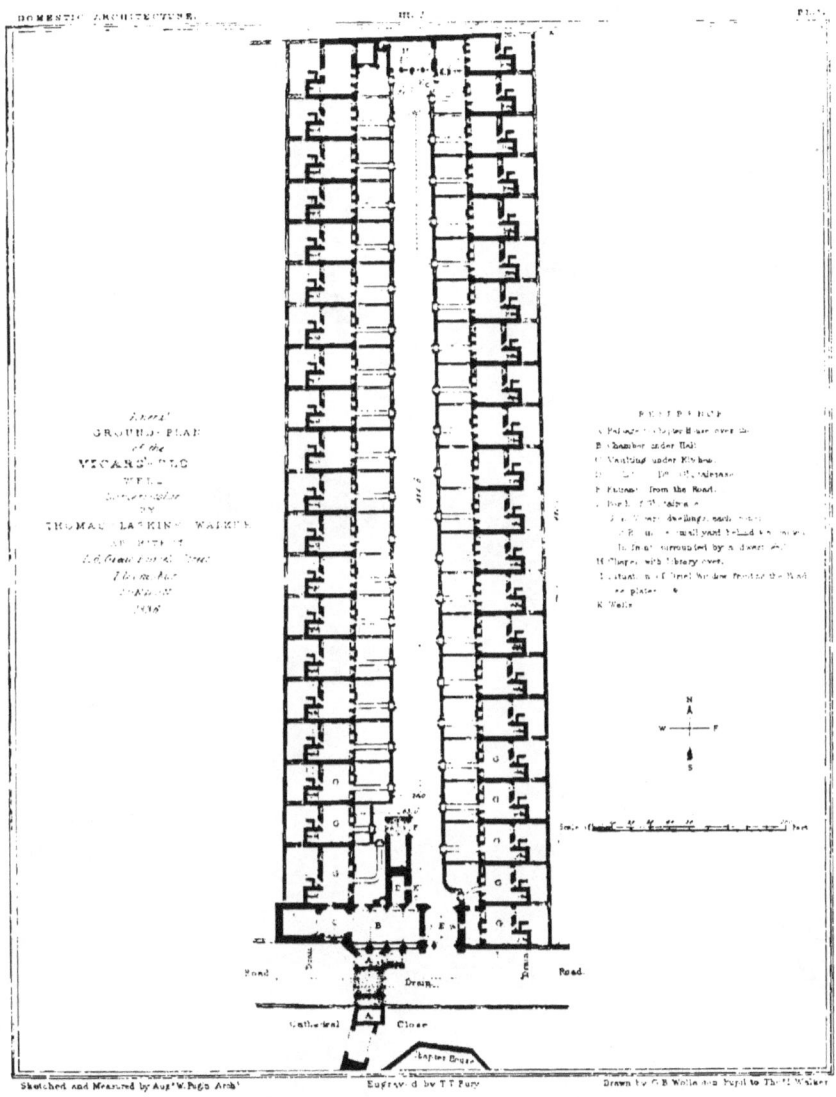

DOMESTIC ARCHITECTURE.

FRONT ELEVATION.   TRANSVERSE SECTION.

VICARS' CLOSE, WELLS.

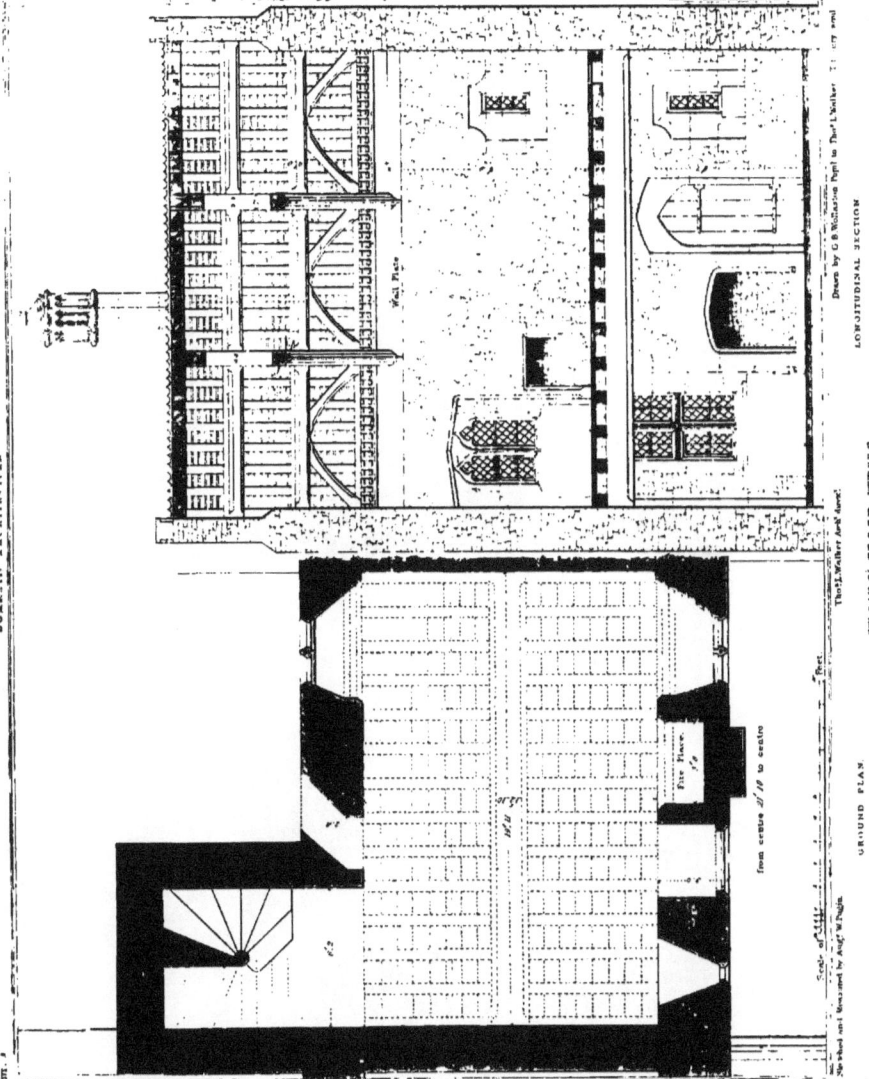

VICARS' CLOSE, WELLS.

GROUND PLAN   LONGITUDINAL SECTION

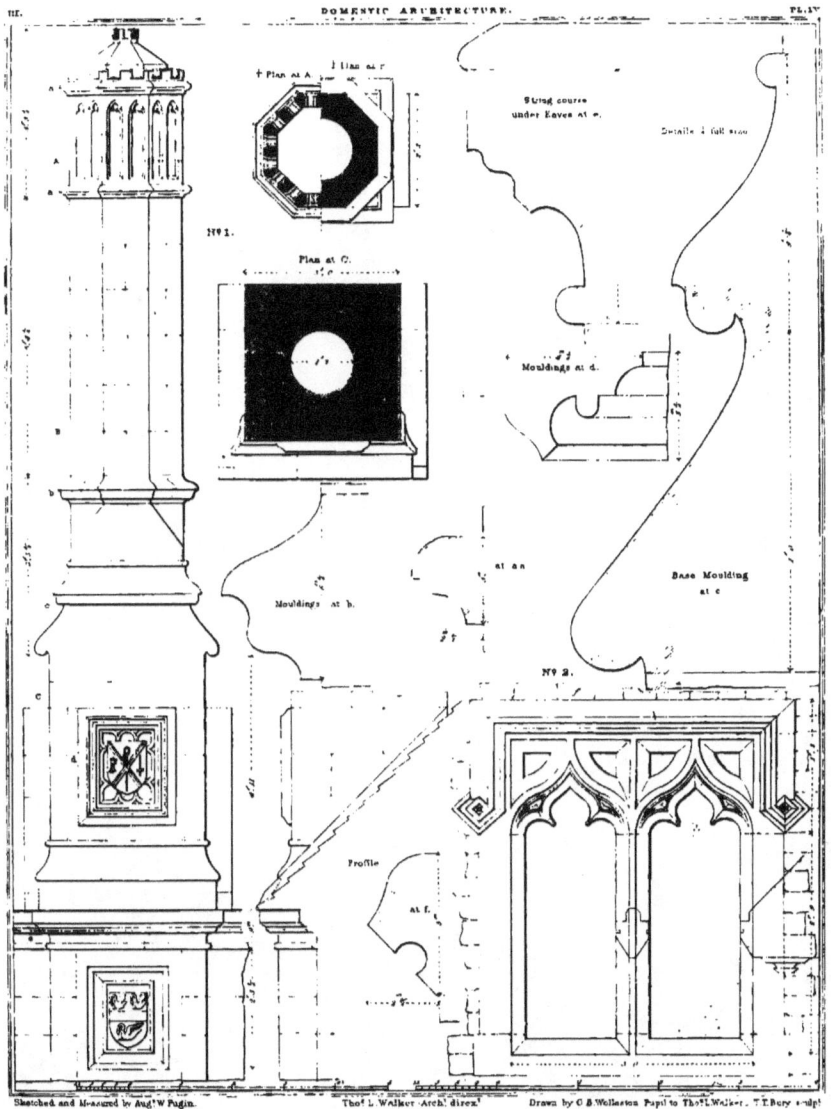

VICARS' CLOSE, WELLS.

DOMESTIC ARCHITECTURE.

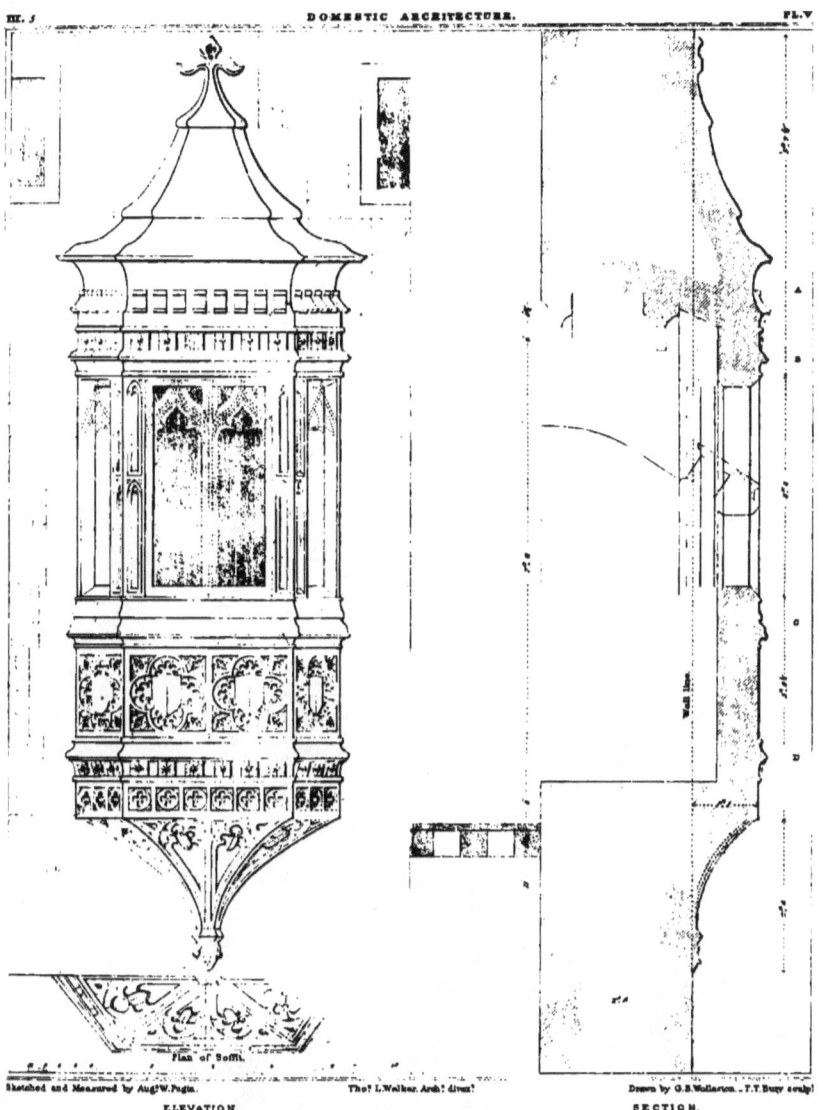

Sketched and Measured by Aug.W. Pugin.   Thos L. Walker, Arch.^t direx.^t   Drawn by G.B.Wollaston. T.T. Bury sculp.^t

ELEVATION.   VICARS' CLOSE, WELLS.   SECTION.
VICARS' DWELLINGS.

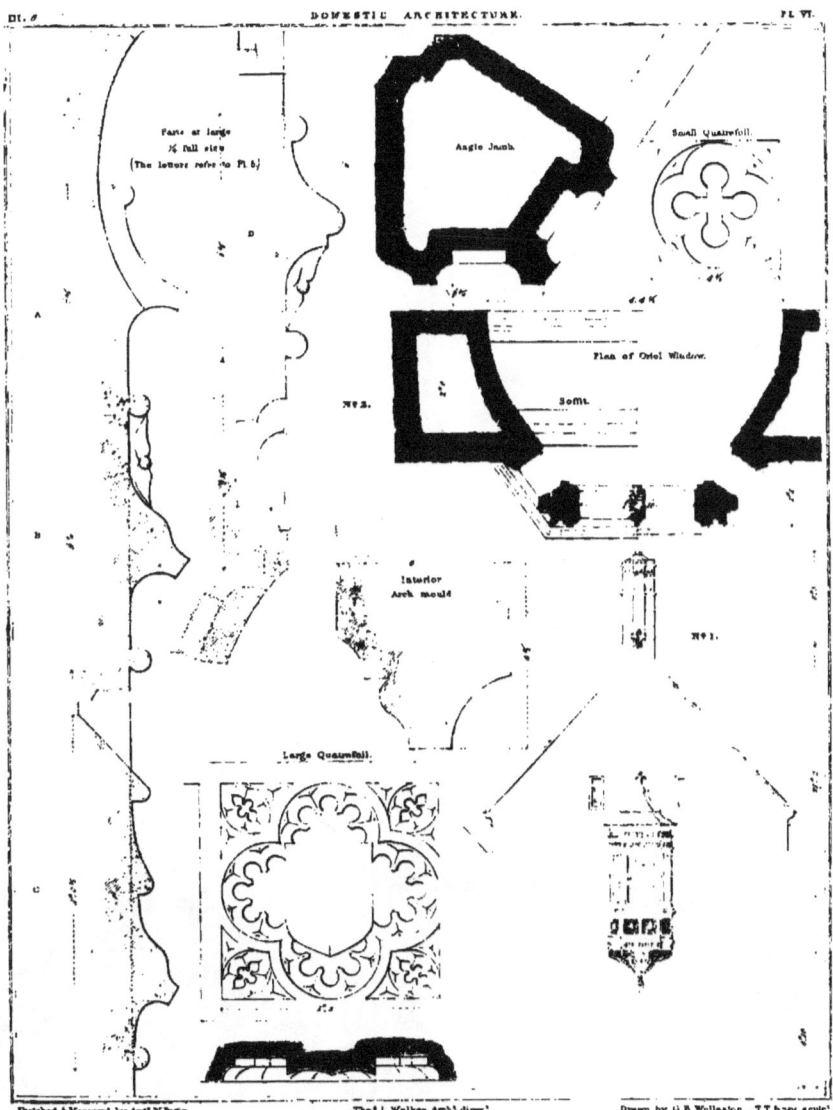

VICARS' CLOSE, WELLS.

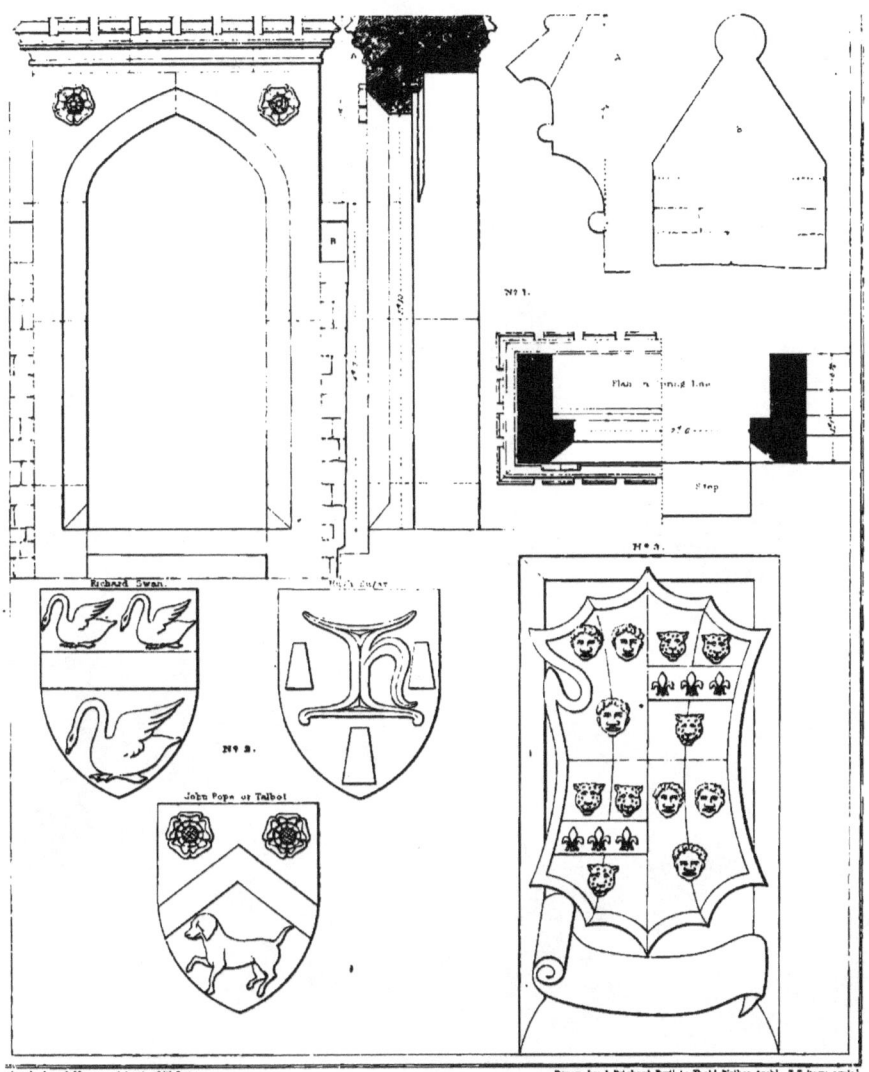

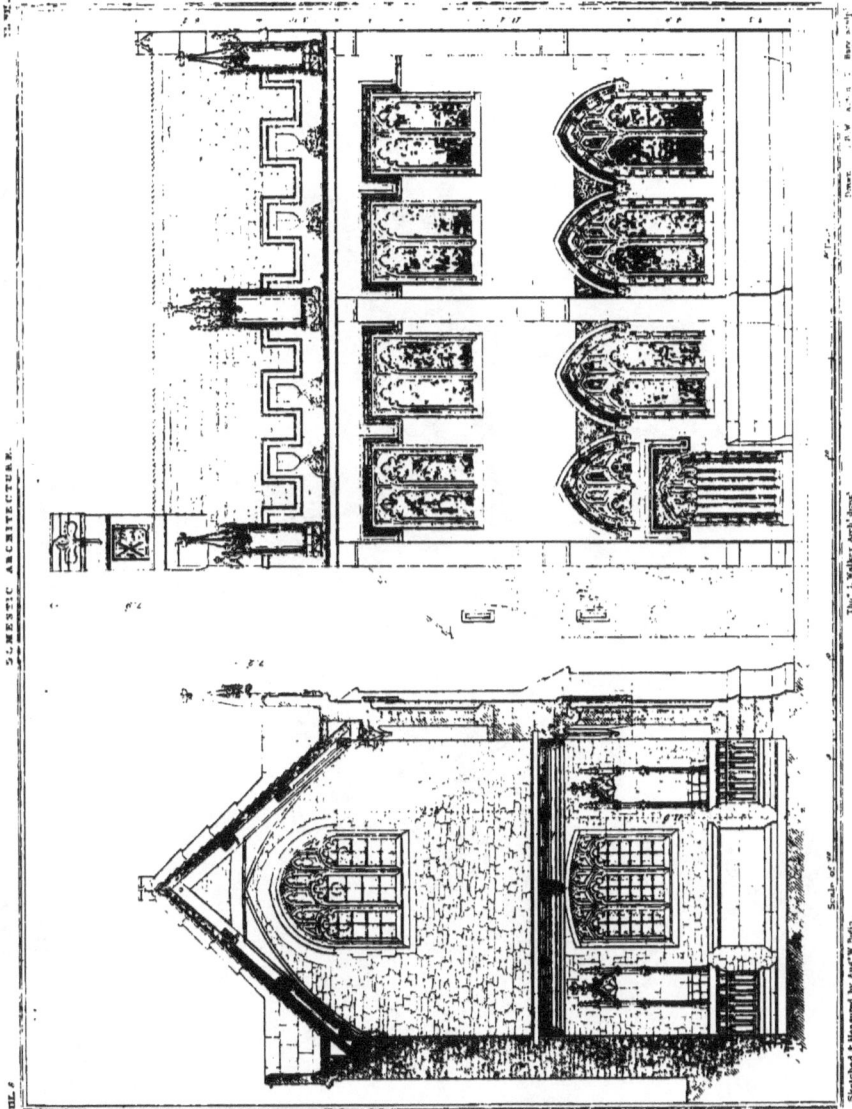

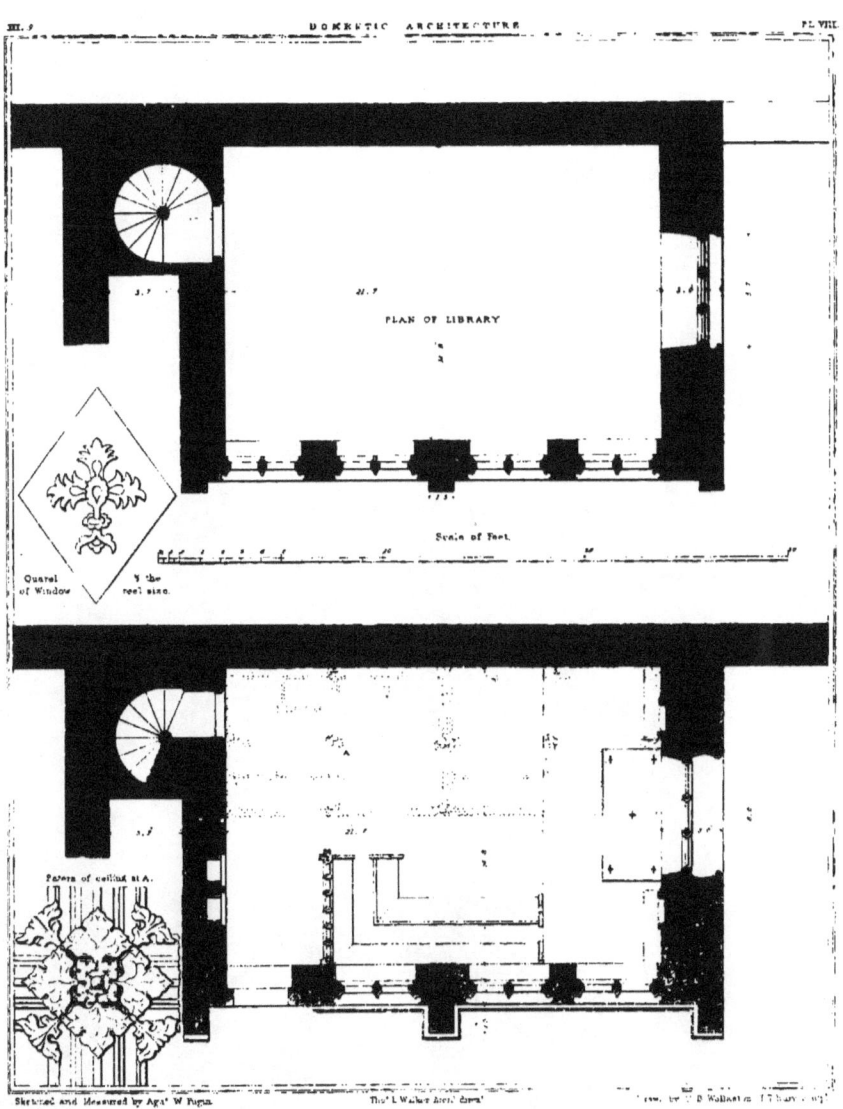

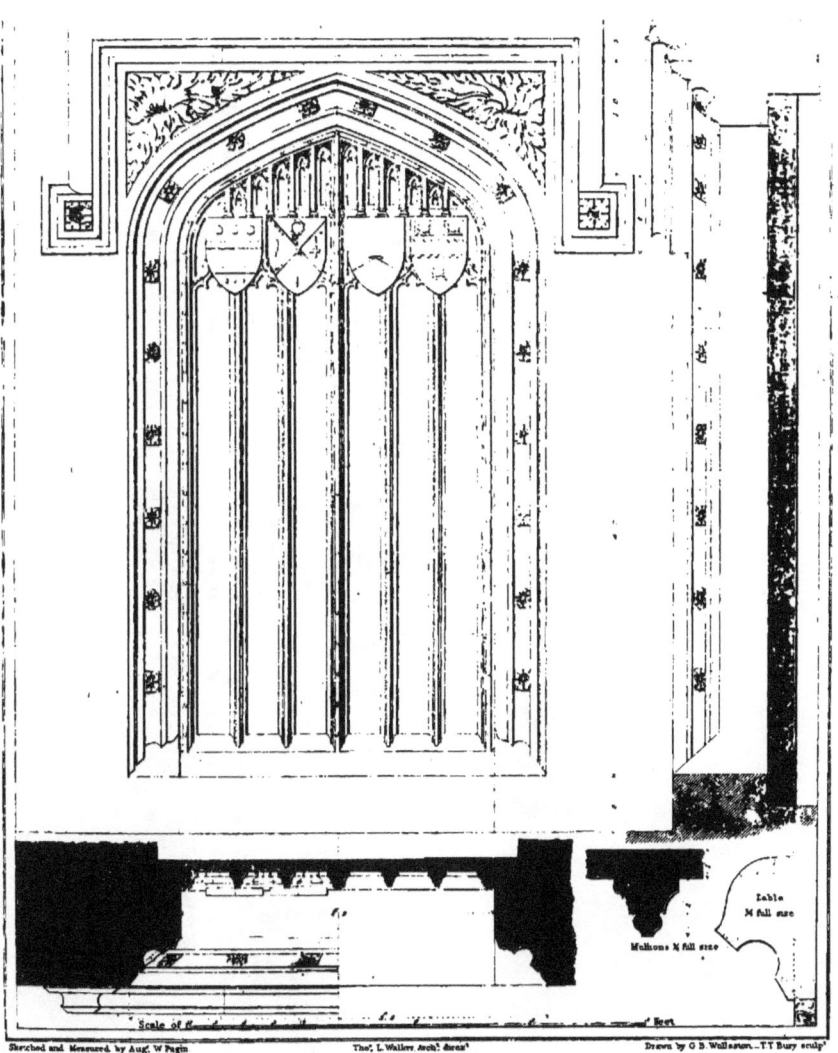

VICARS' CLOSE, WELLS.

VICARS' CLOSE, WELLS.

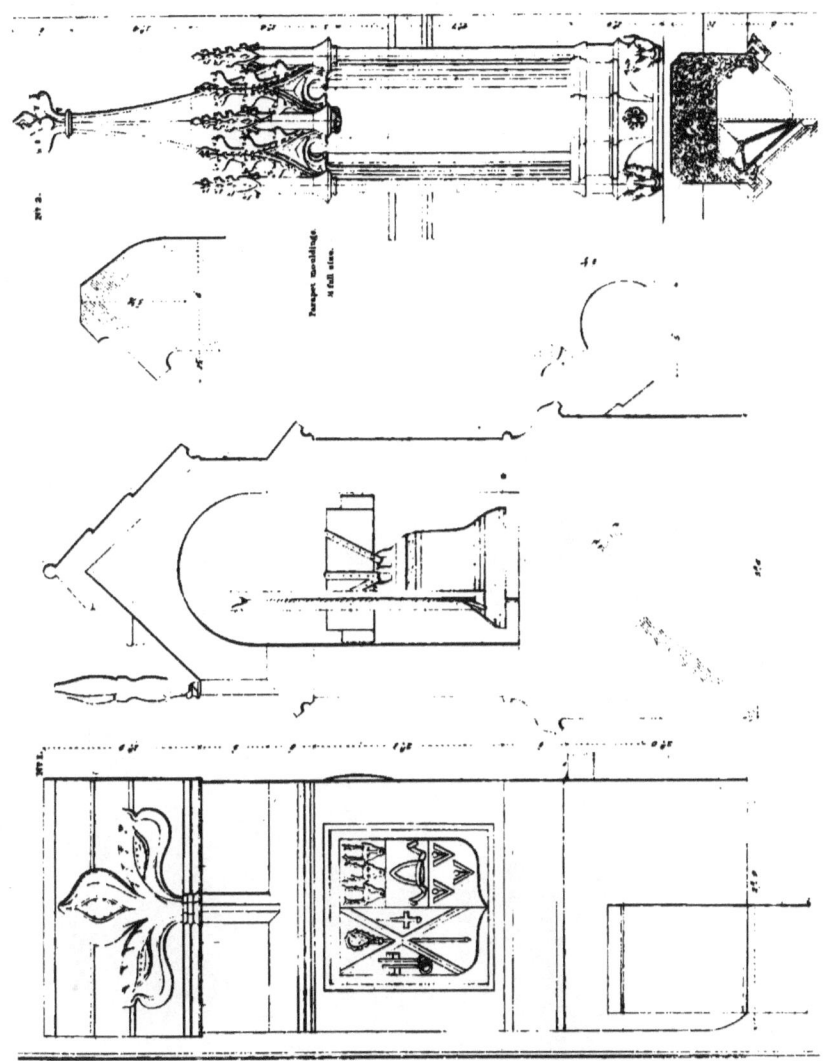

DOMESTIC ARCHITECTURE.

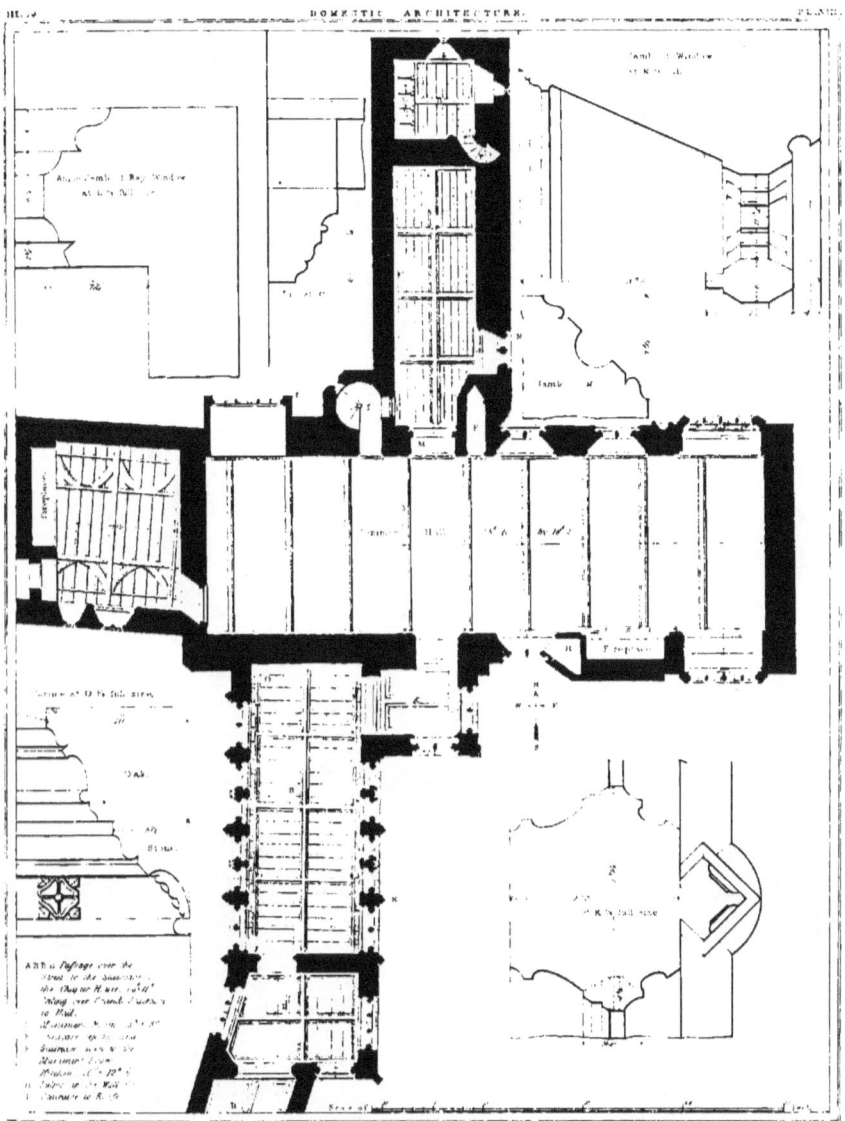

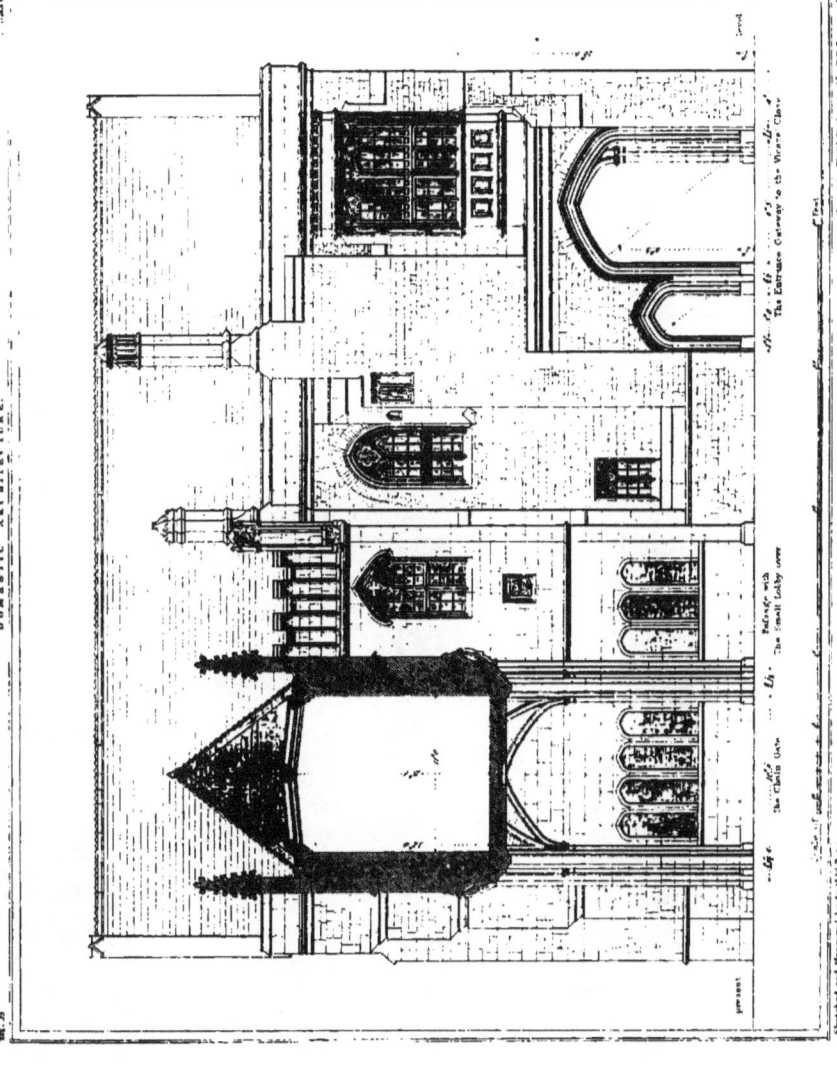

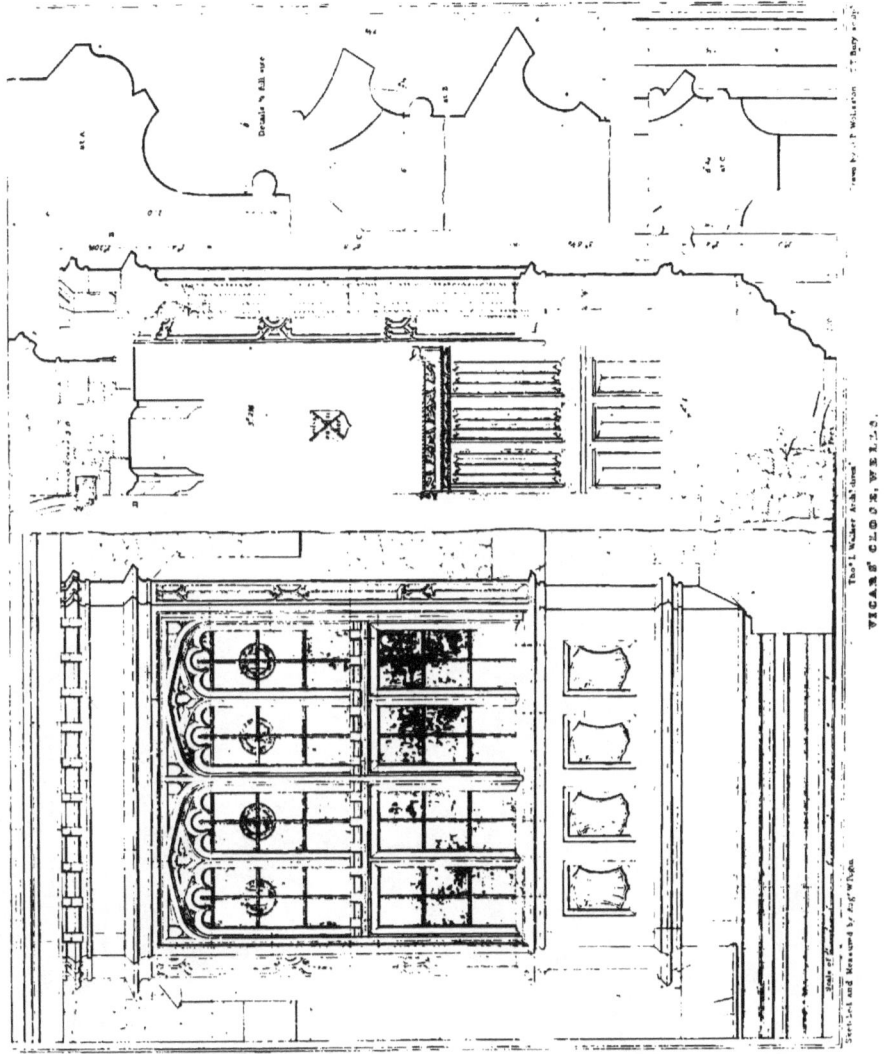

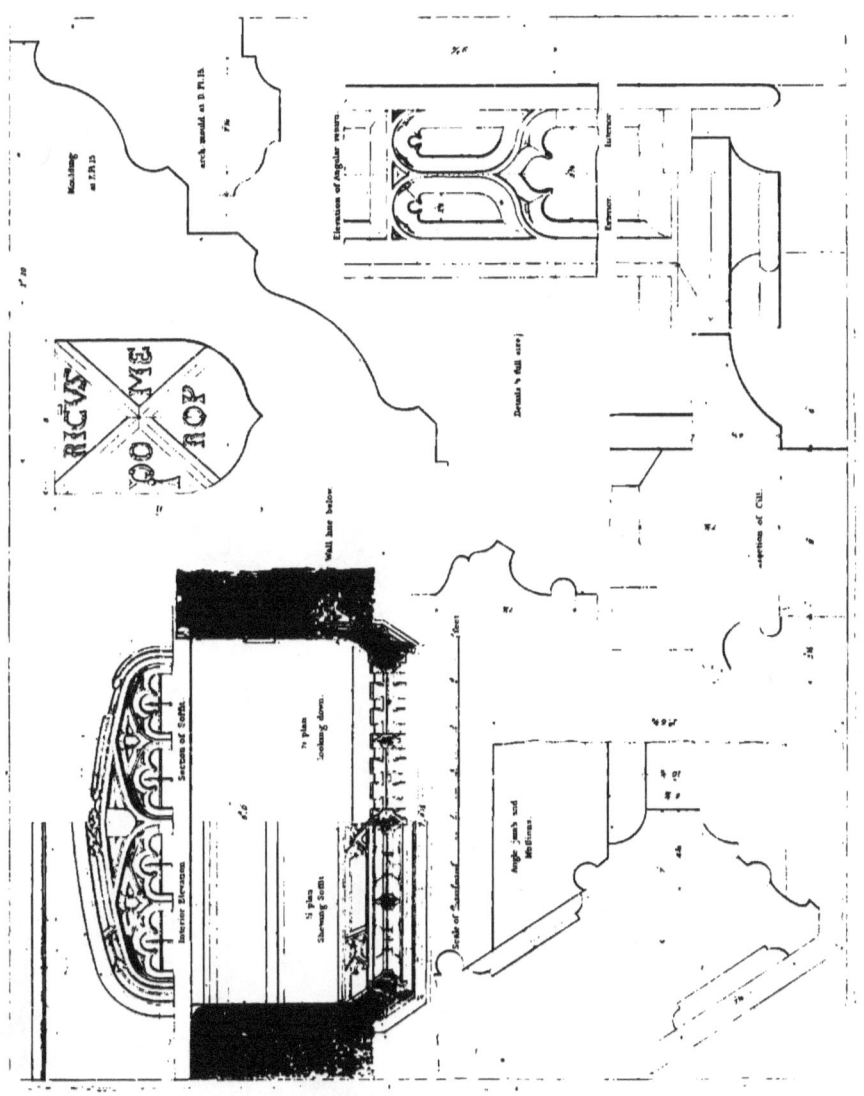

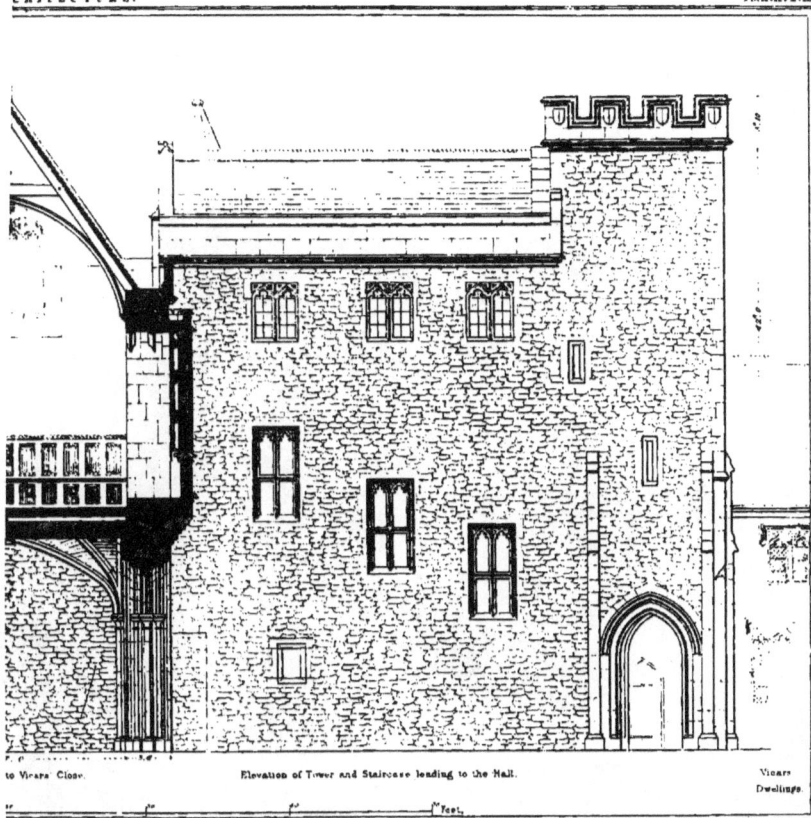

Elevation of Tower and Staircase leading to the Hall.

Drawn by G.B. Wollaston — T.T. Bury sculp.

VICARS' CLOSE, WELLS.

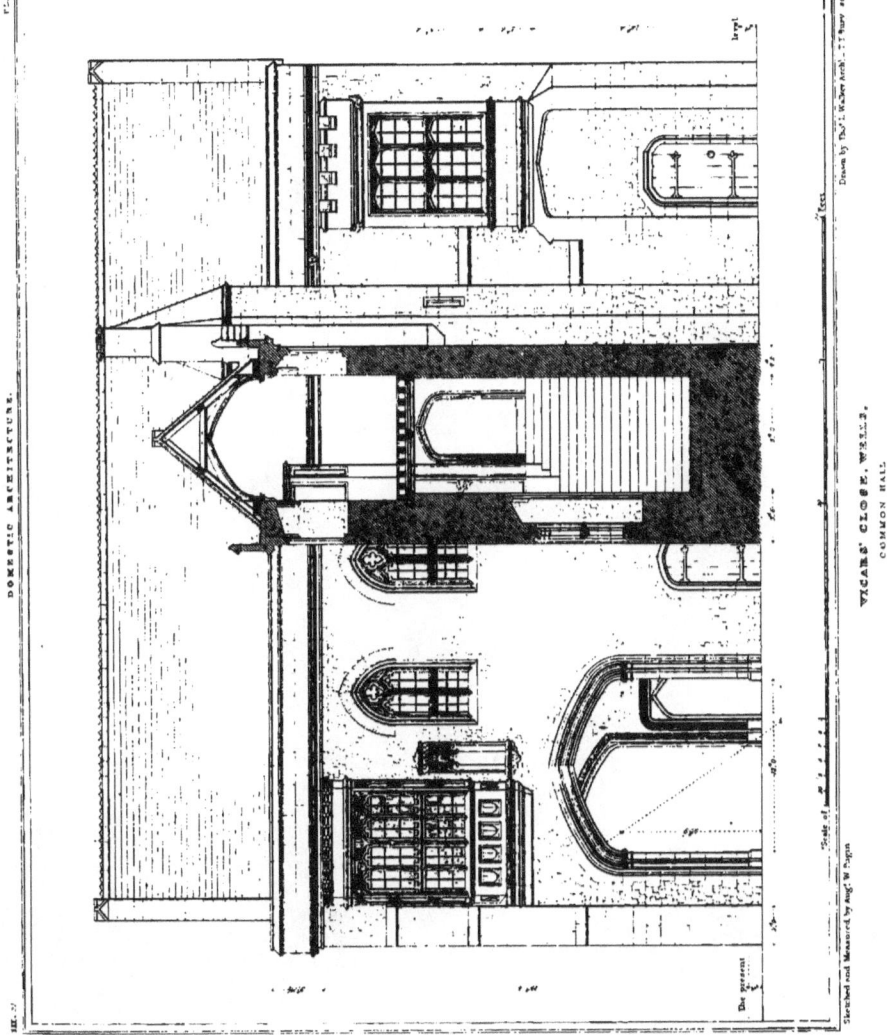

VICARS' CLOSE, WELLS.
COMMON HALL.

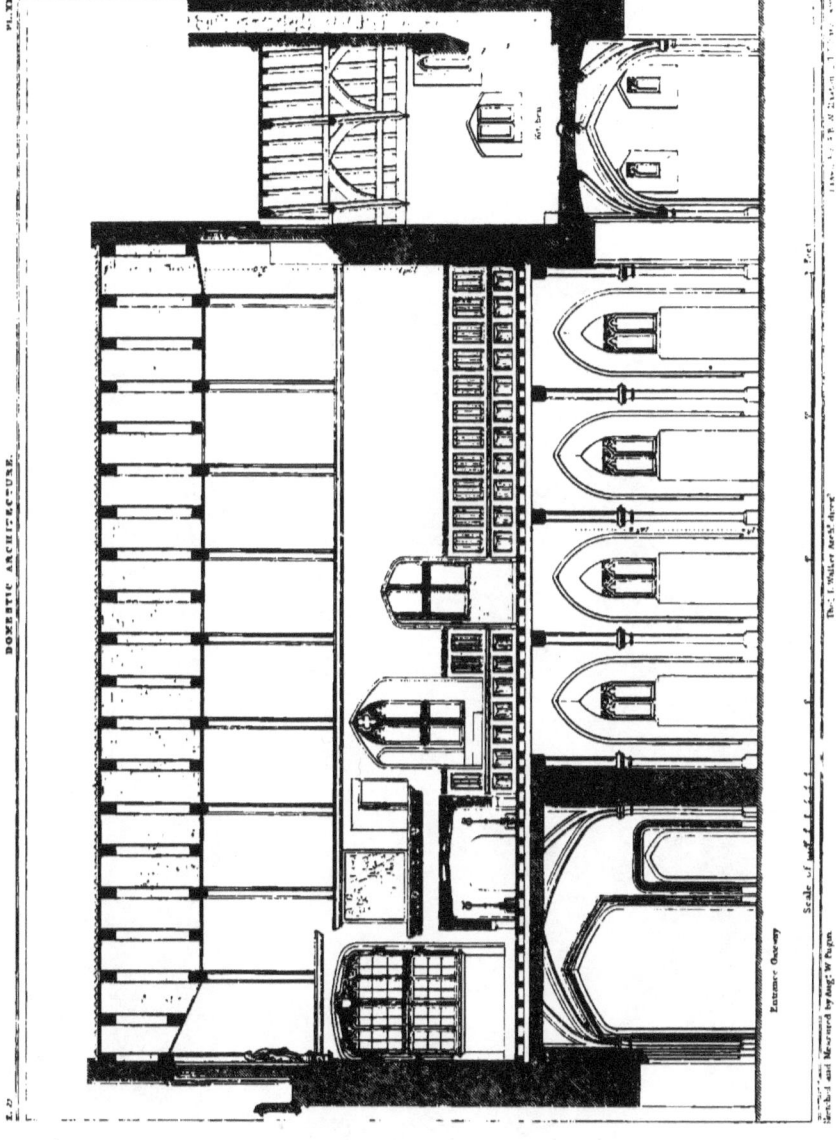

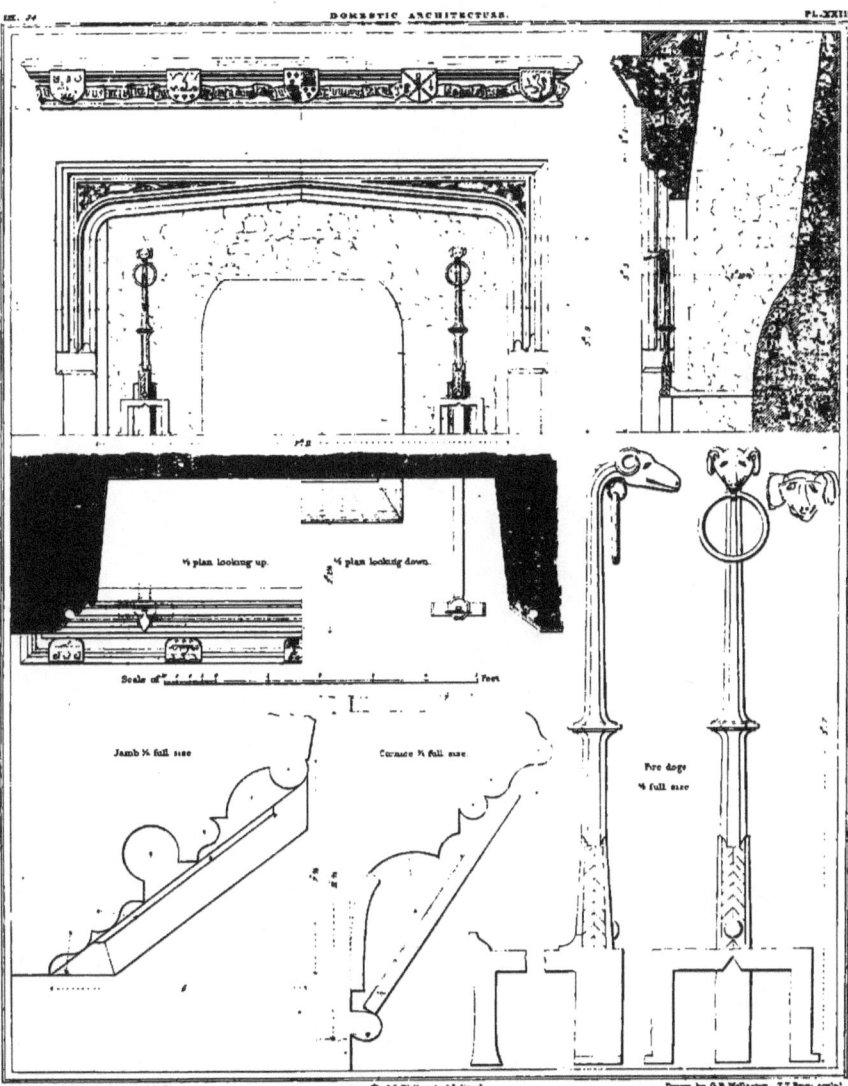

VICARS' CLOSE, WELLS.

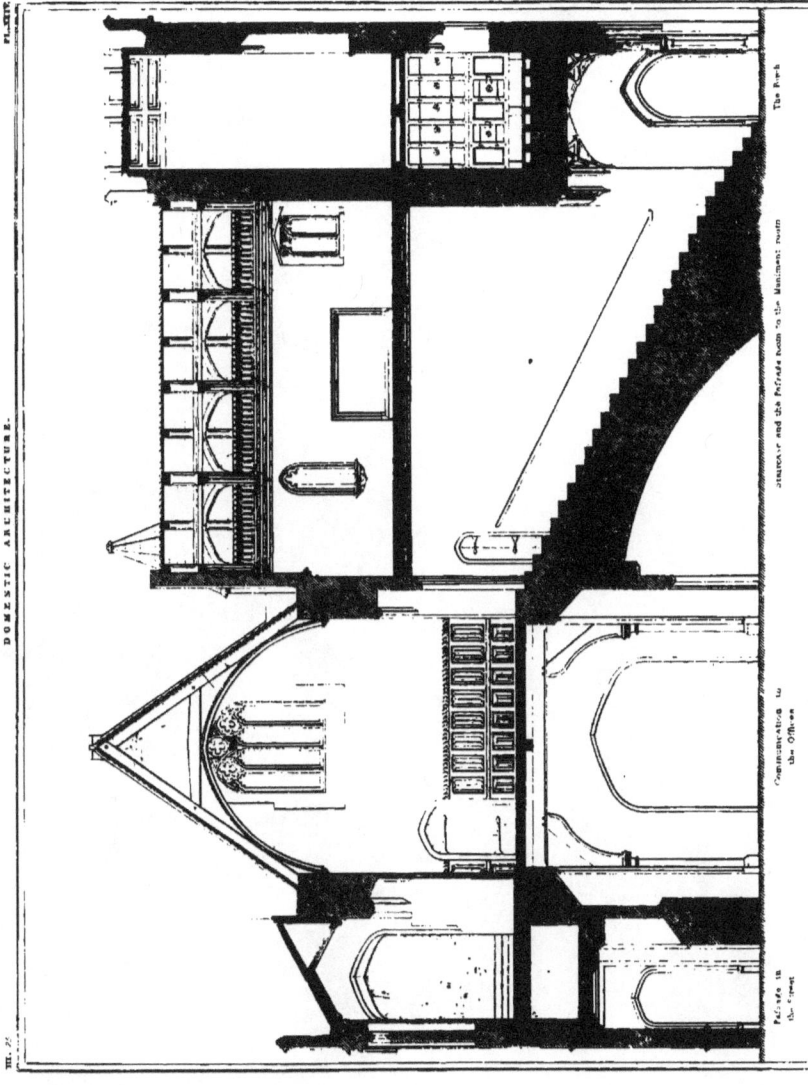

VICARS' CLOSE, WELLS.
THE COMMON HALL.

DOMESTIC ARCHITECTURE

THE

HISTORY AND ANTIQUITIES

OF

The Manor House and Church

AT

GREAT CHALFIELD, WILTSHIRE;

THE PROPERTY OF SIR HARRY BURRARD NEALE, Bart. G.C.B. &c.

ILLUSTRATED BY TWENTY-EIGHT PLATES OF

PLANS, ELEVATIONS, SECTIONS, PARTS AT LARGE, AND
A PERSPECTIVE VIEW;

FROM SKETCHES AND ADMEASUREMENTS TAKEN IN 1836;

FORMING PART II. OF

"Examples of Gothic Architecture,"

THIRD SERIES:

ACCOMPANIED BY

Historical and Descriptive Accounts,

BY THOMAS LARKINS WALKER, ARCHITECT,
HONORARY TREASURER OF THE ARCHITECTURAL SOCIETY OF LONDON.

Edinburgh
JOHN GRANT
31 GEORGE IV. BRIDGE
1895

Examples

of

Gothic Architecture:

THIRD SERIES.

LIST OF PLATES CONTAINED IN PART II.

THE MANOR HOUSE AND CHURCH AT GREAT CHALFIELD, WILTSHIRE.

1. Perspective View from the North West, restored.
2. General Ground Plan.

THE MANOR HOUSE.

3. Ground and First Floor Plans.
4. North Front, and Figures terminating the Gables at large.
5. Longitudinal Section, Details of Roofs, &c.
6. Two Transverse Sections, Figures terminating the Gables at large, &c.
7. Elevation and Section of the Semicircular Oriel Window, North Front.

8.	Plans and Details of the Semicircular Oriel Window, North Front.
9.	Interior Elevation and Details of ditto, ditto.
10.	Window of Bay of Hall, and Window of Hall, ditto.
11.	Elevation and Section of the Octagonal Oriel Window, ditto.
12.	Plans and Details of ditto, ditto.
13.	Plan and Section of the Porch, and Details, ditto.
14.	Plan of the North-East Bay of the Hall, and Details.
15.	Three Square-headed Windows, and Details.
16.	Elevation and Section of the Fireplace in the Hall, and Details of Chimney-shafts.
17.	Elevation of the Oak Screen in the Hall, and Details.
18.	Panelling at large of ditto and Details.
19.	Large Bosses in the centre of the Hall-ceiling, Masks in the Hall, at large, and Details.
20.	Small Bosses, executed in Plaster, at large, and restoration of one compartment of Hall-ceiling.

THE CHURCH.

1.	West Elevation and Longitudinal Section.
2.	Transverse Section, Plan, and Details of the Oak-ribbed Ceiling of the Chapel, and of the Arch-mouldings.
3.	Porch at large, and Details.
4.	Belfry and West Window at large, and Details.
5.	Stone Screen and Details.
6.	Back Elevation of Top of ditto, Coats of Arms, and Details.
7.	Oak Seat and Desk, and Stone Piscina, at large, and Details.

TOMB IN CORSHAM CHURCH, WILTS.

8.	Tomb of Thomas Tropenell, Esq., and Agnes, his Wife, in the Chantry.

A

HISTORICAL ACCOUNT

OF THE

Manor House and Church,

AT

GREAT CHALFIELD, WILTSHIRE.

GREAT, or EAST CHALFIELD,* is a small parish in the hundred of Bradford, Wiltshire, situate between the towns of Bradford and Melksham, and about four miles from each. It is supposed to have been an outpost of the Romans, guarding a road of communication which crossed the main road from the camp on *Kingsdown*, near Bath, to the station, *Verlucio*, and the camp on *Roundaway-Hill*, near Devizes, and thence to have derived its name—CHALDEFELD, implying the *seat or post on the line of passage leading to the heights*; *Cal* meaning *an eminence*—the *h* being inserted by the Saxons to soften the *c* hard; *ed*, a *seat* or *post*; and *feld, the passage*.† Little or nothing remains, however, of the original fortifications; but the straight line of the road can still be traced along the flat, running, in its northerly direction, into the *Fosseway*, which entered Bath from the north-east.

* It is also written 𝕮𝖍𝖆𝖓𝖉𝖋𝖊𝖑𝖉.—COLLINSON's *History of Somersetshire*, Vol. iii. p. 594. 𝕮𝖍𝖆𝖘𝖋𝖊.—HOARE's *History of Modern Wiltshire, Hundred of Heytesbury*, p. 13. 𝕮𝖍𝖆𝖑𝖉𝖋𝖊𝖑𝖉, 𝕮𝖍𝖆𝖑𝖋𝖊𝖑𝖉, 𝕮𝖍𝖆𝖚𝖋𝖊𝖑𝖉.—*Old MS. in the possession of* WILLIAM WALDRON, Esq., *of Lipiat, Wilts*.

† For this communication the Author is indebted to the Rev. J. Skinner, of Camerton, Somerset, who is well versed in Belgic, British, and Roman Antiquities.

In *Domesday Book* it is thus noticed under **Wilteschire**:—

"XXV. TERRA ERNVLFI DE HESDING. IPSE ER. ten. CALDEFELLE. Wallef. tenuit T. R. E. 7 geld. p. II. hid 7 diñi. Tr̃a. ē. II. car. De ea. ē in dñio. 1 hida. 7 diñi. 7 ibi. l. cař. cũ. l. servo. 7 IIII. borđ. Ibi dim moliñ. redđ XVII. deñ 7 VI. āc. "p̃ti. 7 VI. ac̃ siluæ 7 VIII. āc. pasturæ. Valluit IIII. liƀ. Modo. L. soliđ."*

IPSE ER. teñ. in ead. villa tantđ tr̃æ p uno m̃l. Godvin tenuit T. R. E. Ibi tantđ habeī qtũ in supiori c̃tineī 7 tn̄tđ appciaī.†

In Edward the First's days, the Manor of Great Chalfield was a whole knight's fee, and was held, by knight's service, by one Sir William Rous of the Earl of Salisbury, as part of the honour of Trowbridge (which honour belonged to the duchy of Lancaster), free from all services and demands; and, by virtue of this Manor, Rous and the Lords of Chalfield, for the time being, were constables of Trowbridge Castle.‡ To this office belonged a place in Trowbridge called the Logge Place, afterwards the site of a garden called the Logge Plot. Great Chalfield afterwards came into the possession of a family of the name of *Percy*, which, from the arms shewn in Plate VI. *Ecclesiastical Architecture*: viz., *azure*, five fusils in fesse *or*,§ must have been a younger branch of that of William de Percy, a Norman chieftain, who accompanied William the Conqueror into England, who left *four sons* and two daughters. He was succeeded by his eldest son, Alan de Percy, surnamed the *Great*, who was succeeded by his eldest son, William de Percy, at whose decease the eldest branch of the first race became extinct in the male line, and his whole inheritance devolved upon his two daughters, Maud and Agnes; by which circumstance, and the marriage of the latter (the former dying *sine prole*) with Joceline Barbatus, the ancient Percy Arms were lost, although the surname was retained.

---

* DOMESDAY BOOK, 70 A.
† This refers to LITTLE or WEST CHALFIELD.
‡ *Old MS. in the possession of* WILLIAM WALDRON, *Esq. of Lipiat:* "In 4th of King Stephen, when Maud, "daughter to King Henry I. (commonly called Maud the Empress), landed in England with her brother Robert, earl "of Gloucester, Humphrey de Bohun, at the incitation of Milo, earl of Hereford, his wife's father, fortified his Town "of *Trobregge* against King Stephen, in such sort as that it was impregnable."—DUGDALE's *Baronage*, Vol. I. 179.

§ These were the ancient arms of **Percy**, until Agnes, daughter and coheiress of William Percy, married Joceline, younger son of Godfrey Barbatus, duke of Lower Lovain and count of Brabant. Her ladyship would not consent of this great alliance unless Joceline would adopt either the surname or the arms of Percy; the former of which he accordingly assumed, and retained his own paternal coat in order to perpetuate his claim to the principality of his father, should the elder line of the reigning duke at any period become extinct. The matter is thus stated in the great old pedigree at Sion House: "The antient arms of Hainault this Lord Joceline retained, and gave his children the surname of Percy," who afterwards became Dukes of Northumberland.—BURKE's *Peerage and Baronetage*, Vol. II. p. 241. *London*, 1832. See, also, GOUGH's *Sepulchral Remains*, Vol. I. Part XCV. DRAKE's *Antiquities of York*, Plate at p. 535, which are the arms drawn by some curious person from the windows of the Cathedral and Chapter House, in A.D. 1641, most of which were existing when Drake wrote.

In a MS. now in the possession of William Waldron, Esq. relating to Great Chalfield, there is a pedigree given of the *Percys, Knights of Great Chalfield*, but which does not trace the lineage further back than *circa* A.D. 1180. In the former part of it are extracts from a Mr. Dickenson's Vellum Book,* and runs thus: "Here the booke goes on again in another place, and says, y^t y^e" "above Sr William† an Agnes dyed; after whose death ye s^d second son, Sr Harry," "son of ye s^d Will: & Agnes, entered on ye Man^r of Chaldfield, & ye other Man^{rs}," "as son and heir to the said William, who took to wife Eve, daughter of" "John Gifford, Lord of Broughton Gifford, in Wiltshire, who had Sr Roger," "Sr Walter, & Sr William, Knights and Juhan; the said Sr Walter, S^r" "William, and Juhan, dyed without issue, and Eve dyed, after whose decease" "the said Sr Roger entered on ye Man^{rs} at Chaldefeld and elsewhere, as son and" "heir of the Sr Harry, who took to wife Dorothey Ryvers, Lord of Burgate, in" "Southamptonshire."

"Sir Roger and Dorothey had issue Sr Harry Percy, Knight the third, John," "and Emmot; ye s^d John and Emmot dyed without issue; the said Roger" "and Dorothey dyed; and, after their decease, ye said Sir Harry Percy the" "third, as son and heir of the said Sir Roger, entered upon all the Man^{rs}, &c.," "who toke to wife Alianore, daughter of Sir Walter Skydmore, Knight, Lord of" "Upton Skydmore (in A.D. 1301), in Wiltshire, ye s^d Sr Harry & Alianore had" "Issue a daughter called Beatrice, and none other child. Y^e said Alian^{re}" "dyed; Sr Harry, ye son of Sir Roger, overlived, who took to a second" "wife, Constance, bedfellow & cousin to Master Robert Wayvile,‡ Bishop of" "Sailsbury, born to no arms nor lands, wch Sr Harry gave his estate at Chald-" "feld, to Constance, for life, and some grant likewise to ye Bishop." "But" "Constance, marrying a second husband,§ and proving very naughty, & by y^e" "w^{ch}, with too great concessions of her first husband, long and expensive suits" "arose about the Manor of Chaldfield; but, at length, about 24. Hen. 6.,"

* Original MS. at Monks (vellum), in 1744, contained charters and grants relating to twenty-eight parishes. Mr. Waldron made inquiries about it, but unsuccessfully, and supposes that it is now in the possession of a family of the name of Mordaunt.
† This WILLIAM DE PERCI DE CHADENFELD was living in the time of Richard I.—See *Rotuli Curiæ Regis*, Vol. i. p. 245; also, at p. 248, where it is written KALDEFELD; also, pp. 266, 324.
‡ Bishop of Salisbury from A.D. 1330, to 1375.
§ Constance, widow of Sir Henry Percy, must have married Henry de la Rivers; since, from A.D. 1404, to A.D. 1419, according to the *Register at Salisbury*, the patroness of Great Chalfield was "Constantia, nuper uxor Henrici de la Ryver."

B

"Thomas Trapenell recovered the greatest part, and afterwards y⁰ whole," "except y⁰ Constableship of Trowbrige Castle, wᶜʰ of right belonged to y⁰" "Manʳ of East Chaldfield."

In the time of Edward III., Phillip Fitzwaryn held the manors of Chalfield and Trowbridge, and in that year granted a part to the court of Edyngton.*

The next person whom we find patron of the living at East Chaldfeld is "Willᵐᵘˢ Rous, Armiger,"† who was Chamberlain to King Henry VI. in virtue of the Manor of Imber; but that he was ever lawful possessor of the Manor of Great Chalfield, does not appear very probable, since Little or West Chalfield belonged to his family; and in the MS. so often referred to, we find the following passage: "In y⁰ 4th of Hen. 6., concerning the Constableship of Trowbridge" "Castle, a dispute arose betwixt y⁰ Duke of Glouɴester and y⁰ Bishop of Win-" "chester, Cardinal of England, & others, Feoffees to y⁰ Duke of Lancaster, of" "wᶜʰ dutchy Trowbridge was parcell—Rouse, Lᵈ of Chaufield, claimed y⁰ same" "office as appurt. to his Manʳ, and was supported by y⁰ Duke Glosester, who" "brought his Servᵗˢ & Foresters from Pewsham and Blackmore forests, and" "defended Rous's possessˢ at Chaufield, and y⁰ office of Constable. Yᵉ sᵈ" "Duke and Rouse went wᵗʰ a great Retinue (to) y⁰ Parleamᵗ at Lincoln, wᵗʰ wᶜʰ" "y⁰ Cardinal was much offended. At length Rous was forced to quit y⁰ office," "and others by y⁰ Duke of Lancaster placed, tho' Rous &, after him, Trapnell" "sued & made great intrest for the office, cou'd never attain, notwithstanding" "they deemed it their inheritance."

Probably Rous held Great Chalfield under Constance, who was life-interested in it as widow of the last Sir Henry Percy, and may have been obliged to render up the possession to Thomas Tropenell at her death, or soon afterwards, which must have taken place between 1419 and 1425. He was Lord of Imber, and patron of that living from 1414 to 1435. In 16th Henry VI., 1438, by a fine levied, he sold the Manor of Imber and Winterbourne Lymington, with the

---

* He was patron of the living in 1361,—see the *Register at Salisbury*, given at page 11, and in the 40th of Edward III. (1366), he, and his wife, Constance, granted a part of the manors of *Chaldfeld* and *Troubragg*, in *Wilts*, "*Rectori & Fr'ibus Domus de Edynton.*"—See "*Callendarium Inquis' post mortem*," Vol. ii. p. 277. In a document in the Dutchy of Lancaster office, under "*Reasonable aid granted to the King to marry the daughter of Henry IV.*," is the following:—"De Dño de Chaldfeld pro uno feodo in Chaldfeld XX¹."

† In HOARE's *Modern Wiltshire*, he is mentioned as having resided latterly (he died, Aug. 12, 30 Henry VI., and was buried at the church of Greyfriars, London, by the name of William Rous of Emmer, in co. Wilts, Esq.) of East Chalfield, which he held under the Earl of Sarum. But this must be a mistake, as we find, in 1411, John Rous of Immere, patron of the chapel at Chaldefeld (meaning West, or Little Chaldefeld), as the name of Philip Lye, the ecclesiastic, proves.—See the Extract of the *Register of Salisbury*, given at p. 11.

advowson of the Free Chapel at Imber, and half the Manor of Folke, with the advowson in Dorset, to Walter, Lord Hungerford, for an annuity to be paid for his life.*

The following is the pedigree of the Family of Tropenell, as given in the MS. before referred to, which the author has preferred embodying into the historical matter, rather than giving it as an Appendix, since it will the better serve to show the manner in which the estate passed into the different families, either by marriage of the heiress or by purchase:

"This is the pedigree of the name and blood of Tropenelles contained"
"wthin ye shire of Wiltshire, Long before ye time that no mind reneweth,"
"& before ye conquest, unto the making ye book never change'd, one S^r"
"Osbert Tropenell, Knight, before the time y^t no mind reneweth, was"
"Lord of the whole Lordship of Sapworth, with ye Lawday and the pa-"
"tronage of ye Same in the County of Wiltshire, wth other, and had Issue"
"two Sons, Sr James, a knight, & Walter, The said Sr Osbert gave to y^e"
"said Walter, parcel of his Lands in Sapworth, & all his Lands & tenants he"
"had in much Sherston, Litle Sherston, Whadden by Ivy Church & Combe,"
"and deyed. Sr James had issue Daughters, Margarete and Luce, which"
"parted ye said Lordship, Margarete had half with the Patronage, and Lucy"
"had other half with ye Lawday; Margarete took to husband, Hugh Paruns,"
"w^{ch}, both by several deeds appointed apart, Anno dno 1260, gave her part by"
"ye name of her Mannor and Church of Sapworth, unto the house of Monkton"
"Farley, and dye'd. Lucy took to husband Sr Leonard Mantrvers, Knight,"
"Lord of Somerford Mantvers, and had Issue together, John Mantvers, which"
"had the keeping of ye King Edwd to his death, which John gave apart of his"
"Lands he had in Sapworth unto ye house of Monkton Farley, keeping in his"
"own hands the Lawday wth all the remnant thereof; the said Walter Trope-"
"nell, the second son, took to wife Catherine, daughter of Sr William Percy,†"
"Sister to Sr Harry Percy Knights Lords of Much Chaldefeld, otherwise called"
"East Chaldefeld, & had Issue together a son, Philipp, and a daughter, Galiana."
"The said Walter gave his Lands he had in Sapworth to Galiana in marriage;"
"and she, about Anno dno ye year 1267, in her Widowhood, gave the same"

* It appears, also, that he had, two years before (1438) granted all his right in Imber, south part, to the Court of Edyngton.—HOARE'S *Modern Wiltshire, Hundred of Heytesbury*, p. 161.

† This marriage is shewn by the arms on the screen in the church (see No. 1, Plate VI. *Ecclesiastical Architecture*): viz., on the *dexter* side of the shield *gu.* a fesse *ar.* engrailed and powdered with *ermine*, between three griffins' heads erased *of the same*, two and one (sometimes they are placed one and two, see Plate VI.), for *Tropenell*; on the *sinister* side *az.* five fusils in fesse *or*, for *Percy*.

HISTORICAL ACCOUNT OF THE MANOR HOUSE

"Lands unto the house of Monktonffarley:* the said Philipp Tropenell took to"
"wife Isawde daughter to Richard Cotell* Lord of Cotells Atteward, otherwise"
"Little Atteward, and had Issue by her, two Sons, Roger Tropenell and John"
"Tropenell, the said Philipp parted his Lands, and ordained to his eldest"
"Son, Roger, all his lands & tenants he had in Whadden & Combe; and"
"all his lands and ten^{ts} he had in Much Sherstone & Little Sherstone, he"
"gave to his second Son, John Tropenell, Roger took to wife Christian,"
"daughter to Sr John Rous,† Lord of Immer, and had Issue together,"
"John Tropenell, which took to wife Agnes daughter to James Lye, Lord"
"of Liniford and had Issue together Harry Tropenell who took to wife"
"Edeth daughter to Walter Roche‡ and younger Bro^r to Sr John Roche,"
"Knight, sones to John the Roche of Bromeham, Wiltshire, Harry & Edeth"
"had Issue together, Thomas Tropenell, Esqr. which had the Liverys of King"
"Harry ye 6th & K. Edward ye 4th Lords of the said Much Chaldefeild, wh^{ch}"
"Thomas Tropenell took to wife Margarete, daughter to William Ludlow,§"

---

* Patron of Atteworth, A.D. 1298.—See SIR THOMAS PHILLIPP's *Institutions in Wiltshire*, p. 1.

† This marriage is shewn on the next shield: viz., on the *dexter* side, the *Tropenell* arms, and, on the *sinister* side, impaled *az*. and *gu*. three lions rampant *argent*, powdered with *ermine*, armed with *gules*, for *Rous*. There is an altar tomb, of good workmanship, in a chantry, formerly belonging to the Tropenells, at the north side of the church at Corsham, under which Roger Tropenell and his ,wife lie buried. It is, in design, very similar to that shewn in Plate VIII. *Ecclesiastical Architecture*, but smaller. Two sides of it are seen, the other two being placed against the north and east walls; the south side has three quatrefoils, in which are as many oblong shields, with a mantle falling over at top and bottom. The shields are slightly curved. The centre one, on the south side, bears the *Tropenell* and *Rous* arms impaled in one; the left hand (the heraldic *dexter*) bears the *Tropenell* arms, and the right (the heraldic *sinister*) has the *Rous* arms. The west end has one quatrefoil, in which is a shield, similar to the others, bearing the *Rous* arms. The east end must have been ornamented, and probably had the *Tropenell* arms. The north side seems never to have been ornamented, but designed to abut against the wall.

‡ This marriage is shewn on the same screen, at No. 3, on the same plate: viz., on the dexter side of the shield, the *Tropenell* arms as before, and, the *sinister* side, *az*. three roaches *ar*. within a bordure *or*. for *Roche*.

§ This marriage is also shewn on the same, at No. 4: viz., as before, on the dexter side the *Tropenell* arms, and on the *sinister*, *or*. a chevron *sa*. between three bears' heads erased of the same, for *Ludlow* of Hill Deverill. Sir Richard Colt Hoare gives the latter, in his *History of Modern Wiltshire*, among the arms of the families in the *Hundred of Heytesbury*, and also the same, but martins', instead of bears', heads, in another page. In the pedigree there given of *Ludlow*, the fourth daughter of *William Ludlow*, the first of that name, as of *Hill Deverill*, marries *Thomas Trapnell*, or Tropenell, of Chavile, co. Wilts, Esq. The Christian name of this lady is not mentioned; but it must have been *Agnes*, and not *Margaret*, since *Margaret*, who was the eldest daughter, married *William Sandes*, and at a court held at Corsham "upon the Morrow of Saint Bartholomew the Apostle, in the *twentyeth* Year of the reign of *King Henry*,"
"the Sixth after the Conquest, came Thomas Tropenell, who holds of the Lord to him and his Heirs, according to"
"the custom of the mannor, &c. One Mess^e and one Yard Land, with the appurts in Newton called le Eyres, and"
"surrendered into the hands of the Lord the Messuage and Yard Land afores^d, with the appurts, to the use of him-"
"self and *Agnes* his wife, Robert Hungerford, Knight, and Robert Hungerford, Esqr. (their Attorneys). This must"
have been on his marriage, as he was admitted tenant to the same Messuage "At a court held there on Monday"
"next after the feast of the Body of Christ, in the *sixteenth* Year of the Reign of King Henry, the Sixth after the"
"Conquest," which seems to have been his first purchase, for which he paid "to the Lord for a Herriot, 12 shillings,"
"according to the antient custom," and "for a Fine 13 shillings and 4 pence."—*Copies of Court Roll and Surrenders of Lands, &c., in Corsham, in the same MS.*

"Lord of Hill Deverell. In the last year of Edward IV. Mr. Tho' Tropenell, of" "East Chalfield, was living, which was in y* year 1483, who probably lived many" "years after."* Here the author imagines the pedigree to be incomplete, as the Thomas Tropenell who married the fourth daughter of William Ludlow, butler to the kings, Henry IV., V., and VI., must have been the projector of the Manor House at Great Chalfield, and had livery of the estate from King Henry VI. and King Edward IV. He recovered it, after infinite litigation, in the 24th year of the reign of Henry VI., A.D. 1446; whereas the Thomas Tropenell, who was father to Jane married to Mr. John Eyre, we find patron of the living, A.D. 1535, eighty-nine years afterwards, which would make him about one hundred and fifty years of age; in 1526, a John, and in 1528, a Thomas, presented to the living; both of whom must have been sons to Thomas who married Miss Ludlow. The former must have been the elder, and died *sine prole*, and the latter must have been father to Jane, married to Mr. John Eyre, who jointly presented to the living in 1555. Thomas married Elianore, daughter of Thomas Englefield, of Englefield, knight,† and "had issue together, two sons," "Humphrey and Christopher, and two daughters, Anne and Mary. John Trope-" "nell of Sherstone (this is second son to Philip Tropenell) had issue, John and" "Agnes, wedded to Thomas Ivy, Lord of Sherstone, which had issue together," "John Ive, otherwise named himself John Trapnell, and Harry a younger son." "But Tho' leaving behind him Issue, only one Son & two daughters, the son," "being at Mans estate dyed by an unfortunate accident as he was hunting: he" "put a pair of dog couples over his head, persued his sport, &, leaping over a" "hedge, the end of the dogg couple, wch hung at his back, took hold of a" "bough, kept him from ground untill he was strangled. His two sisters," "Ann & Mary, coheirs, the eldest married Mr. John Eyre, the other, Mr." "Young, of Little Dunford,‡ in the County of Wilts, wch estate went to the" "Youngs by y^t marryage. Mr. Eyre, by ye eldest sister, had a son, William," "and six daughters.§ The eldest daughter marryed Mr. Green, of Milton in" "Somersetshire; another, Mr. Beausham, of Cottles, in ye parish of Attward,"

* He died A.D. 1490; was feoffee to Robert, Lord Hungerford, A.D. 1487; and had a son named Christofer.—See SIR THOMAS PHILLIPP's *Institutions in Wiltshire*, pp. 170, 174.

† See pedigree of Thomas Englefeld, at p. 83, I'h. 9, in *College of Arms*, which varies much from this MS.; as *Thomas de Tropnelle ar.*, who married *Eleanore Englefeld*, had four daughters: viz., *Anne*, mar. to *Ayers*, of *Wiltshire*; *Elizabeth*, mar. to *W^m*. *Ogane*, yoman; *Mary*, mar. to *John Younge*, of *Wiltshire*, and *Eleanore*, mar. to *Andrew Blackmor*, yoman, and only one son, viz., *Giles de Tropnelle*, who died younge.

‡ In a pedigree of Younge, of Dorneford, this marriage is given; but *Egidius Trapnell de Chaufield*, and not *Thomas*, is given as the name of the father of Mary. This, however, must be a mistake; as the pedigree of Englefeeld, cited above, clearly shews it is the same person.—See 1. C. 22, 26^b. in *College of Arms*.

§ In BURKE's *History of the Commoners of Great Britain*, four daughters only are mentioned.

"or Attford, in Wilts; Mr. Scroope, of Castle Combe, another; one other to"
"Mr. Burdet, a family in Berks; one to Mr. Dantsey, in Gloucestershire; one"
"to Mr. Quintine, of Corton, in Hilmarton parish, Wilts. The son, afterwards"
"Sr William, marryd Anne, daughter of Sr Edwd Bainton, of Bromeham,"
"Wilts^r, by whome he had three sonnes, John, afterwards Sr John, Edwd, &"
"William, afterw^{ds} Sr Edwd & Sr William. Sr John had Chaldfield, and dyed,"
"leaving no Issue. Edward, the second son, dyed unmarryed. S^r W^m his"
"youngest son, had Nestone, wch S^r W^m left one son, William,* whose Issue male"
"failing, ye Estate Nestone came to his daughter, Mrs Jane Eyre, who marryd"
"Sr John Hanham, Bar^t., of Wymbourn, Dorsetshire, who inherited Great"
"Chalfield, Nestone, &c. & sold Chalfield to M^r. Hall. Sr Wm Eyre of Chal-"
"field, after ye death of Anne, his first wife, marryd ye daughter of Alderman"
"Jackson, of London, by whome he had two sons, Robert & Henry. To"
"Robert he gave Little Chaldfield, or West Chaldfield, lately sold to Mr Baynton,"
"who left it to his youngest son, Thos. Baynton; & Mr. Thos. Baynton's wife"
"had a daughter by Mr Hall: he gave her all his estate; and this lady marryd"
"ye marquis of Dorset,† was mother to the last duke of Kingston, who sold"
"Great Chalfield to Neale.‡ He had also three daughters, Anne, Lucie, &"
"Olive. Anne married Jno, eldest son of Sr Walter Long, of Draycut, Bar^t;"
"Lucie marry'd W^m. Stafford, of Marlewood, in Gloucestershire, Esq. Olive"
"dyed unmarried, 1695."

> "As leafs from trees, mankind do drop away,"
> "So sonnes of mortals fleurish and decay:"
> "What mortals build, time does in Rubbish lay,"
> "As fates decree ye destinies obey."

William Percy and Agnes, the first mentioned in the pedigree of Percy, must have had a daughter, Catherine, who married Walter Tropenell, second son of

---

* In 14th of Charles the 1st (1638), the manor and the patronage of the church at Great *Chawfield*, was a whole knight's fee, annexed to the Duchy of Lancaster, and was held by Richard Gurnard, and the heir of Sir William Eyre, together with the constableship of Troubridge Castle; and then consisted of a thousand acres of land in Chalfield, Holt, and Lynefford.—*An Account of the Knights' Fees, and Parts of Fees, in the County of Wilts, annexed to the Duchy of Lancaster. Roll in the Duchy of Lancaster Office.*

† This ought to be *Dorchester*, son of Evelyn Pierrepoint, fifth earl of Kingston, created Marquis of Dorchester, 1706, by Queen Anne, and Duke of Kingston by George I., which title became extinct upon the death of Evelyn, then duke of Kingston, 23d September, 1773, who "must have married the daughter of Mr. Hall by the wife of" "Thos. Baynton."—See DUGDALE's *English Peerage*, vol. ii. pp. 18, 19, *Extinct Peerage, London,* 1790. Also BURKE's *Extinct and Dormant Peerage*, p. 420.

‡ Robert Neale, Esq., of Shaw House, near Melksham, Wilts, was a descendant of the O'Neales, dukes of Tyrone, Ireland.—See the Pedigree, *D.* 6. 14. *in College of Arms;* also, *Keating's History of Ireland.*

Sir Osbert Tropenell, Knight. As, in the pedigree of the Tropenells, "the said" "Walter, the second son, took to wife Catherine, daughter of Sʳ William Percy," "sister to Sir Harry Percy, Knights, Lords of Much Chaldefeld, otherwise called" "East Chaldefeld," and by this marriage and the failure of male issue to Sir Harry Percy, the third knight of that name, the estate, after much litigation, was recovered by Thomas Tropenell, Esq.,* who married Agnes, fourth daughter of William Ludlow, Lord of Hill Deverell, and who, by the arms now existing on a shield in the roof of the noble banqueting hall at Great Chalfield, shewn in Plate XIX., which are those of Ludlow of Hill Deverell, as, also, by those on the elegant stone screen in the church, shewn at No. 4, Plate VI., must have been the projector of THE MANOR HOUSE at GREAT CHALFIELD, which is the immediate subject of research; and than which there cannot be found a more interesting example of *Domestic Gothic Architecture.*

Thomas Tropenell, and Agnes, his wife, lie buried under a magnificent altar-tomb, in a chantry, formerly belonging to his family, in Corsham church, Wilts,† which is shewn in Plate VIII., *Ecclesiastical Architecture*, on which the *Tropenelle* and *Ludlow* arms appear, together with the motto which he seems to have adopted: viz., **Le joug tyra bellement,** which we also find on the ceiling of the hall at Great Chalfield in various places, and introduced in various ways (see Plates XIX. and XX.), but always with the representation of a yoke, such as was formerly used for oxen, forming the nominative case to the verb *tyra.* Whether this was expressive of the tenure under which he held the manor, or whether it applied to politics, or to agricultural pursuits, is not easy, at this remote period, to determine; but it proved sadly prophetic of the melancholy manner in which his race became extinct, in less than a century afterwards, as mentioned in the pedigree above cited.

The author has to regret the absence of any kind of document as to the real date of the erection of the building, beyond those he has given; which, however, sufficiently warrant him in ascribing it to the latter end of the reign of Henry the Sixth. Since then, nothing has been added to its beauties. The long range of offices to the right, and the barns, seem to have been built in Queen Elizabeth's time; and, in the guest chamber, a very elaborate fireplace was inserted, by which the hand of destruction first went to work, in cutting up,

---

* He was feoffee, in A.D. 1453, to Robert Lye, and, in A.D. 1486, to Robert, Lord Hungerford.—See SIR THOMAS PHILLIPP'S *Institutions in Wiltshire.*

† This Chantry Chapel seems to have descended with the estate of Neston, as Mr. Fuller of Neston is the present proprietor.

into the oak-ribbed roof, to admit of this singular design of meretricious taste, which forms a very striking contrast to the elegant semicircular oriel window in the same room, shewn in Plates VII. VIII. and IX.; and which contrast would be quite sufficient, independent of any other proof, to convince the advocates of what is generally termed *Elizabethan Architecture*, of the infinite superiority of good taste prevalent in the fifteenth century. Buildings, in which the original offices were contained, were then pulled down to the south of the left wing, at *x. x. x. x.* Plate III., by which the present external south wall, which was originally an internal division, has been exposed, and the head of the furthest truss to the south was cut away, to form a hip to the roof, by which means the rafters have pushed out, and endangered the east wall. The present possessor, Sir Harry Burrard Neale, to whom this estate came by his marriage with Grace-Elizabeth, daughter and co-heiress of Robert Neale, Esq., whose father was the purchaser from the Duke of Kingston, anxious to preserve this truly venerable fabric, has intrusted the author with the necessary repairs.

The CHURCH at Great Chalfield, which is dedicated to All Saints, bears evident signs of greater antiquity than the present Manor-House; and, in 1308, a *chapel* existed here, to which "Walterus de Chaldefeld" presented "Wm de Cumbe," the walls of which, the author presumes, still remain, forming the body of the present church,—the west window having been an insertion, and the bell turret an addition of a later date. The porch, also, which is peculiar, and of elegant design, seems to have been added, together with the present west doorway, about the time of Henry VII. Thomas Tropenell, who built the manor-house, erected a beautiful chantry chapel to the south, and enclosed it with a rich stone screen, of excellent workmanship, adorned with the arms of his family, shewing its descent from the *Percys*, to the time of erection (see Plates V. and VI., *Ecclesiastical Architecture*, and descriptions). A chancel must have existed eastward of the present church, which has been rebuilt, and, in 1775, added to, southward, to the extent of the chantry chapel, when an arch was cut through the east wall of this chapel, by which the cornice of the ornamental oak ceiling was injured. The floor of the church was raised one foot eight inches, in 1765,[*] and the *whole*

---

[*] The Parchment Register, now in the church, commences in 1545, 25 January, "In die conversionis Sancti Pauli," and the following are the entries concerning the church repairs:—
"The church of Chalfield Magna was set in good repair, A.D. 1719:—viz., the roof was new laid, and a large buttress set up on the north side; and the body of the church was new ceiled."

"JOHN LEWIS, *Rector*."
"THO^s. MILES, *Church Warden*."

church white-limed and painted. By the former, the base of the stone screen, which had before been removed to its present position, namely, under the arch between the church and the chancel, was buried; the screen itself was much injured, and some elegant fresco paintings on the walls of the chantry chapel were covered, portions of which now are visible; and, although the present worthy rector, the Rev. Richard Warner, is most anxious to have these renovated, they are so completely destroyed by this barbarous practice, that they must only remain as proofs of the magnificence of past ages. Mr. Warner has done much towards restoring other portions of the church, particularly the west window, and has enriched the other windows with stained glass.

The following is a list of the Patrons and Rectors of Great and Little Chalfield, as given in Sir Thomas Phillipps' "Institutiones ex Registro Novæ Sarum Episcopi:"—

	CAPELLA VEL ECCLESIA.	PATRONUS.	CLERICUS.
1308	Capell. Chaldefeld	Walterus de Chaldefeld	Wm de Cumbe
	Capell. Chaldefeld	Walterus de Chaldefeld	Robertus de Broghton
1316	Capel. Chaldefeld Magna	Rogerus de Percy	Johannes de Mere
1338	Cap. Chaldefeld Magna	Henricus le Percy	Johannes de Chaldfeld Magna
1338	Capel. Chaldefeld Magna	Henricus de Percy, Dominus de Chaldfeld Magna	Henricus de Lodyngton
1341	Capel. Chaldefeld	Henricus Percy	Johannes Pilk
1348	Capel. Est Chaldefeld	Henricus Percy, Miles	Johannes Gore *p. m.* Johannis Pilk
1349	E. Chaldefeld Magna	Henricus Percy, Miles	Johannes Pacy, *p. r.* Johannis Gore
1354	E. Chaldefeld Magna	Henricus de Percy, Miles	Ricardus Trymenet, *p. r.* Johannis Spacy
1361	E. Chaldfeld Magna	Philippus *fils.* Waryn, Miles	Thomas Alayn (*qui resignavit Chaldefeld Parva*)

"The Chancel was set in good repair, Anno Domini 1722, cost £3 : 5 : 8. J. LEWIS, *Rector.*"
"The Chancel was again repaired, A.D. 1747. J. LEWIS, *Rector.*"
"The floor of Chalfield Church was raised one foot and eight inches, and now laid, new forms were set up, and" "*the whole church white-limed* and painted, and a canopy placed over the pulpit, A.D. 1765."
"CLEM^t. GLYNN, *Rector.*"
"The Chancel was again repaired : viz, the roof new laid and ceiled, the floor raised one foot and three inches," "and the seats painted, A.D. 1765 ; cost £15 : 14 : 1."
"C. GLYNN, *Rector.*"
"J. MILES, *Church Warden.*"

	CAPELLA VEL ECCLESIA.	PATRONUS.	CLERICUS.
1362	E. Chaldefeld Parva	Prior de Worspryng, ob minor. ætatem Johannis filii Thomæ Perci	Johannes Wilde, p. m. Reginaldi de Berleigh
1388	E. Chaldfeld Parva	Johannes Percy de Chalfeld	Philippus Lye, p. r. Johannis Wilde
1404	E. Chaldefeld Magna	Constantia, nuper uxor Henrici de la Ryver	Johannes Mascal
1410	E. Est. Chaldefelde	Constantia, quæ fuit uxor Henrici dela Ryver, Militis	Walterus Wylmot, vice Johannis Mascal
1411	F. Est. Chalvelde	Constantia, relicta H. de la Ryver, Militis	Johannes Plebs, p. r. Walteri Wilmot
1411	E. Chaldefeld (Parva)	Johannes Rous de Immere, Armiger	Johannes Wyseman, vice Philippi Lye
1417	E. Chaldefeld Magna	Constantia, Relicta Henrici de la Ryver, Militis	Johannes Plebs, permut. cum Wmo Beckebury
1419	E. Est Chaldefeld	Constantia Domina de Est Chaldefeld	Johannes Hillewyke
1419	E. Est Chaldefeld	Constancia, nuper uxor Henrici de la Ryver	Radulfus Benet, p. m. Johannis Illewyk
1425	E. Est Chaldefeld	Wmus Rous, Armiger	Tho' Broun
1437	———West Chaldefeld	Johannes Boorne	Ricardus Beauchamp
1445	E. Est Chaldefeld	Episcopus, per laps.	Robertus Benet
1488	E. Chalfield Magna	Episcopus, per laps.	Thomas Langporte
	E. West Chalfeld	Episcopus, per laps.	Thomas Hedley
1494	Capel. de West Chaldefeld	Episcopus, per laps.	Ricardus Norton, p. m. Thomæ Sqwier
1507	Capel. de Chaldfeld Parva, alias West Chaldfeld	Johannes Westbury	Edwardus Huggyns, p. r. Ricardi Norton
1518	E. Chaldefeld Magna, al. Est Chaldefeld	Thomas Tropenell, Armiger	Willielmus Haxe, p. m. Johannis Rede
1525	E. Omnium Sanctorum Chaldfeld Magna	Thomas Trapnell, Armiger	Wmus Haye, permut. cum Johanne Floke
1526	E. Chaldfeld Magna	Johannes Tropnell, Armiger	Johannes Jeffery, p. r. Johannis Floke
1528	E. Chaldfeld Magna	Thomas Tropnell, Armiger	Gulmus Robynson, p. r. Johannis Jefferys
1535	E. Chalfeld Magna	Thomas Tropnell, Armiger	Thomas David, P. R. Gulmi Robynson
1537	Capella de Chalfeld Parva	Wmus Button, Gen: ex concess: Haivisiæ de Westbury, Vid.	Johannes Thyn, p. m. Edwardi Higgons

	Ecclesia.	Patronus.	Clericus.
1555	E. Chaldfild Magna	Johannes Eyre & Anna uxor ejus	Radulphus Hyll, p. m. Thomæ Davys
1575	E. Chaldfield Magna	Johannes Eyre, Armiger	Johannes Ap-Jones, p. r. Edwardi Procter
1593	E. Chaldfield Magna	Regina, per lapsum	Nicholaus Lymbye
1598	E. Chalfield	Wmm Eyre, Miles	Francis Staune
1603	E. Chalfield Magna	Wmm Eyre, Miles de Chalfield	Robertus Bradshawe,* p. d. Francisi Staune

* The following is a copy of an extract from the Registry at Salisbury:—
"Extracted from the Registry of the Lord Bishop of Sarum.—1671."

"Chaldfield } A Terrier of all such Tythes, Profits, and Priviledges as belongeth to the Parsonage of Chald-"
"Magna. } field Magna, in the countie of Wilts, and Dioce of Sarum."

"First, We returne, that there is noo House or outhouses, within our Pish of Chaldfield Magna, that belongeth to"
"the Parsonage, save only one Chamber in the Mannor House, which is commonly called the Minister's"
"Chamber; But antiant men have reported, that they have heard from other antiant men that were before"
"them, that said that there was a Parsonage House which stood in a Ground near the Mannor House, called"
"Parsonage Closse, als Pen Closse."

"Alsoe, Wee returne, that, upon the Report of Antiant Men, Long since dead, there have ben Glebe Lands"
"belonging to the Parsonage of Chaldfield Magna, But that any of this incumbant's predecessors, for many ages"
"past, did ever possess or enjoy them, we never heard, neither is there any Terrier to be found thereof (albeit"
"diligent search have ben made in the courts at London, and else where, by the incumbent."

"Alsoe, We have heard, that one Mr Bradshaw, who was Parson of our said Pish before the Present Incumbent,"
"had his dyett, the keeping of a House, and Sixteen Pound p. Annum, of the owners of the said Mannor of"
"Chaldfield Magna, in Lieu of his Tythes due out of the said Mannor, for the space of Forty Years, and that"
"the p'sent Incumbent hath had, for the space of forty yeares, a composition of two and thirty Pounds yearly,"
"paid him by the owners of the said Mannor in Lieu of his Tythes, and the keeping of a Horse (and besides"
"exempted) and discharged from all taxes and payments whatsoever (except the Tenthes payable to the King's"
"Matt, and procroscums to the Lord Bishop."

"Alsoe, the p'sent Incumbent hath the Tythes of a Farme, called Moxham's Farme, lying within the said Pish,"
"worth to him five Pounds ℔ annum, and the Tyth of a Ground lying within the same Pish, called Bowood,"
"worth ten Shillings ℔ annum."

"Alsoe, the present Incumbent hath received forty Shillings by the yeare from the owners of West Chaldfield,"
"which do usually come to his Church.—John Wilton, Rector.—Christofer Moxham."

"Magna Chalfield.—There is now only paid from the tenant of John Hall, Esqr., whose name is John Sartain, the"
"sum annualy of thirty-two Pounds.—Of Christopher Moxham is received annualy, four Pounds. Witness o'"
"Hands, May 21, 1705.—John Deacon, Rector.—Christ. Moxham, Churchwarden."

"Chalfield Magna.—A true Note and Terrier of all such Tithes, Profits, and Privileges as belong to the Rectory of"
"Chalfield Magna, in the County of Wilts, and Diocese of Sarum."

"First, We return, that there is no House or Outhouses, nor Glebe Lands, belonging to the Parsonage of Great"
"Chalfield."

"Also, We return, that the present Incumbent is paid a composition of Fifty Pounds ℔ Annum, by equal half-yearly"
"payments, in Lieu of all Tithes arising and becoming due from the Manor of Great Chalfield, and is exempted"

14   HISTORICAL ACCOUNT OF THE MANOR HOUSE

	CAPELLA VEL ECCLESIA.	PATRONUS.	CLERICUS.
1029	E. Chalfield, *Magna*	W^{mus} Eyre, *Miles*	Johannes Wilton, *p. m.* Roberti Bradshaw
1678	E. Chalfield, Magna	Johannes Hall, *Armiger*	Michael Poulton, *p. m.* ―― Wilton
1689	E. Chawfield	Johannes Hall, *Armiger*	Johannes Deacon
1707	E. Chaldfield Magna	Johannes Hall, *Armiger*	Thomas Weeks, *p. m.* Johannis Deacon
1711	E. Chalfeld Magna	―― *Comes* Kingston	Gulielmus Skammell,* *p. m.* Thomæ Weeks
1712	E. Chaldfield Magna	W^{mus} *Comes* Kingston	Johannes Lewis, *p. r.* Gulielmi Skamell
1761	E. Great Chalfield	Evelyn, *Duke of* Kingston	Clement Glynn, *p. m.* John Lewis
1809	E. Chaldfield Magna	*Sir* Harry Burrard Neale of Walhampton, Co. Hants, *Bar^t*	Richard Warner,† *p. m.* Clement Glynn

The living is a discharged Rectory in the archdeaconry and diocess of Salisbury, valued in the King's Books at £6. The population of the parish, together with the extra-parochial Liberty of Little Chalfield, was, at the census of 1831, 83 souls. The estate was assessed to the Property Tax of 1815, at £2,920.

"and discharged from all Taxes and payments whatsoever, except the King's Land Tax and Procurations to the "
" Lord Bishop."
" Also, The present Incumbent is paid the yearly sum of three Pounds and ten Shillings, in Lieu of Great and "
" Small Tithes, arising and becoming due on certain Lands in this Parish, belonging to John Blagden, of Grey's "
" Inn, London, Esqr., and now in the occupation of Farmer John Reynolds."
" Also, The present Incumbent hath the Tithe of Hay, Wool, and Lamb, arising on certain Lands in this Parish, "
" belonging to James Moxham, of the City of London, Sugar Refiner; but the agistment Tithes due for "
" dispasturing barren cattel on the same Estate, are not yet settled."
" Also, The present Incumbent is paid the yearly sum of nineteen Shillings in Lieu of the Tithes of a Field in this "
" Parish, called Bowood."
" Also, We return that the Rectory of Great Chalfield hath been augmented with four hundred Pounds, two "
" hundred Pounds of which were from the Governors of the Bounty of Queen Anne, and the other two hundred "
" Pounds the Benefaction of the late Robert Neale, of Corsham, Esqr. the Interest of which, paid yearly, "
" amounts to eight Pounds."
" Witness our hands, the fourteenth day of July, in the year of our Lord one thousand seven hundred and "
" eighty-three.—CLEMENT GLYNN, Rector.—JAMES FRICKER, Churchwarden.—WILLIAM PAIN."
" The above are true Copies and Extracts taken from the Originals, and examined by me,"
"EDW. DAVIES, N.P.—*D. Registrar*."

* Removed to Tetbury in 1712.
† The Rev. Richard Warner, F.A.S., Hon. Mem. of the Imperial Cæsar. Soc. of Nat. Hist. at Moscow, and of the Dutch Soc. of Sciences at Haerlem, &c. &c. ; is Author of "*Hampshire Extracted from Domesday Book*," "*Antiqui-*

tates Culinariæ," "*An Attempt to ascertain the Situation of the Ancient Clausentum,*" "*The History of Glastonbury Abbey,*" and many other works, both on Antiquity and Divinity.

On a tablet, on the south wall in the body of the church, is the following inscription to the memory of the mother of Mrs. Warner:—

Sacred
TO THE MEMORY OF
MRS. ELIZABETH PEARSON,
DAUGHTER AND HEIRESS
OF JOHN LEAKE, ESQ.
OF SALTER'S HILL, SHROPSHIRE;
RELICT OF THOMAS PEARSON, ESQ.
OF TETTENHALL, STAFFORDSHIRE;
AND MOTHER OF ANNE
(HER YOUNGEST DAUGHTER)
THE WIFE OF THE
REV. RICHARD WARNER,
RECTOR OF THIS PARISH:
FULL OF FAITH, HOPE, AND CHARITY,
SHE PUT OFF THIS MORTAL
TO BE CLOTHED WITH IMMORTALITY,
ON THURSDAY MORNING,
THE 12TH DAY OF APRIL, 1832.
BLESSED ARE THE DEAD WHICH DIE
IN THE LORD, FROM HENCEFORTH,
YEA, SAITH THE SPIRIT, THAT THEY
MAY REST FROM THEIR LABOURS, AND
THEIR WORKS DO FOLLOW THEM.
REV. XIV. 13.

DESCRIPTION OF THE PLATES.

THE MANOR HOUSE AND CHURCH AT GREAT CHALDFIELD, WILTS.

PLATE I. THE FRONTISPIECE.

THIS is a *Perspective View*, taken from a point marked ☉ on the General Plan, Plate II., shewing the *Manor House* and the *Church*, restored in those parts which are now either destroyed or altered. A window has been inserted under the right hand Oriel of late years; but the one shewn is as it is supposed originally to have existed, the label being still perfect. The tops of the chimney-shafts are restored from existing documents. In the left wing, a small window has been inserted between the semicircular Oriel and the two-light window on the ground floor, but is omitted in this view, as forming no part of the original design. The wall, which divides the consecrated ground of the Churchyard from the fore court, is shewn pulled down in parts to display the west front of the Church, and the left wing of the Manor House. The entrance from the fore court into the churchyard does not exist, but is introduced, instead of a common wicket, to harmonise better with the other portions.

PLATE II. THE GENERAL PLAN.

This Plate shews the *Plan* of the *Ground* and buildings, which lie within the fortifications; no remains of the original works of the Romans are now discernible. The front is guarded by a *Moat* and *two bastions*, which latter are, in plan, portions of circles, but which, from wooden lintels still remaining over the openings of the loopholes, cannot be of very great antiquity; probably these were rebuilt on old foundations, as, from the thick wall having been taken down at the south of the Church to the point marked *x*, we may safely suppose a fortress to have existed here, prior to the present Manor House; for, if the line of this wall were continued, it would cut into a space which has been occupied by buildings forming part of the house, but now pulled down. The approach at present is by a stone bridge over the moat, where the original entrance existed, as the jamb-mouldings of the *Outer Gateway* still remain, and a drawbridge probably occupied the place of the present stone one. The *Entrance Gateway* to the fore-court is near the extremity of the long range of offices, which extend from the house to within twenty feet of the front wall. The arches of this gateway are much older than the offices themselves, which must have been built about Queen Elizabeth's time, together with the barns, and other out-buildings. The old work extends to a little above the archways. Another *gateway* has existed at the furthest extremity of this range of buildings at *y*, and another at *z*, the latter was the entrance to an *inner court*, the buildings of which are now entirely destroyed. The *Church* stands in an area of irregular figure, now forming the *Churchyard*. The Manor House, from its situation with regard to the Church, must have been built since the latter, as it is not very probable that the architect would wish to obscure a view of the principal front. To the left is a *Mill*, impelled by the water from the Moat, and this building, though modernised, is of great antiquity; and, even at the time of the Domesday survey, *half a mill* existed here, the *other half* probably belonged to the Manor of West or Little Chaldfield. At the back is a *moat* or *fish pond*, which is supplied by natural springs; it is 51 feet wide, and 538 feet long; out of it two smaller *fish ponds*, each 83 feet by 31 feet, are supplied; it empties itself into a *rivulet* which flows parallel with its length, which also receives the water from the mill. The level of the moat at the back is many feet lower than that in front, and that of the rivulet is still lower. The space between the house and the moat, or fish ponds, at the back, is planted out as an orchard. From the rivulet the ground rises rapidly southwards.

THE MANOR HOUSE.

PLATE III. shews a *Ground Plan*, and a *First Floor Plan*, of the Manor House, to a scale of one inch to twenty feet. The *Ground Plan* is expressed by a darker tint, and occupies the top and right hand side of the Plate. Those walls, which are shewn in dotted lines at *x x x x*, have been pulled down, by which the *Staircase*, which led up to the rooms in the left wing, has been removed. The ground floor consists of a *Banqueting-Hall*, 40 ft. 2½ in. by 20 ft. 2½ in. and 20 ft. high, which is entered by a richly groined *Porch*. In this porch, to the right hand, is a *very small loop-hole*, for the convenience of receiving letters, or ascertaining who wished to enter, before the cumbrous *oaken bar* should be withdrawn. Even that precaution was not deemed sufficient, as a *small wicket* was cut in the sturdy *oak door*, across which the bar could be withdrawn, without admitting of the large door to open, the better to guard against intruders. An *oak screen*, very similar to that at Haddon, reaches across the Hall near the door, and forms a *passage*, at the other end of which a door entered into the inner court; outside of this door a *Porch* has existed, but is now pulled down. From the portion of the Hall divided off by the screen, a door led to the left, into the *Dining-room* and *Staircase* now existing. Behind the dining-room is a long narrow room, with a fireplace and two loopholes; below the further loophole, the oak bar of a *Gateway*, now destroyed, ran into the wall; so that this must have been a kind of *Porter's dwelling*, from which a *passage* led to the extremity of the building westward, having loopholes, to enable the Porter to survey those persons who approached the inner court. Out of the dining-room, a door enters, into what is supposed to have been the *Priest's Dwelling*. At the eastern end of the Hall are two *Bays*, richly groined, which communicated with the *Domestic Offices*, now pulled down, and the *staircase* leading to the rooms on the first floor of the left wing, which was approached through a strongly *groined apartment*, lighted by one very narrow window at each side of the buttress supporting the semicircular oriel. At C, a door still exists, which is presumed to have led into the staircase, as the wall at that point has evidently been an interior partition; these being the only rooms without fireplaces, must have served as *passage rooms* to the staircase and offices. The long range of building to the right, built about the time of Queen Elizabeth, contains *Stables*, and other *Offices*, and seems to have been designed to screen the *Barns* and other *Farm buildings* from the front of the house. The *First Floor Plan* is in a lighter tint at the bottom of the Plate, and shews the rich *ceiling of the Hall*; in the left wing, *the Guest Chamber*, and a *small dressing-closet*; this room is lighted by the elegant *semicircular oriel window* at one end, and a four-lighted square-headed window, and another two-light one now blocked up in the east wall; at the further end are two openings, which originally have been *doorways*, leading to other rooms now pulled down. Opposite the small dressing-closet, out of the Guest Chamber, was a similar one over the corresponding Bay of the Hall, from which a *door*, at D, led into the rooms, now pulled down. From these dressing-closets, whatever was passing in the Hall, could be distinctly seen and heard, by means of a small opening in each, disguised in the Hall by a mask (see Plate XIX. and description). In the right wing is a spacious *bed-room*, 29 ft. 4 in. by 17 ft. 9 in., lighted by an *octagonal Oriel Window*, towards the north, and a two-light window and loophole to the west (at C, in this room, is a similar look out into the Hall), out of which was another *small dressing closet*; and from this, and the corresponding one, led two *small staircases* into the roof of the Hall, whereby a private communication might be kept up, without the necessity of going down one staircase, traversing the Hall, and up another. This room, and the guest chamber, seem to have been originally open to the rafters of the roof, as the purlins and braces are moulded, see Plate V. Other explanations are given on the Plate.

PLATE IV. The *North Front*, and the *Figures which terminate the Gables.* This, the principal front of the Manor House, is more regular in design than ancient buildings generally; yet the playfulness of outline is not lost sight of. The richness of the two *Oriel Windows*, the spirit expressed in the figures, and the elegant *Chimney-shaft*, make it a highly interesting subject of study; the beauty of the details will be appreciated in the following Plates. The *two figures* which are on the gables of the Banqueting-Hall, are in the armour of the time of Henry VI., as also the one on the gable of the left wing, which circumstance gives additional weight to the presumed date of erection.*

PLATE V. shews a *Longitudinal Section* through the Hall, the line of which is dotted on the Plans, Plate III. In the Hall are seen the *Entrance Door*, with the *Oak bar* drawn across, and the *small wicket*; the *Screen*; the *Music Gallery* now destroyed; the *Windows*; the *Fireplace*, and the *Archway* into the north Bay, over which is a *mask*, concealing a small look-out from the dressing-closet. To the left is the *Guest Chamber*, and *room* under; below is shewn a section of the *Groined room*; to the right, the *Dining-room* and *Bed-rooms* over; at *c c*, in the roof of the Hall, are the *entrances* to the *small staircases*, leading into the *Dressing-closets*: a compartment of the *roof of each wing* is given at the bottom of the Plate, with its own details. To the left is the base of the *chimney-shaft* at D, and in the centre of the Plate is a *jamb*, found, on the level of the first floor, in the south wall of the left wing, which proves that wall to have been an interior partition; a *section of the base* is also shewn.

* For this information, the author is indebted to the opinion of Sir Samuel Meyrick, F.S.A., than whom no person possesses a better knowledge of ancient armour. In answer to an inquiry on this subject, the author was honoured by the following note :—

"23 *Mount Street, Grosvenor Square,*
3d *May,* 1837.

"Sir Samuel Meyrick presents his respects to Mr. Walker, and, in reply to his inquiry, begs leave to say, that the figures are of the time of Henry VI., *i.e.*, about the fifteenth century. Those in armour wear on their heads the salade; but the other figure has the head-piece, either not correctly represented, or the upper part is modern. It seems to be intended for the visard salade, which, as well as the simple salade, was worn in the time of Henry VI. at any rate, the feet are of the period."

D

DESCRIPTION OF THE PLATES.

PLATE VI. shews two *Transverse Sections* across the Hall, the lines of which are dotted on the Plans, Plate III.; that to the right shews the *Bays* and the *Dressing-closets* over, with the *look-out* through a mask from each into the Hall. At the bottom of the Plate are shewn the *Griffins*, which terminate the small gables of the North Front, holding a shield with the *Tropenell Arms*. These figures are of excellent workmanship, and are designed with great spirit. To the right are given the details of the *carpentry* of the roof of the Hall, and the *oak mouldings* of the ceilings in the dressing-closets.

PLATES VII. VIII. and IX. illustrate the *Semicircular Oriel Window* in the left wing, north front. PLATE VII. shews the *Exterior Elevation* and *Section*; PLATE VIII. *Plans*, sections of *Mouldings*, and the *pateras* in the lower string course; PLATE IX. the *Interior Elevation*, and *various details*. The ornament, which crowns this window, is shewn on a larger scale, and is peculiarly beautiful in effect, though not, perhaps, in drawing; it is extremely light, and appropriate in application: by the bold manner in which it is pierced, and the undulating form of the leaves, any heaviness, which otherwise would exist, is done away: it is commonly termed the *Strawberry-leaf ornament*: but this example differs from any the author has seen, as the circular portions of the leaves, instead of being convex, are concave, which adds greatly to the richness of the whole. The *soffit* inside is richly groined in fanwork, a half plan of which is given in Plate VIII. The *pendants*, which terminate the groining, are peculiar, spreading over the arch moulding. The heads, at the bottom of the Plate to the right, form the brackets of the corbelling outside; see Plate VII. The original *iron fastening* to the window is given half the real size.

PLATE X. gives, at No. 1, the *Window* in the Bay of the Hall, and, at No. 2, the *Window* of the Hall, north front. The labels are terminated by squares placed diagonally, enriched with a leaf in the centre; the *details* explain themselves.

PLATES XI. and XII. shew the *Octagonal Oriel Window* in the right wing. Plate XI. gives an *Elevation* and *Section*: the arms which finish this window at top, are those of *Tropenell*, but seem of later date than the rest of the work; under the *Corbelling* which is panelled, the *label* of a *square-headed window* still exists; the dotted lines shew what the head of the window is supposed to have been, with a strong mullion in the centre, similar to that given in Plate XV.,

No. 2. Plate XII. shews *Plans* double the scale of the Elevation, taken at three different heights, *jamb* and *mullion*, sections of *mouldings* at large, &c.

PLATE XIII. gives the *Entrance Porch* and the *Oak Door* of the Hall. The section shews the *small window* or *loophole*, through which letters might be received in the dining-room, or visitors might be reconnoitred before an entrance was granted them. The Porch is richly groined; two of the *Corbels* consist of angels bearing shields with the *Tropenell Arms*. The primitive *oak bar*, wherewith to secure the door, is still existing. The door consists of two thicknesses of oak; the joints of the outer thickness are laid vertically, and those of the inner horizontally, and are bolted together with large iron nails: the *jambs* of the arches and other details, are given to a larger scale. The *iron handle* of the small door is also shewn.

PLATE XIV. gives a plan and details of the *North Bay* of the Banqueting-Hall, which is also groined; the *rib of the groining* is richly moulded, and is shewn one-fourth full size. In the centre is a shield with the *Tropenell Arms*. The *South Bay* is similar to this, except that the shield in the centre of the groining which is given in this plate, differs in form; it, also, bears the *Tropenell Arms*. At the top of the plate to the right, are shewn the *water table of the buttresses*, and the *set-off* of the base of the great Chimney-shaft; to the left, are *bracket mouldings*, supporting a staircase in the corner (at A) of the North Bay, which leads from the dressing-closet to the roof of the Hall. Other *details* are given, and are referred by letter.

PLATE XV. gives, at No. 1, a small *Square-headed Window* in the dressing-closet, over the South Bay, see Plate VI.: at No. 2, one half of a *long window* in the east wall of the left wing; and at No. 3, one half of a similar *window*, but of later date, in the priest's dwelling. The *jambs* and *mullions* are given at the top of the plate to the right.

PLATE XVI. gives the *Fireplace* of the Hall, and details of the same. The *Spandrils*, which had been plastered up when the author visited Great Chalfield, are shewn to a larger scale, and are very peculiar in character. At the bottom of the plate, are details of the *Great Chimney-shaft* of this fireplace, see Plate IV.: to the left of this, and immediately over the eaves of the small gable, a covering has originally existed for the *Small angular Staircase*, but is now destroyed: this accounts for the irregular way in which the base of the chimney-shaft is finished, and for the precaution taken in cutting a small gutter in the stone-work.

PLATE XVII. shews an Elevation of the *Oak Screen* of the Hall; which does not seem ever to have had doors, as the pinnacles and buttresses of the octagonal uprights, are returned in profile; probably, Arras was hung across the openings: the octagonal uprights, support a beam into which the joists of the Music Gallery floor were morticed, and on which the front of the Gallery rested. This screen has been very similar to the one in the Hall at Haddon;* but the front of the Music Gallery has been destroyed, while that at Haddon is entire. Details are given at the bottom of the Plate referred to the Elevation by letter.

PLATE XVIII. *Details of the Oak Screen;* one of the octagonal uprights is shewn, and the *tracery heads* of the panelling, which in each division are different, are of very superior workmanship. This screen has been very richly painted and gilt; but, from the various coats of white-wash, it is now hastening rapidly to decay; indeed, the bases were with great difficulty made out. The *pinnacle* is shewn one-half full size, and the *mouldings* one-fourth full size.

PLATE XIX. shews at the top, the *motto* adopted by Thomas Trapnell or Tropenell, Esq., the projector of the Manor House, which is **Le joug tyra belement**, the representation of a yoke forming the nominative case to the verb **tyra; belement** is an old French word, *bellement* meaning *well* or *effectually;* so that it might be rendered, *the yoke drew well,* or *the yoke sat lightly.* The yoke is painted white, as, also, the scroll on which the words *Tyra belement* are painted, (the T is pink, and the other letters blue,) on a deep red ground. In the centre of the plate, are shewn the *oak bosses* which ornament the tie-beams of the Hall ceiling. The three centre bosses formerly had shields with coats of arms; the first to the right, still exists as shewn, and bears the *Ludlow Arms* of Hill Deverell, Wilts; viz. *Argent,* a chevron between three bears' heads erased, *sable;* which are those of *Agnes,* wife of Thomas Tropenell, Esq., and fourth daughter to *William Ludlow.* In the centre, it may be presumed, were the *Tropenell* and the *Ludlow* arms on one shield, shewing

* See "RAYNER'S *Account of Haddon Hall,*" illustrated with lithographic plates, imperial 4to.

the marriage; and to the left, the *Tropenell* arms on another shield, as on the tomb in the Chantry at Corsham Church, represented in *Plate VIII., Ecclesiastical Architecture:* these bosses have been richly painted and gilt, as, also, the moulded *tie-beams* and *cornice* shewn at the bottom of the plate, to the left, in section. The *Masks* concealed small openings into the dressing-closets; one seems to represent a *King* with asses' ears, the other a *Bishop;* the eyes and mouths are pierced, so that a person might overlook the Hall without being seen; the head at the top of the plate is for a similar purpose, and overlooks the Music Gallery from the large bed-room.

PLATE XX. *Plaster bosses of the Hall ceiling.* These bosses are shewn one-fourth full size, and are run in plaster with a dark core: they, together with the ribs which subdivided the squares of the Hall ceiling, formed by the tie-beams and the corresponding mouldings in the centre, were taken down a few years ago, as they threatened danger to the inmates, and were presented to the present venerable Bishop of Bath and Wells, of whose valuable collection in the Crypt at the Palace of Wells, they now form part; they shew the *motto* introduced in various ways. At the bottom of the plate is one compartment of the ceiling, which is shewn as it is presumed to have existed with these bosses applied; some represent *oak leaves,* some the *water lily,* and others bear the letters ihc,—*Jesu hominibus crucifixo.*

THE CHURCH.

PLATE I. shews the *West Elevation* and the *Longitudinal Section.* The *Stone Screen* which at present divides the chancel from the body of the Church, is placed in its original situation, which is under the arch between the Chantry Chapel and the body of the Church. The arch in the chancel is modern, and being a segment of a circle, a block of stone has been left to hide the awkwardness of the arch mouldings cutting obliquely on the capitals. The levels of the floor have been raised at different times, but the original levels are here shewn. The walls of the body of the Church are certainly more ancient than the other portions, and must have been those of the original Chapel, which existed here as early as A.D. 1308. The *West Window,* the *Porch,* and the *Bell-Turret,* have been additions, about the time of Henry VII.

PLATE II. gives a *Ground Plan* of the whole Church as it now exists, and a *Transverse Section* through the Church and *Chantry Chapel*, which latter has a good *oak-ribbed ceiling*, ornamented with pateras and *coats of arms*. In the centre of this ceiling, the *Tropenell* Arms and the *Ludlow* Arms on one shield, evidently shew that the Chapel was an after addition to the Church, by the same person who built the Manor House. The other two shields bear the *Tropenell Arms* singly. That part of the *Chancel* which is immediately eastward of the body of the Church is rebuilt on old foundations; but that part eastward of the Chapel, was added by Robert Neale, Esq., as the tablet over the small door, with the initials R. N., and the date A.D. 1775, indicates: by this addition, the segmental arch in the south wall of the Chancel, and the elliptical one in the east wall of the Chapel, were made, which do not add at all to the beauty of the building; indeed, by the latter, the oak cornice of the Chapel has been injured. The walls of the Chapel were adorned with fresco paintings, which have been destroyed by white-wash: they seem to have been historical subjects from the Bible: the details are referred by letter.

PLATE III. shews the Elevation, Section, and Profile of the *Porch*, which, though of late date, is of elegant design; the soffit is enriched by panels with tracery heads; the *details* are referred by letters.

PLATE IV. gives, on one side, one-half the Elevation and one-half the Section of the *Bell-Turret* and *Crocketted Spire;* plans of the same at three different heights and details. The other side of the Plate shews the *West Window* and its details. Round the bell is the following inscription:—RP ANNO DOMINI 1622, and the royal arms of England as at that time worn.

PLATE V. shews the elegant *Stone Screen* which divided the Chapel built by Thomas Tropenell, Esq., from the body of the Church; the part shewn in dotted lines is now destroyed, but is restored from portions of the small spandrils still left. This screen has been disencumbered of its coats of white-wash by the present Rector. It consists of a small door, 2 feet 6 inches wide, and two tiers of three panels on each side, the upper tier being open; and is surmounted by a cornice enriched with the *vine leaf*, over which are five *shields* bearing the different arms of the family of *Tropenell*, which the next Plate will better explain; at the bottom of the plate are details; to the left, the *cornice* in section; to the right, a section of the *sill* and *base*, and plans of the *jamb* and *mullion*.

PLATE VI. *Details* of the *Stone Screen.* At the top of the plate is the *cornice* towards the Chapel, and below it are details referred by letter to this and Plate V. In the centre, are the five shields which shew the Tropenell Arms, and those of the families with which they intermarried. The centre, No. 3, bears the *Tropenell Arms* singly; viz. *Gules,* a fesse engrailed and powdered with ermine between three griffins' heads erased *argent.* No. 1 bears the *Tropenell* Arms on the *dexter* side, and the *Percy* Arms on the sinister, which are *azure,* five fusils in fesse *or;* this shews the marriage of Walter Tropenell with Catherine, daughter of Sir William, and sister of Sir Harry Percy, Knights, who owned Great Chalfield, by which marriage and the failure of male issue to the third Sir Harry Percy, the estate devolved on Thomas Tropenell. No. 2, on the *dexter* side, the *Tropenell Arms* as before, and on the sinister, the *Rous* Arms, viz. *Azure,* three lions rampant *ermine;* this shews the marriage of Roger Tropenell, the grandson of Walter, with Christian, daughter to Sir John Rous, of Imber. No. 5, on the dexter side, the *Tropenell* Arms as before, and on the sinister side, the *Roche* Arms, viz. *Azure,* three roaches *argent,* within a bordure *or,* and shews the marriage of Harry Tropenell, grandson to Roger, with Edeth, daughter to Walter Roche, younger brother to Sir John Roche, Knight, sons to John the Roche of Bromham. No. 4, the *Tropenell* Arms as before, on the dexter side, and the *Ludlow* Arms, on the sinister side, which shews the marriage of Thomas Tropenell, son to Harry, with Agnes (not Margaret, as stated in the pedigree), fourth daughter of William Ludlow, of Hill Deverell, Wilts, by whom this screen and the Chapel which it enclosed was erected; he died in 1490, and was buried with his wife in the Chantry Chapel, at Corsham Church, under the magnificent altar-tomb shewn in Plate VIII. At the bottom of the plate are the *pateras* in the quatrefoils at the top of the screen towards the Chapel, which are beautifully executed.

PLATE VII. shews an *Oak Seat* and *Desk* in the present Chancel at large, with details, and a *Stone Piscina,* now in the south wall of the modern Chancel, but which the author presumes has been removed from the body of the Church.

TOMB IN CORSHAM CHURCH, WILTS.

PLATE VIII. shews the elegant ALTAR TOMB in the Chantry Chapel at Corsham Church, which formerly belonged to the family of Tropenell, and is that of *Thomas Tropenell, Esq.*, and *Agnes* his wife. On the cornice is a prayer for the safety of their souls, which runs thus:—**I.H.S. Ihus Nazarenus filius Dei, filius David, filius Mariae Virginis, salvet nos.** *May Jesus, the Saviour of mankind, Christ of Nazareth, son of God, son of David, son of the Virgin Mary, save us.* In the moulding under, between the Pateras, the *motto*, **Le joug tyra belement**, is repeated on all sides [the representation of a yoke, forming the nominative case to the verb **tyra**, as at Great Chalfield]; in the quatrefoils are shields, bearing, on the north side, the first to the left, the *Ludlow Arms*; the centre bears the *Tropenell Arms* in dexter, and the *Ludlow Arms* in sinister, on one shield; the right bears the *Tropenell Arms*. The west end has two quatrefoils with shields; the one to the left, bears the *Ludlow Arms*; the other, the *Tropenell* and *Ludlow Arms* impaled; the south side is similar to the north; the shields at the east end bear, the one to the left, the *Ludlow Arms*, the other, the *Tropenell* and *Ludlow Arms* impaled. This tomb has been richly painted and gilt, and the arms have been emblazoned, but few traces can now be seen of its former splendour; the ground of the quatrefoils has been of a rich blue, the letters, the motto, the cusps, and the pateras, have been gilt, but the black outlines only of the letters now remain, which makes them difficult to be deciphered.*

* On account of the sketches of this tomb having been rubbed, the arms, though in themselves correctly drawn, have been misplaced; but the author having visited Corsham, is enabled to give the above correct description.

PART II. EXAMPLES OF GOTHIC ARCHITECTURE. THIRD SERIES.

TO SIR HARRY BURRARD NEALE, BART.
AS THE PRESENT
ADMIRAL OF THE BLUE. K.C.B. &c. &c.
POSSESSOR & PATRON
this restored A. A. View of the
Manor House and Church,
AT GREAT CHALFIELD,
WILTSHIRE, *is inscribed*
by his most humble

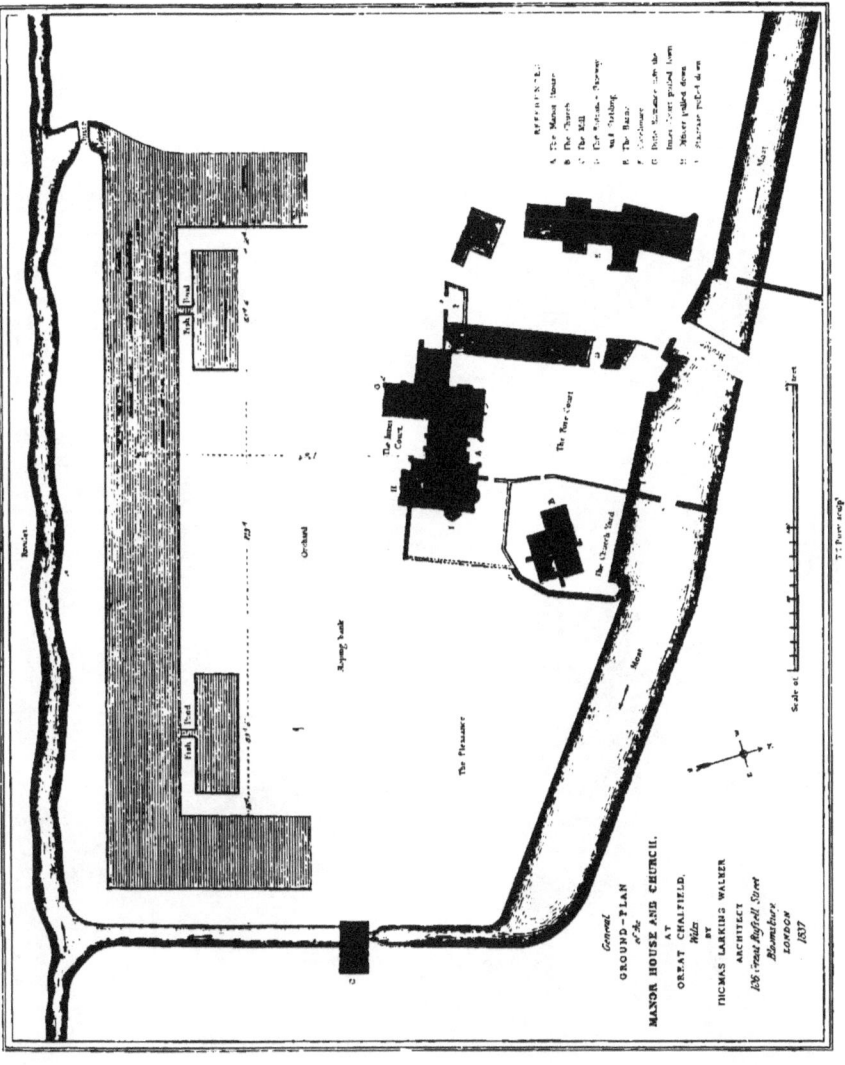

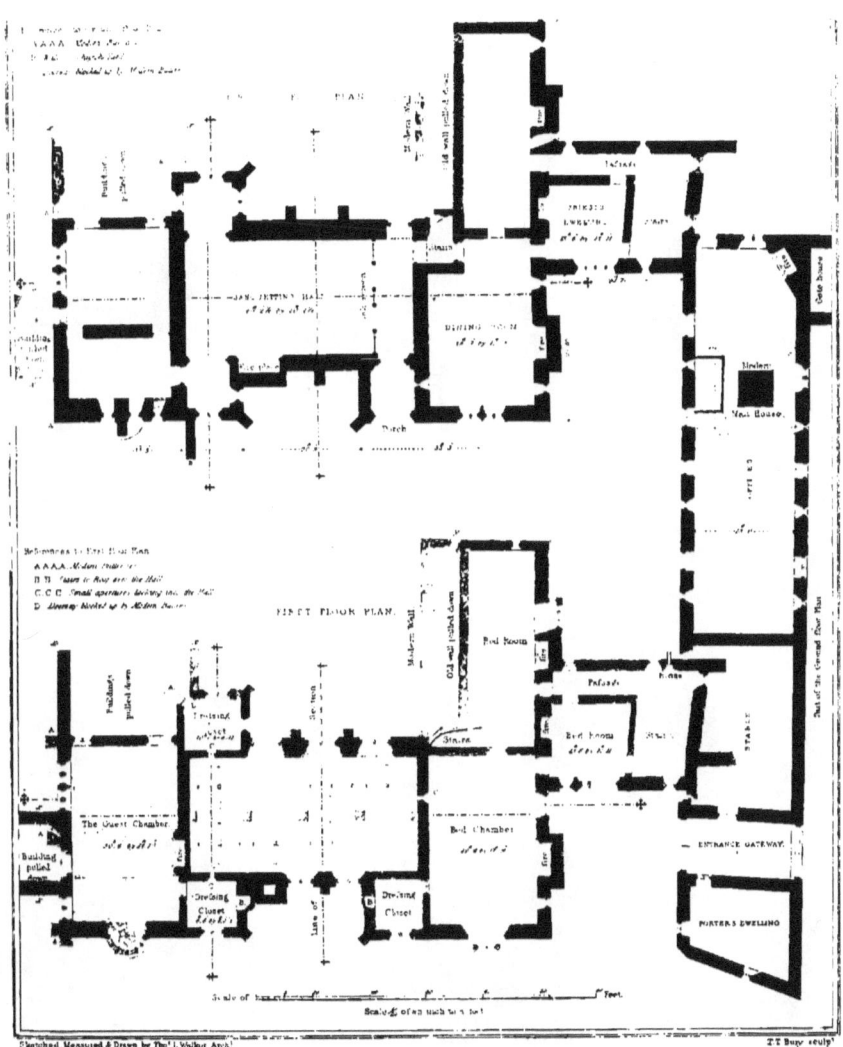

DOMESTIC ARCHITECTURE

HALL OF HOUSE, GREAT CHALFIELD, WILTS.

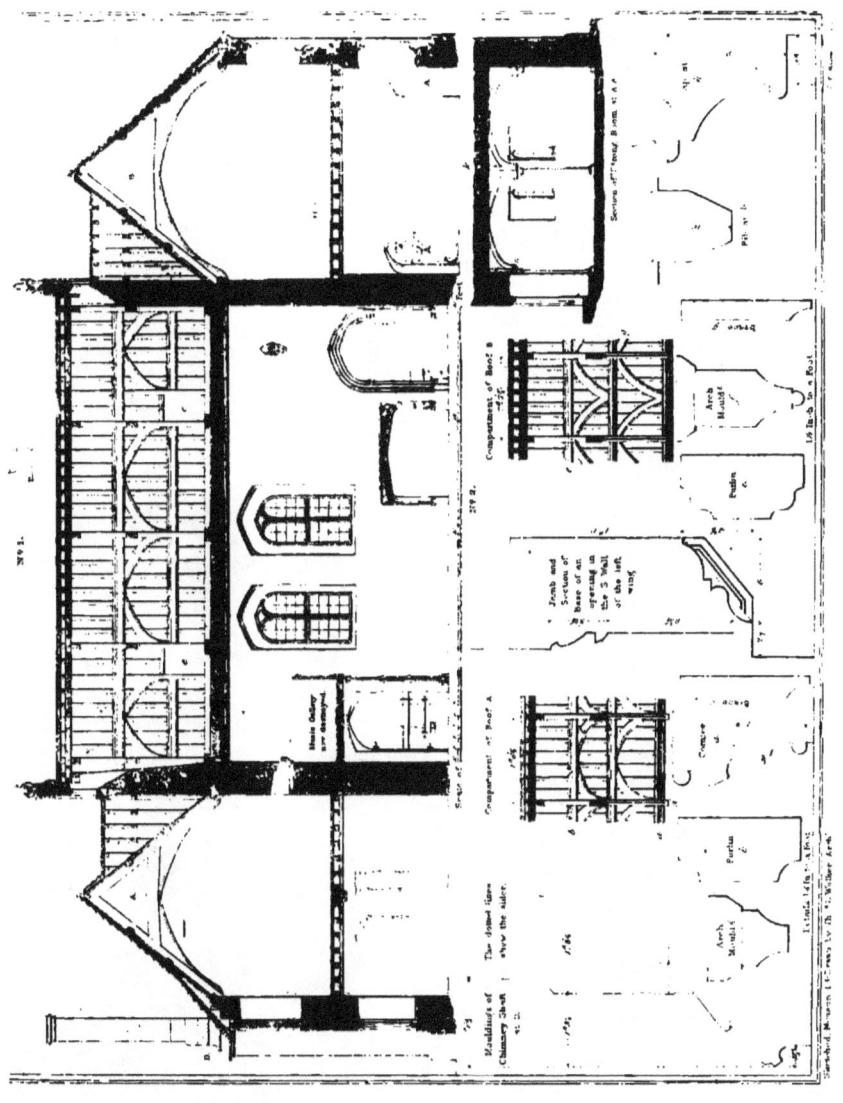

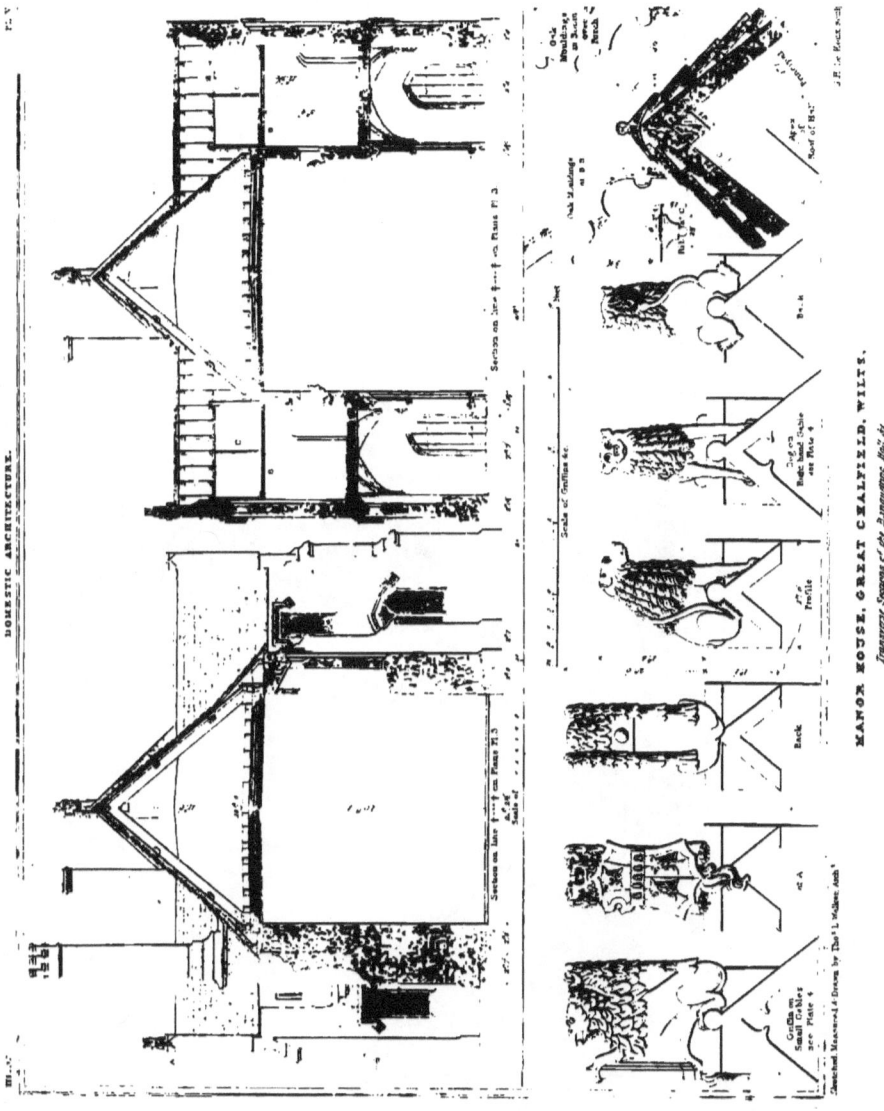

MANOR HOUSE, GREAT CHALFIELD, WILTS.
Transverse Sections of the Banqueting Hall, &c.

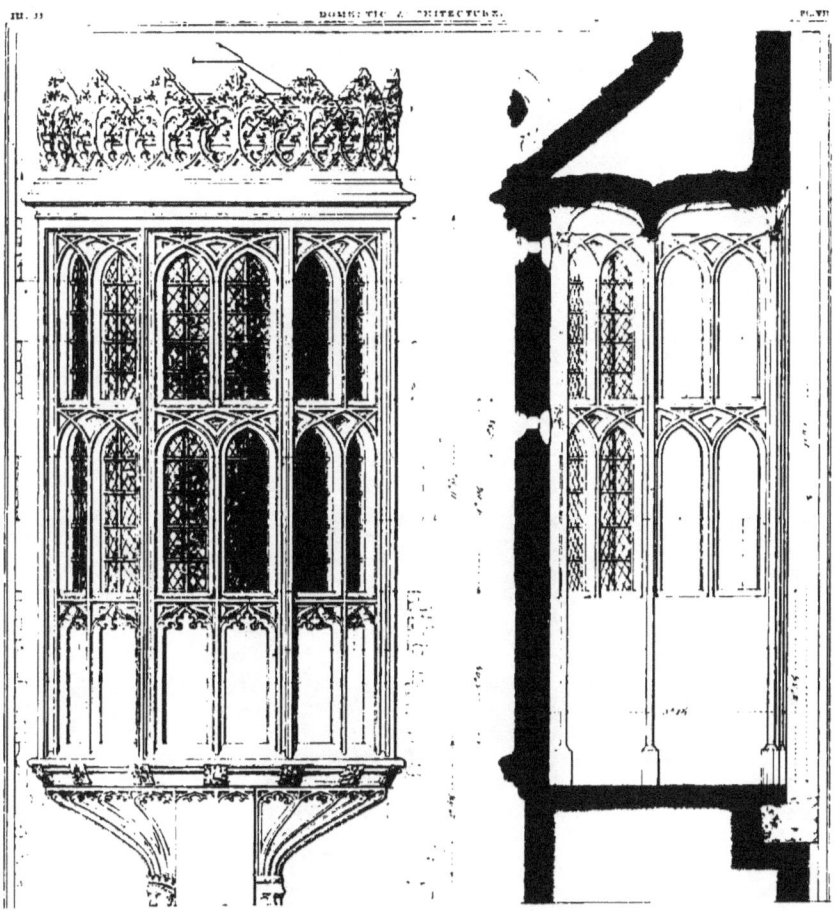

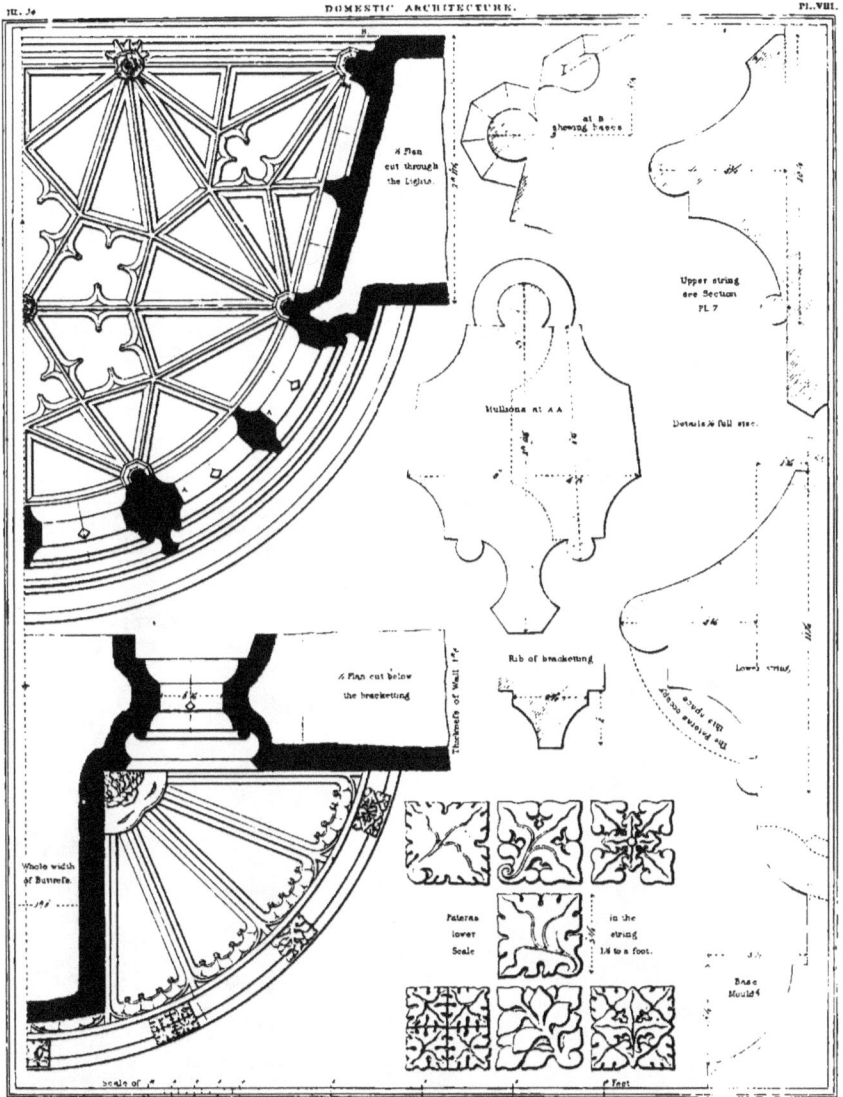

MANOR HOUSE, GREAT CHALFIELD, WILTS.

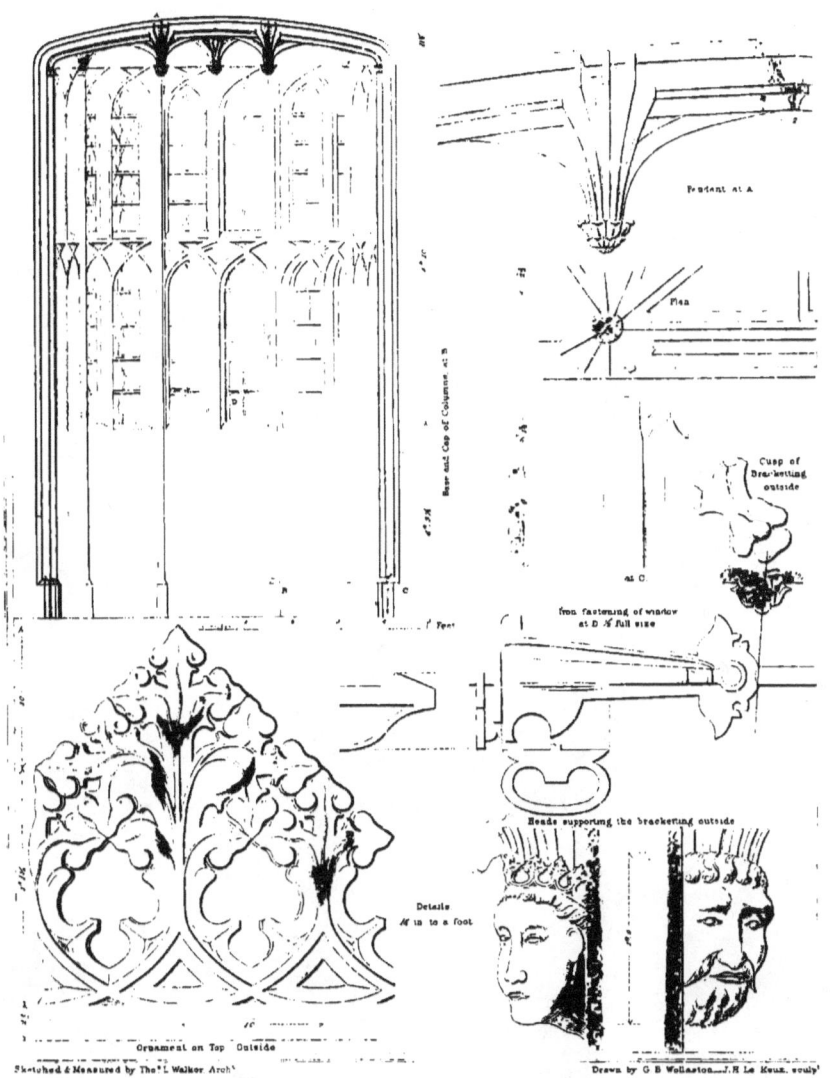

MANOR HOUSE, GREAT CHALFIELD, WILTS.

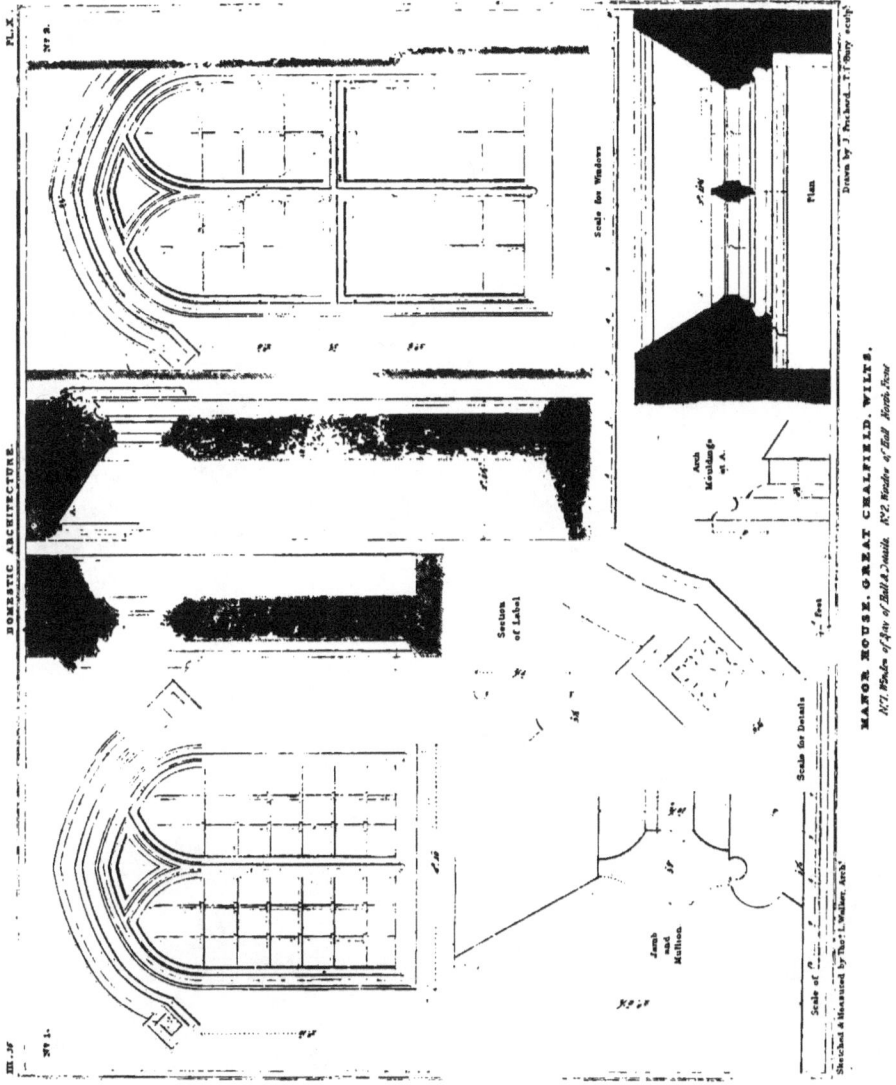

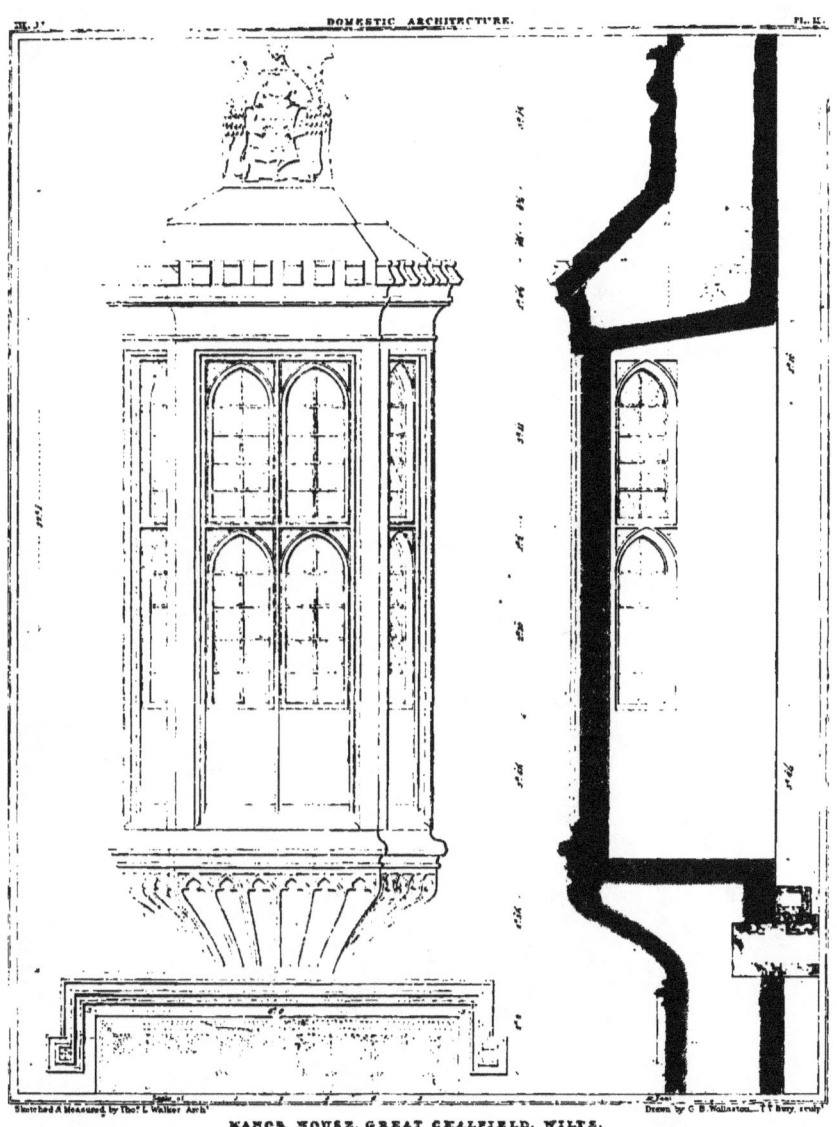

MANOR HOUSE, GREAT CHALFIELD, WILTS.

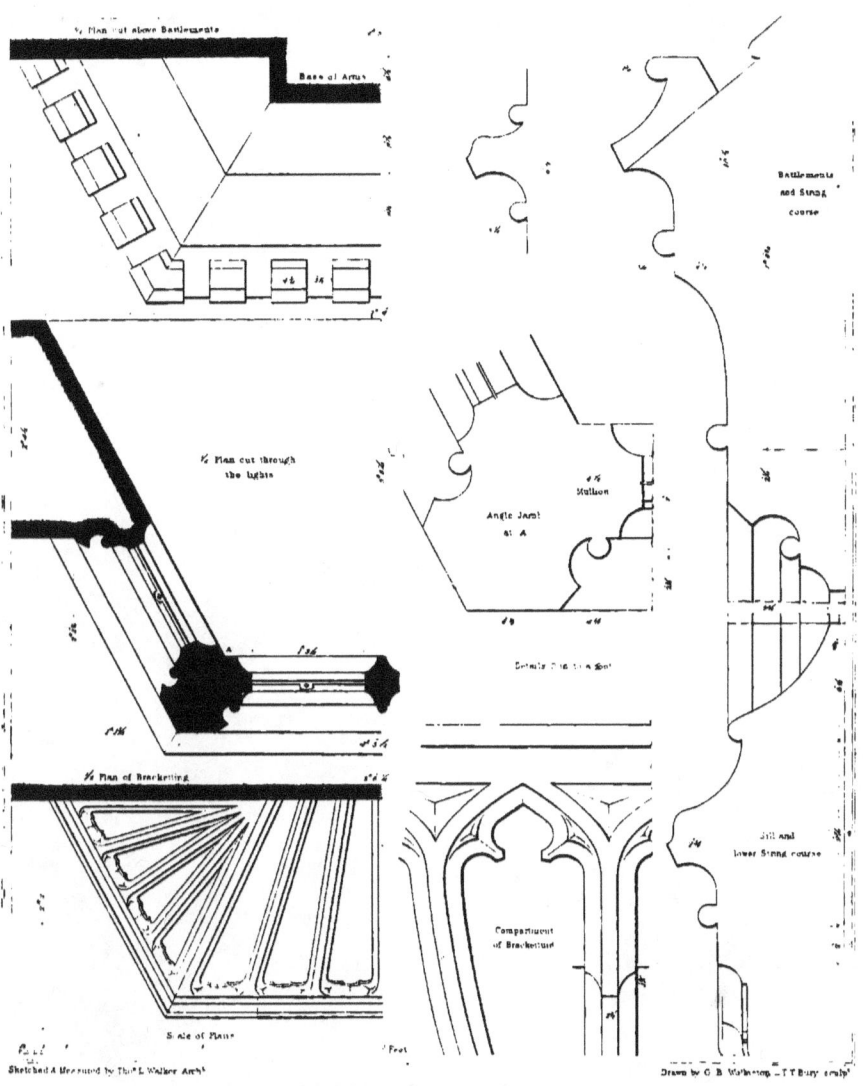

MANOR HOUSE, GREAT CHALFIELD, WILTS.

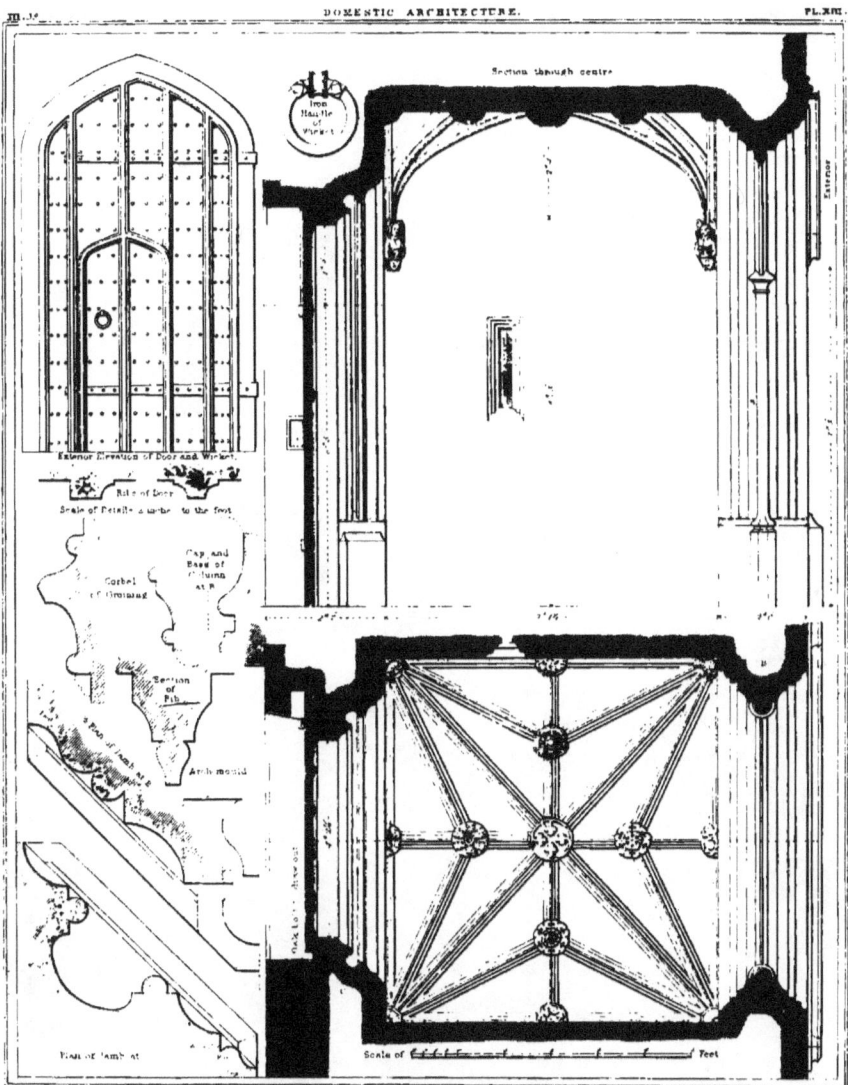

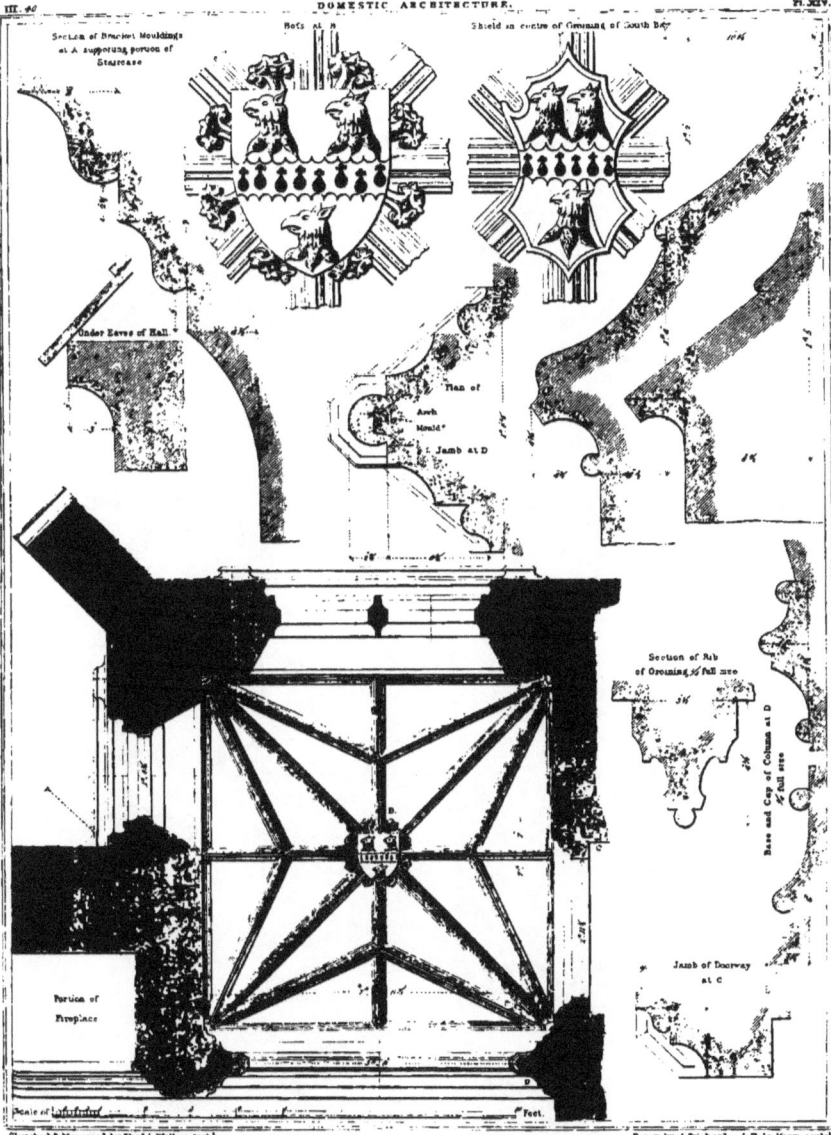

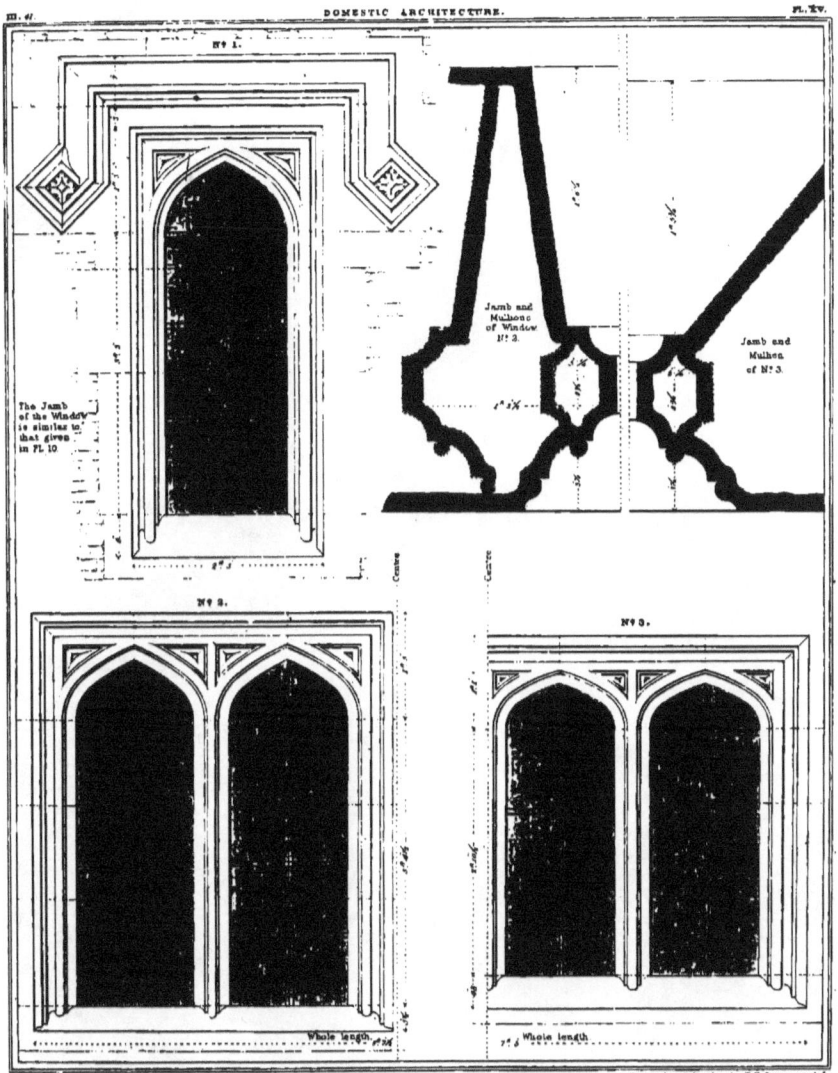

MANOR HOUSE, GREAT CHALFIELD, WILTS.

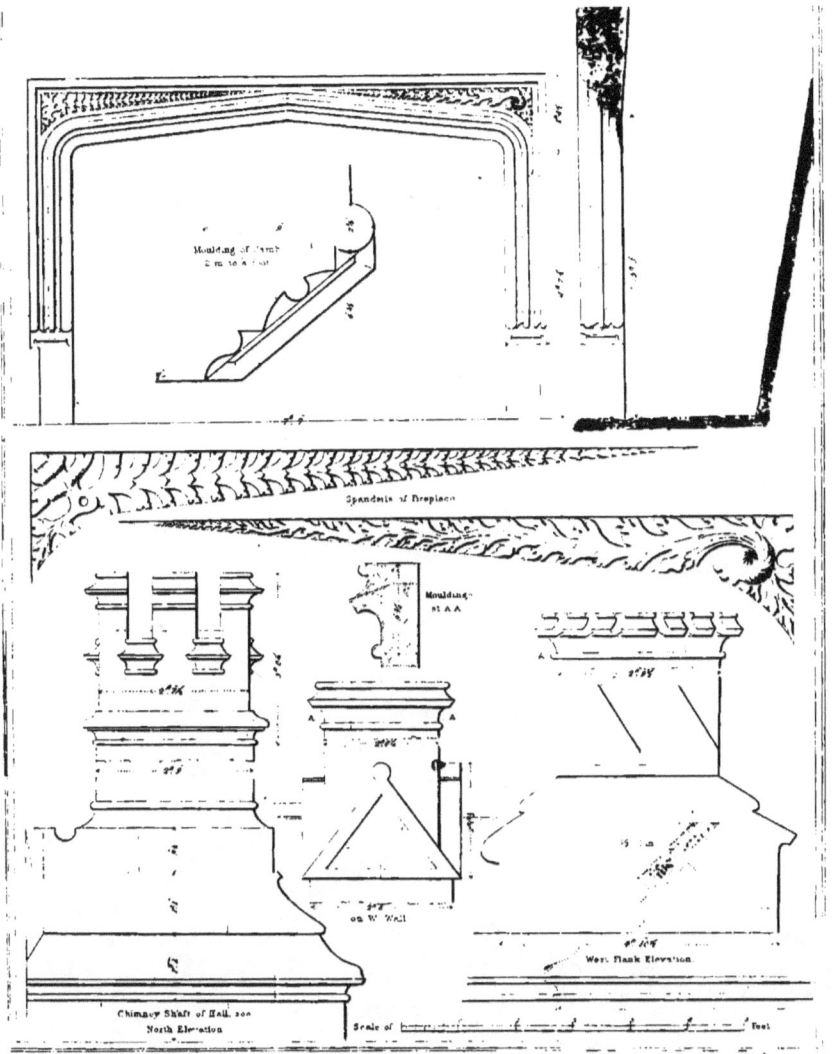

MANOR HOUSE, GREAT CHALFIELD, WILTS.

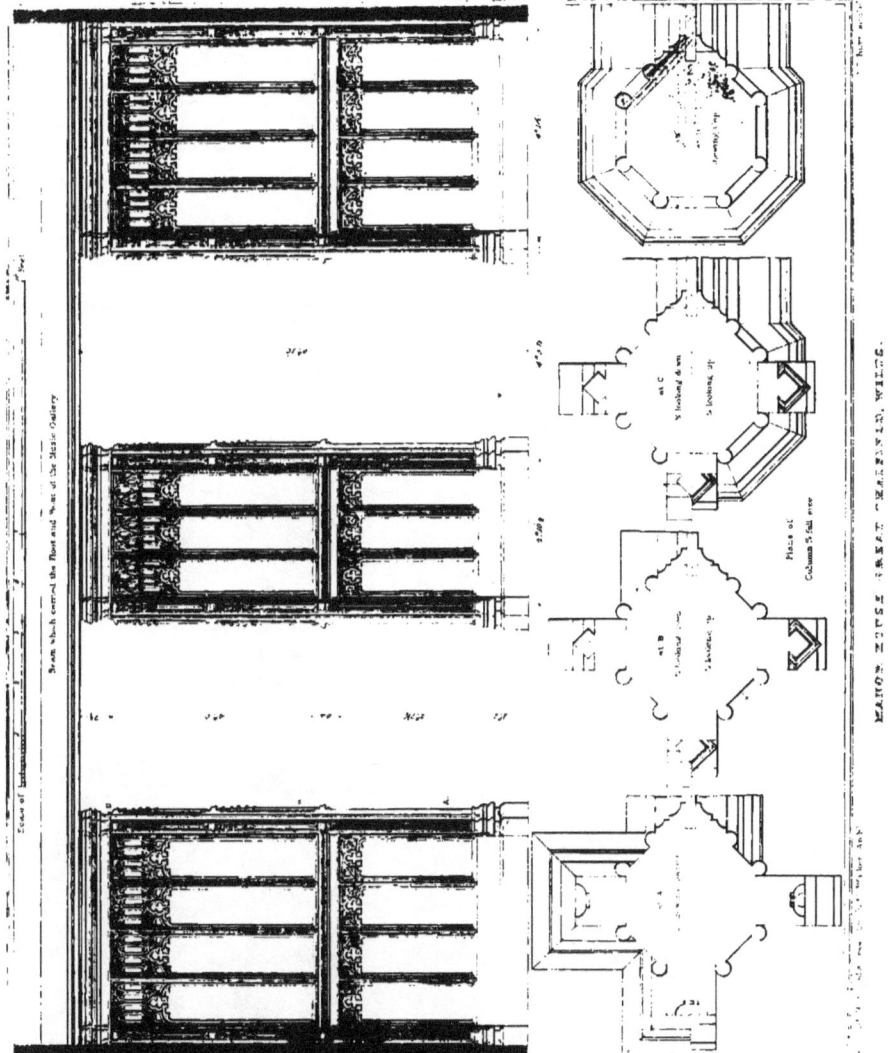

MANOR HOUSE, GREAT CHALFIELD, WILTS.
Details of the Oak Screen in the Banqueting Hall

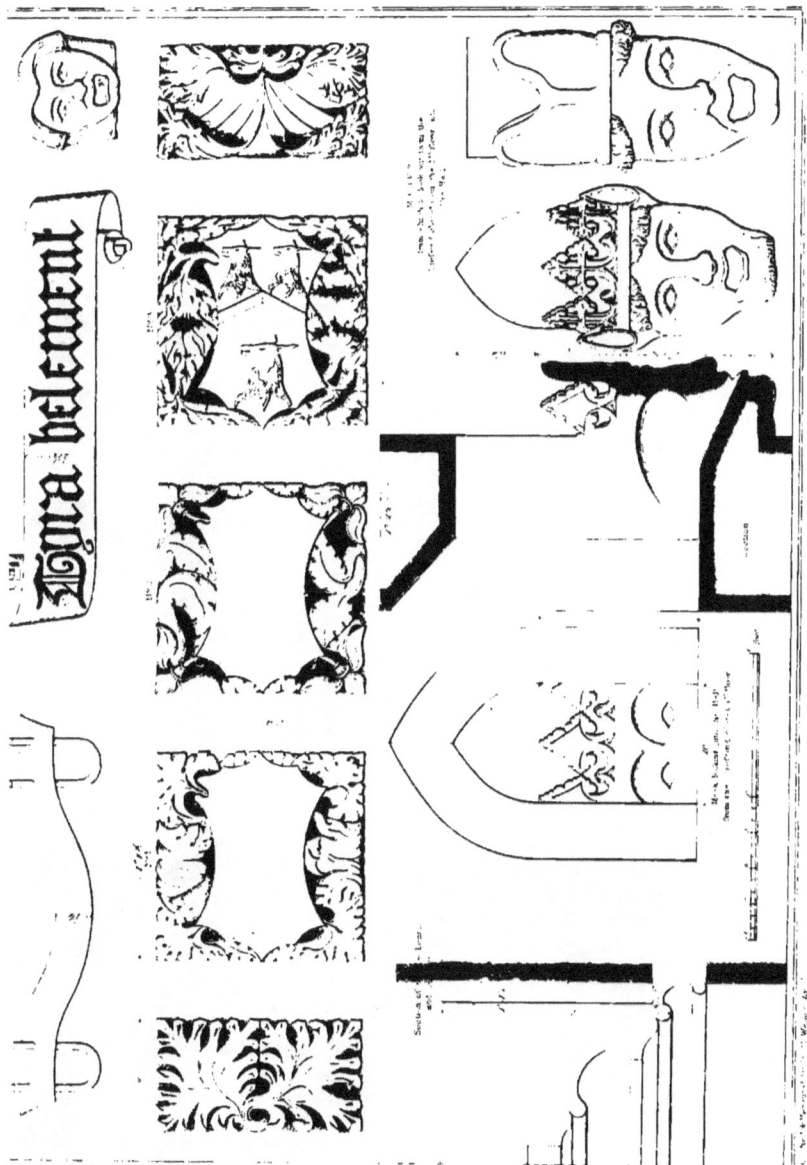

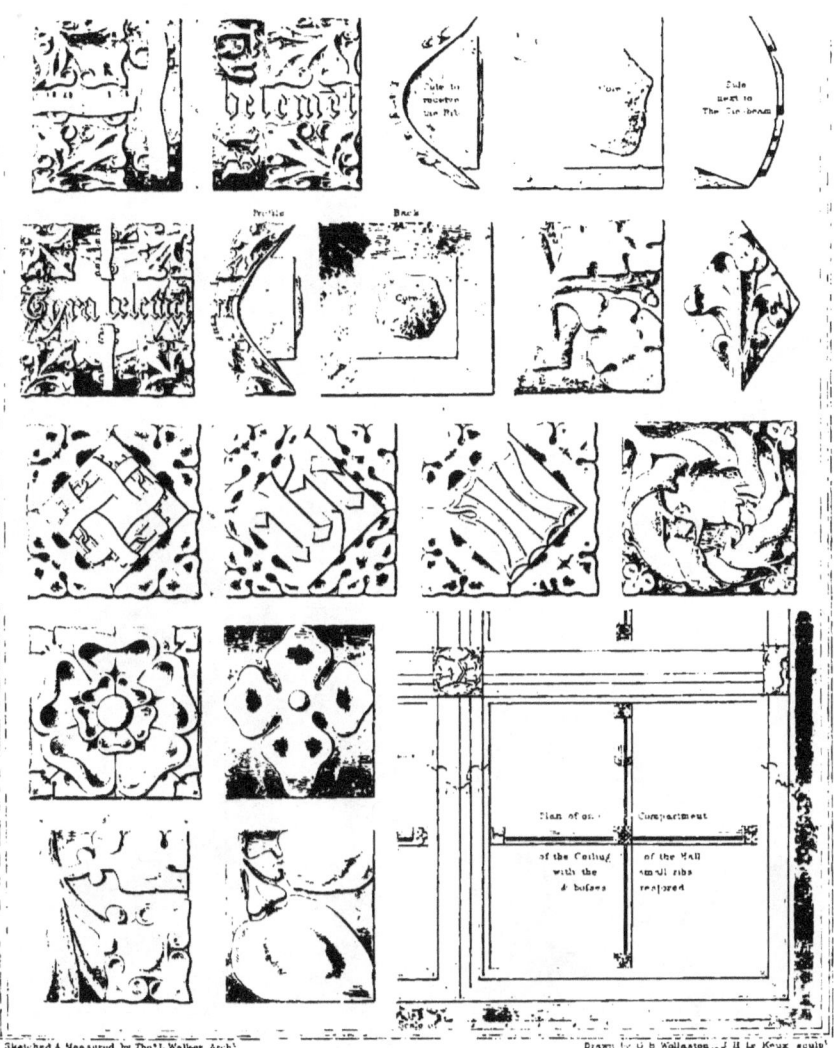

ECCLESIASTICAL ARCHITECTURE.

WEST ELEVATION

LONGITUDINAL SECTION

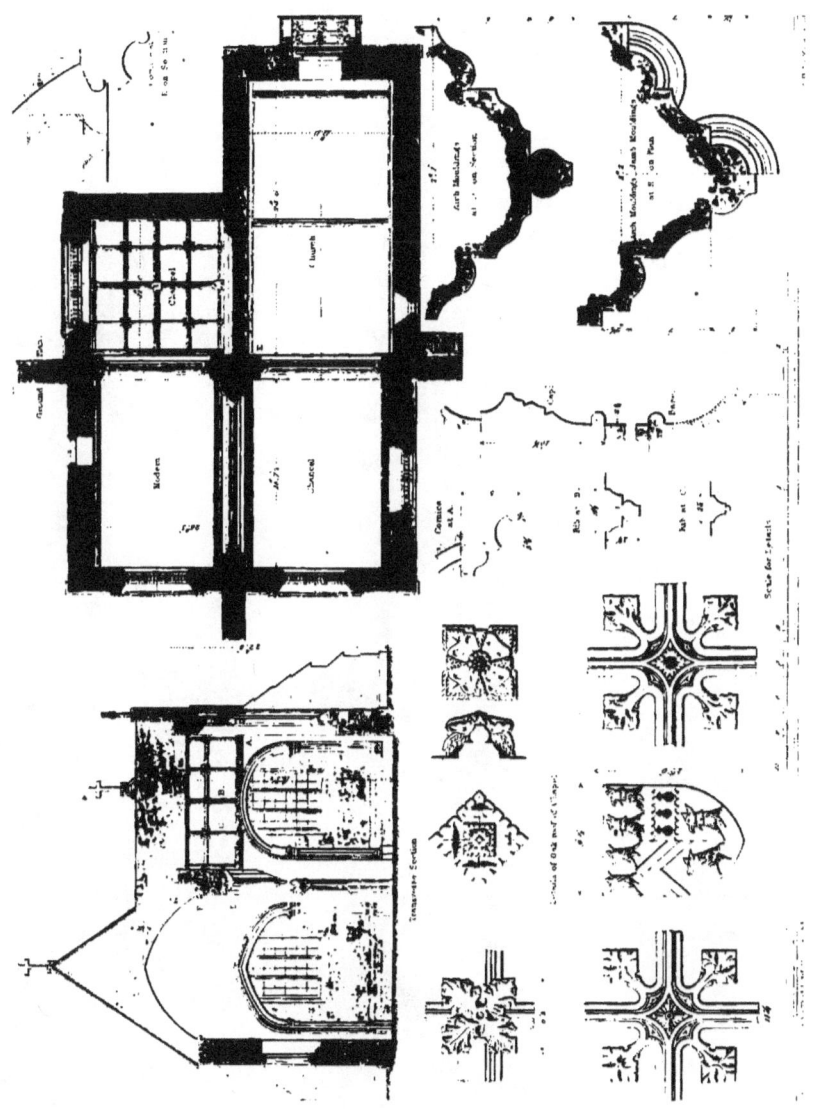

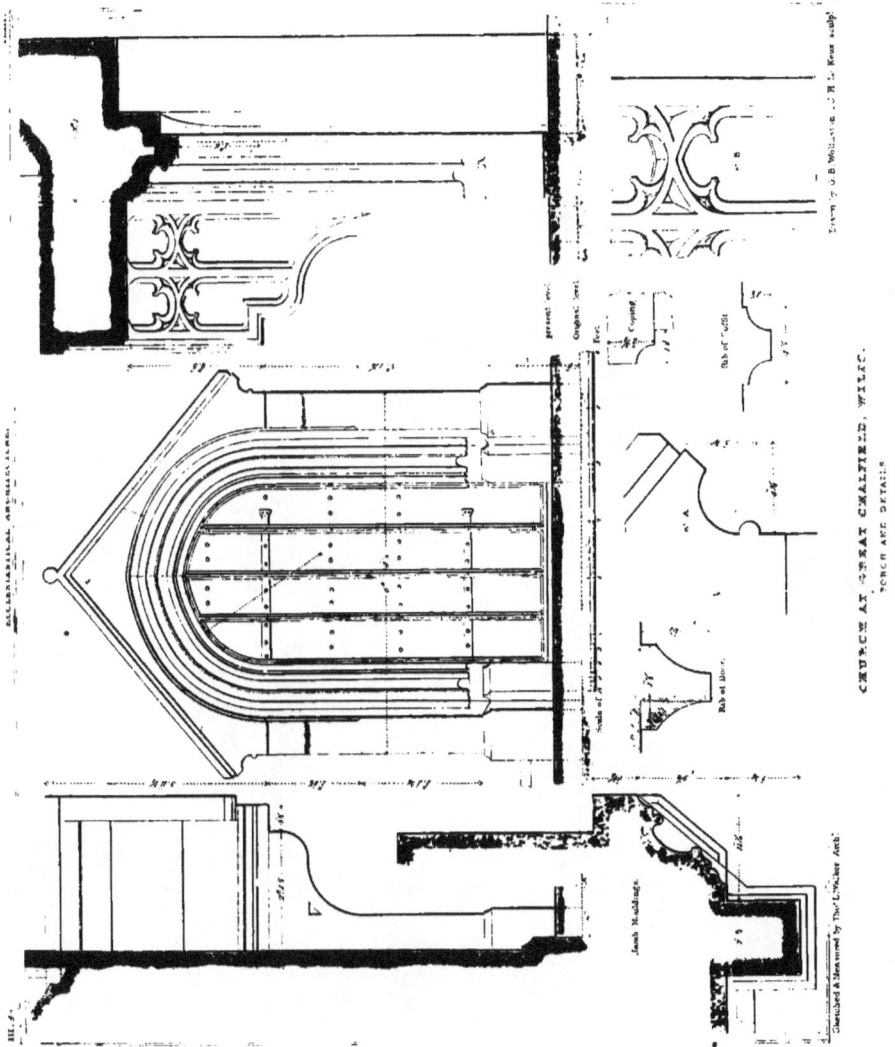

CHURCH AT GREAT CHALFIELD, WILTS.
PORCH AND DETAILS

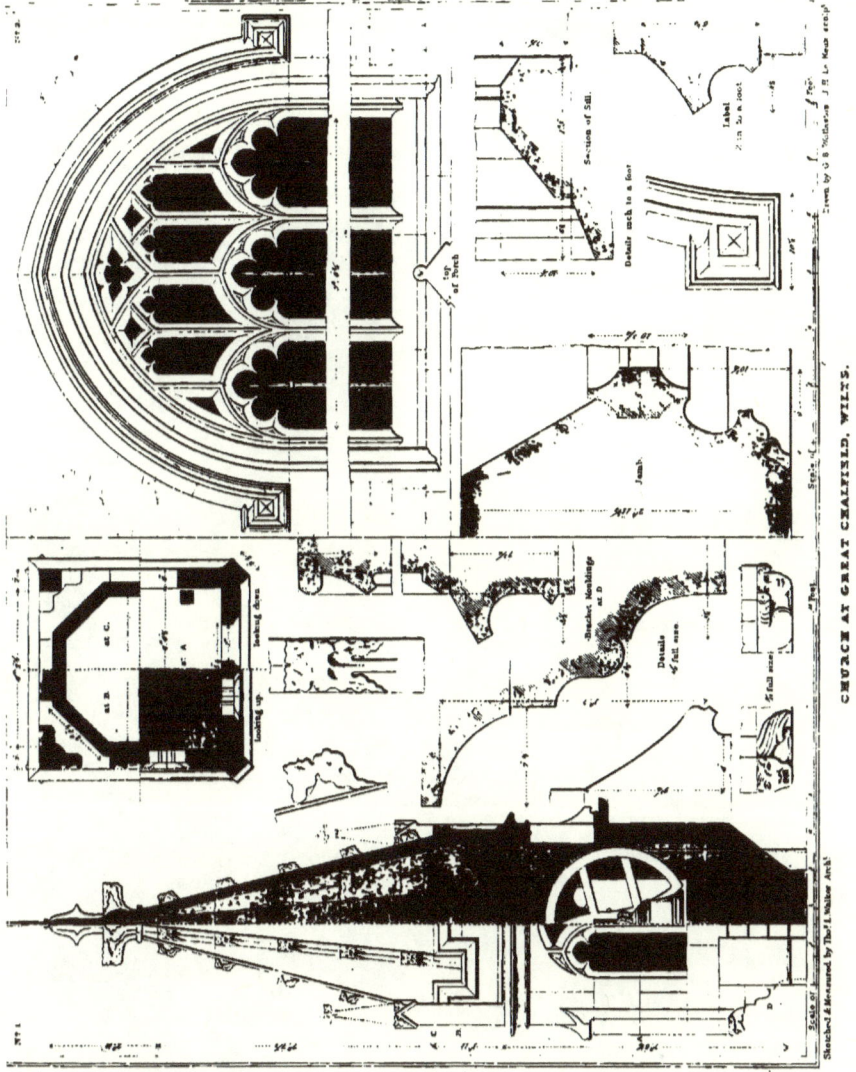

CHURCH AT GREAT CHALFIELD, WILTS.

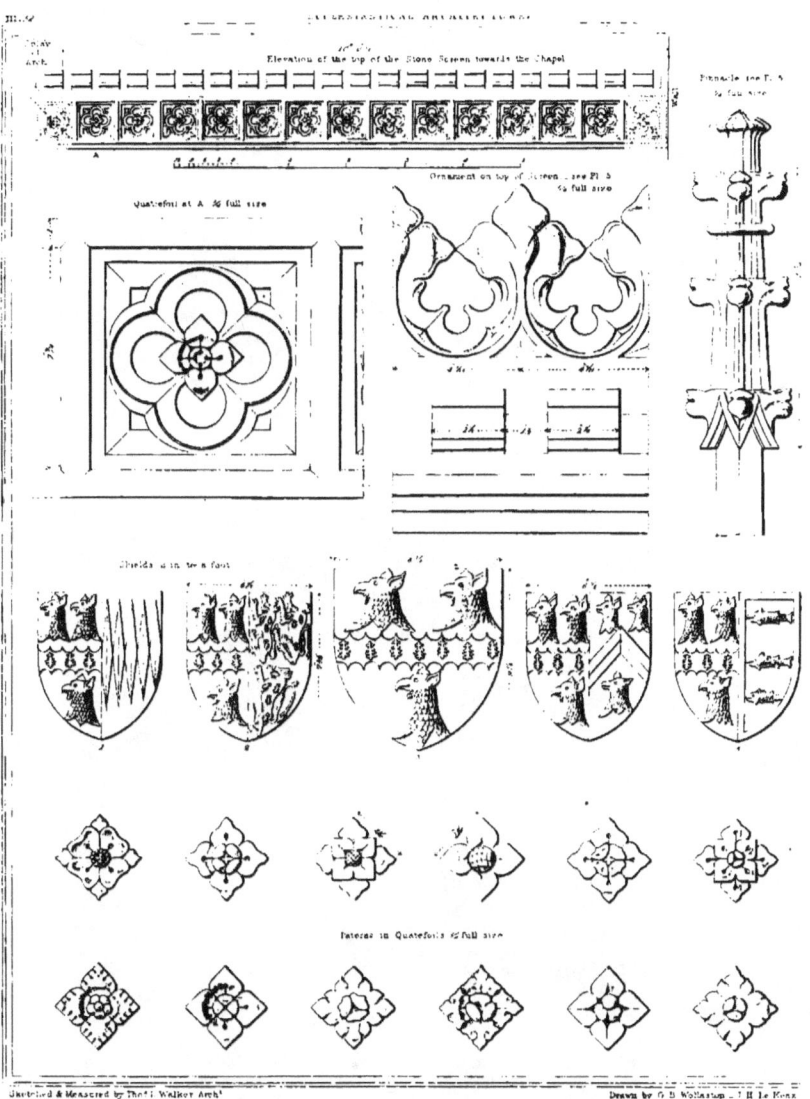

CHURCH AT GREAT CHALFIELD, WILTS.

THE

History and Antiquities

OF

THE MANOR HOUSE, AT SOUTH WRAXHALL,

AND

THE CHURCH OF SAINT PETER,

AT

BIDDESTONE, WILTSHIRE;

THE FORMER THE PROPERTY OF WALTER LONG, Esq. M.P.

ILLUSTRATED BY TWENTY-TWO PLATES OF

PLANS, ELEVATIONS, SECTIONS, PARTS AT LARGE, AND
PERSPECTIVE VIEWS, TOGETHER WITH WOODCUTS;

FROM SKETCHES AND ADMEASUREMENTS TAKEN IN 1837:

FORMING PART III. OF

"Examples of Gothic Architecture,"

THIRD SERIES:

ACCOMPANIED BY

Historical and Descriptive Accounts,

BY THOMAS LARKINS WALKER, ARCHITECT,

HONORARY TREASURER OF THE ARCHITECTURAL SOCIETY OF LONDON.

Edinburgh
JOHN GRANT
31 GEORGE IV. BRIDGE
1895

Examples

of

Gothic Architecture:

THIRD SERIES.

LIST OF PLATES CONTAINED IN PART III.

THE MANOR HOUSE AT SOUTH WRAXHALL, WILTSHIRE.

1.	Perspective View from the South-West.
2–3.	Ground Plan.
4–5.	First Floor Plan.

THE ENTRANCE GATEWAY.

6.	Elevation towards the Road, and Ground Plan.
7.	Longitudinal Section and Plan of Porter's Dwelling.
8.	Elevation and Section of the Oriel Window.
9.	Plans and Details of Ditto.

b

The Banqueting Hall, &c.

10.	Elevation of the Hall and Drawing Room towards the Court.
11.	Porch and Details.
12.	Window of North-West Bay, and Details.
13.	Window of Hall, and Details.
14.	Longitudinal and Transverse Sections of the Hall.
15.	Details of the Roof of the Hall.
16.	Gap Mouths, and Details of the Roof over the Drawing Room.
17.	Interior perspective view of the Drawing Room.
Wood-cut at page 6.	Tomb in South Wraxhall Church.

CHURCH OF SAINT PETER, AT BIDDESTONE, WILTSHIRE.

1.	South Elevation and Ground Plan.
2.	Bell Turret, and Details of Ditto.
3.	Porch, and Details of Ditto.
4.	Interior Door, Piscinas and Details.
5.	Windows, and Details of Ditto.
Woodcut at page 19.	Bell Turret of Saint Peter's, at Biddestone, in perspective.
Ditto ditto.	Bell Turret of Saint Nicholas', at Biddestone, in perspective.

A

HISTORICAL ACCOUNT

OF THE

Manor House at South Wraxhall,

WILTSHIRE.

In consequence of the "*litle Maner at Wrexley*," as Leland* calls it, having anciently formed part of the Manor of Bradford, which was among the many temporalities attached to the Abbey of Shaftesbury previous to the dissolution of religious houses in Great Britain by Henry VIII., the records concerning it are very few, and those which do exist throw but little light on the early history of what afterwards constituted the *reputed Manor*† of South Wraxhall.

The Manor of Bradford was granted to the Abbess and Convent of Shaftesbury by King Etheldred,‡ which was confirmed to them by Richard I. and Edward I.; § and mention is made of Wraxhall in the Chartulary of the Abbey, Harl. MSS. 61, in which "Agnes de la Ferci," whose name occurs as abbess in 1252, 1257, and 1267,‖ "with consent of the convent, granted and" "confirmed to God and the blessed Mary Magdalene of Fernlegh,¶ and to"

---

* *Itinerary*, Vol. II. fol. 30 (p. 25, Oxon, 1711).
† As it did not form a distinct manor at the time of passing the famous statute, known as "The third of Westminster," viz. "*Quia emptores terrarum*," 18th of Edw. I. A.D. 1290; it could only be recognised as, what was termed, "*a reputed manor.*"—*Barrington on the Statutes*. 4to. Lond. 1775. p. 167.
‡ See the "*Chartulary of the Abbey of Shaftesbury.*"—*Harl. MSS.* 61, fol. I.
§ On a plea, "de Quo warranto," temp. Edw. I., the Abbess of Shaftesbury contended that her right to the Manor of Bradford was derived from a grant by Richard I., and the jury determined that the title was undisputed. *Placita de Quo Warranto.*—Rot. 47.d and 50.
‖ Dugdale's Monasticon, Vol. II. p. 473.
¶ Monkton Farley, about a mile from South Wraxhall.

"the monks serving God at that place, the gift which Martinus, Capellanus" "de Wrekeshalle made them; viz. a messuage which the said Martinus held" "of them, in villa de *Wrokeshale*, with half a hide of land, pasture and" "appurtenances,"* for which they were to pay a certain rent. This may refer to a building, presumed to be *St. Adwyne's*, or *St. Edwyne's Chapel*,† which still exists in a field adjoining the Manor House: it possesses evident signs of great antiquity, and, from an immense chimney coeval with the building, which is of early English character, seems at one time to have afforded a rest for the weary pilgrim on his way to the shrine of Joseph of Arimathea, similar to that of Chapel Plaister.‡

Wraxhall is next mentioned in the twenty-fifth year of the reign of Edward III., when the Abbess and Convent of Shaftesbury "manumitted" "Thomas Scathelok their *villain* of the Manor of Bradford, and granted to" "him, and Editha his wife, daughter of Roger le Porter, one messuage, and" "two virgates, and nine acres of land, and four acres of meadow, with" "appurtenances in Lyghe and *Wrokeshale*, within the Manor of Bradford, and" "common pasture for their cattle upon 116½ acres of land in the said *villes*" "within the aforesaid manor, and upon 100 acres of pasture within the town-" "ship of Lyghe."§

It came into the possession of the family of *Longe*, or *le Long*, prior to the reign of Henry VI., but by what means is not recorded, and, in consequence of it having been church land, it is difficult, at this remote period, to ascertain. Leland says, in his *Itinerary*,—

---

* *Harl. MSS.* 61, fol. 92.

† "The Rectory, or Chapel in South Wraxall, called St. Adwynes, *alias* St. Edwynes, *alias* St. Jewens, was pur-" "chased by John Long, sometimes of Haugh, and afterwards of Mounckton, Co. Wilts, Esq., of Henry Thynne and" "Edward Pille, by indenture, 20th Nov. 1629, which he afterwards devised by will, dat. 15th Jan. 1652, pr. 13th" "May, 1654, to his son, John Long."—See "*Belts's MS. Genealogical Collections relative to the Family of Long*," in the possession of Walter Long, Esq. of Rood Ashton, M.P., p. 18.

In the valuation taken, temp. Henry VIII, of the temporalities belonging to the Priory at Monkton Farley, is the following, which relates to South Wraxhall, viz.—

"Wraxhall-cum-Box—Redd' assis' in Wraxhall ... 0 3 0"
"Wraxhall—Redd' custum' tenen' .... 1 3 0"

Dugdale's Monasticon, Vol. V. p. 32.

‡ See an account of Chapel Plaister, with a plate, in the *Gentleman's Magazine* for Feb. 1835, p. 143.

"In those times (besides the Jollities already mentioned), they had their Pilgrimages to *Walsingham, Canterbury,*" "&c., to several Shrines, as chiefly hereabouts, to *St. Joseph's of Arimathea*, at his Chapel in Glastenbury Abbey. In" "the Roads thither were several Houses of Entertainment, built purposely for them; among others, was the House" "called The *Chapel of Playster*, near *Box*, and a great House called . . . . ., without *Lafford's Gate*, near *Bristol.*" —*Aubrey's Miscellanies* P. 34 of an introduction to a History of the Northern Division of Wilts. Lond. 1714.

§ *Rotatl. de anno vicesimo quinto Edwardi III.*—53, 2nd Nos. in Turri Lond.

"ᵃMr. *Long*ᵃ hath a litle Manor about a mile from *Munketon-Farley* at *Wrexley*."
"The Original setting up of the House of the *Longes* cam, as I lernid of Mr."
"*Bonehom*, by this meanes:"
"One *Long Thomas*, a stoute felaw, was sette up by one of the old Lordes *Hungre-*"
"*fordes.* And after by cause this *Thomas* was caullid *Long Thomas*, *Long* after was"
"usurpid for the Name of the Family."
"This *Long Thomas* Master had sum Lande by *Hungrefordes* procuration."
"Then succedid hym *Robert* and *Henry.*"
"Then cam one *Thomas Long* descending of ᵇ*Younger* Brother, and could skille of"
"the Law, and had the Inheritances of the aforesaid *Longes.* Syr *Henry* and Sir"
"*Richard Long* were Sunnes to this *Thomas*." †

And Camden gives a similar tradition, in accounting for the origin of surnames, confirmatory of Leland's hearsay, in the following words:—" In respect of" "stature, I could recite to you other examples, but I will onely adde this" "which I have read, that a young Gentleman of the house of *Preux*, being of" "tall stature, attending on the Lord *Hungerford*, Lord Treasurer of *England*," "was among his fellows called *Long H.*, who afterwards preferred to a good" "marriage by his Lord, was called *H. Long*, that name continued to his" "posteritie, Knights and men of great worship."‡

There seems little doubt but that credit is to be given to these statements, more especially as Camden, who does not quote Leland, but must have *read it* in some other author, gives the *original surname* of the *long* person, and mentions that *a good marriage* was the means by which the Lord Hungerford set him up. They disagree, certainly, as to the *Christian name*, in which, most probably, Camden is right, for his authority being so minute in the other details, was not likely to be incorrect in such an essential.

The first recorded possessor of *South Wraxhall* was ROBERT LONGE, who was in the commission of the peace in 1426, and M.P. for Wilts in 1433. He is stated to have married *Alice*, daughter of *Reginald Popham*, of North Bradley, Wilts, by whom he had issue three sons, Henry, John, and Reginald. In the 25th year of the reign of Henry VI. A.D. 1447, *Henry* was found to be his

---

ᵃ Sir Henry *supr. lin. scribitur* in Autogr.   ᵇ A younger B.
* Sir *Henry Long*, in another place, "Thus rydyng I lefte *Avon* streame, aboute a 2 Miles on the lifte Hand. I" "markid 2 Places between *Malmesbyri* and *Chippenham* notable. *Draicote* wher Sir *Henrye Long* hath a fair Manor" "Place, and a Park about a Mile from *Avon* Streame. *Draicot* is a 5 Miles from *Malmesbyri*, and a 2 Miles from" "*Chippenham.*"—*Itin.* Vol. II. fol. 28 (p. 23, Oxon. 1711).
† *Ibid.* Vol. II. fol. 30 (p. 24, Oxon. 1711).   ‡ *Camden's Remaines*, by J. Philipot, p. 142.

B

heir, and to be upwards of thirty years of age, while Thomas Wayte was found to be the heir of *Margaret*, his wife, and to be upwards of twenty-four years of age; so that he must have married, for a second wife, this Margaret, who was relict of Edward Wayte, of Draycot Cerne, and daughter of *Philip Popham*, of Berton Sacy, in Hampshire;* which may account for two coats of the arms of Popham having been in the Manor House, one without, and the other with a crescent, the sign of cadence. The style of the hall, which is the most ancient portion of the "*Longe Howse,*" would lead one to imagine that this Robert was the projector, but no record can be found to assure us of the exact time in which it was built; and the armorial bearings, in many instances our best evidence, are of little assistance in this inquiry, as they were clearly put up at a later period. They consist of shields, sculptured on the brackets supporting the arched timbers of the hall-roof, which, from their style, cannot be anterior to the reign of Henry VII. or VIII.† The roof itself, which is richly ornamented with quatre-foils between the principal rafters, seems coeval with the exterior. ‡

A visit to these abodes of "the old English gentleman" cannot but impress the contemplative mind with reverential awe, and a desire to investigate the manners and customs of the times in which they were reared. They, for the most part, assimilate in their general arrangements, which, even in Aubrey's time, were kept up in the north: he says—" In *Scotland*, still the Architecture of a Lord's "
" House is thus, *viz.* a great open Hall, a Kitchen and Buttery, a Parlour, over "
" which a Chamber for my Lord and Lady; all the rest lye in common, *viz.* the "
" Men-servants in the Hall, the Women in a common Room." Then it was that "
" the lords of manours kept good houses in their countries, did eat in their "
" great *Gothick* halls at the high table, or oriele,§ the folk at the side tables ; "
when " the Halls of Justices of the Peace were dreadful to behold, the Skreens, "
" garnished with Corslets and Helmets, gaping with open Mouth, with Coats "
" of Mail, Lances, Pikes, Halberts, brown Bills, Batterdashers, Bucklers, and "
" the modern Colivers and Petronels (in King Charles the 1st's Time) turned into "

---

* Esc. 25 Hen. 6, No. 16.   † See Pl. XV.   ‡ See Pl. X. and XIV.

§ "*Oriele,*" he says, " is an Ear, but here it means a little Room at the upper End of the Hall, where stands a "
" Square or round Table, perhaps in the old Time was an Oratory ; in every old *Gothic* Hall is one, *viz.* at *Dracot,* "
" *Lekham, Alderton,* &c. The Meat was served up by *Watch-Words.* Jacks are but an Invention of the other Age ; "
" the poor Boys did turn the Spits, and lick^d the Dripping-Pan and grew to be lusty Knaves. Here in the Hall, were "
" the Mummings, Cob-loaf-stealing, and great number of *Christmas* Plays performed."

" Muskets and Pistols. Upon any Occasion of Justing or Tournaments in those "
" Days, one of these great Lords sounded his Trumpets (the Lords kept Trum- "
" peters, even to King *James*), and summon'd those that held under them. "
" Those again sounded their Trumpets, and so down to the Copyholders," or
villains. " No younger Brothers then were, by the Custom and Constitution "
" of the Realm, to betake themselves to Trades, but were Churchmen, or Re- "
" tainers, and Servants to great Men, rid good Horses (now and then took a "
" Purse), and their Blood, that was bred at the good Tables of their Masters, "
" was, upon every Occasion, freely let out in their Quarrels; it was then too "
" common among their Masters to have Feuds with one another, and their "
" Servants, at Market, or when they met (in that slashing Age), did commonly "
" bang one another's Bucklers. Then an Esquire, when he rode to town, "
" was attended by eight or ten Men in blue Coats, with Badges. The Lords "
" (then Lords in Deed as well as Title) lived in their Countries like petty "
" Kings, had *Jura Regalia* belonging to their Seigniories, had their Castles "
" and Boroughs, and sent Burgesses to the *Lower House;* had Gallows within "
" their Liberties, where they could try, condemn, draw and hang; never went "
" to *London* but in Parliament-Time, or once a Year to do their Homage and "
" Duty to the King. Every baron and gentleman of estate kept great horses "
" for a man at arms. Lords had their Armouries, to furnish some hundreds "
" of Men."*

The next possessor of Wraxhall was HENRY LONGE, Esq., mentioned above as the eldest son and heir; he was Sheriff for Wilts in 1457, 1476, and 1483.† We find him named in the will of Margaret Lady Hungerford, as feoffee, together with Thomas Tropenell,‡ in 1476: he married, first, Johanne, daughter of J. Ernleigh; secondly, Margaret, daughter of John Newburgh of Lulworth, in Dorsetshire; and, thirdly, another Johanne, who survived him; but by neither had he any issue. The two former are mentioned in his will as " *nuper uxores mei*," which bears date at *Wroxall*, 1st May, A.D. 1490, he " commends his soul to God the Father Almighty, the blessed Virgin Mary, " and all Saints," and requests that his body be buried in the Church of

* *Aubrey's Miscellanies.* Pp. 28, 29, and 30, of an Introduction to a history of the Northern Division of Wilts.
† In *Harl. MSS.* 433, p. 35. " Henry Long, late Shireff of the Countie of Wiltess," is said to have received a pardon from Richard III. A.D. 1485, also, " Thomas Tropenell, of Chaldefeld, in the Countie of Wilts, Esquire, hath' " a generall pardonne."
‡ Thomas Tropenell was also Feoffee to Robert Lord Hungerford, A.D. 1487.—See Historical Account of Gt. Chalfield. *Part II. Examples of Gothic Architecture.* "*Third Series,*" p. 7.

"*Wroxhall, coram altâ cruce;*" and, among many other bequests, *in pios usus*, he leaves "to the parochial Church of *Wroxhall* xxs. for vestments."[*]

The maiden surname of his widow is not known, but, from a monument still existing in the *Long's Chapel* at Wraxhall Church, which bears the arms of *Long* impaling *Berkeley* quarterly with *Seymour* (to the memory of a widow, as the crimping of the cap sufficiently testifies), who must have been a Berkeley by an heiress of Seymour, it may be safely presumed that this monument, with which the chapel is coeval, was erected by

SIR THOMAS LONGE, KNIGHT (who inherited the estates of his uncle), to the memory of his aunt; and that she was a daughter of *Thomas Berkeley* by *Elizabeth*, daughter of *Thomas Seymer*,[†] this being the only match on record the dates of which will warrant the marriage with a *Long*. This monument, of which a woodcut is subjoined, is of late date, as may be seen by the style of mouldings, the sculpture of the figures, and the form of the shields.[‡] The figure is partly restored, as shewn by the dotted lines.

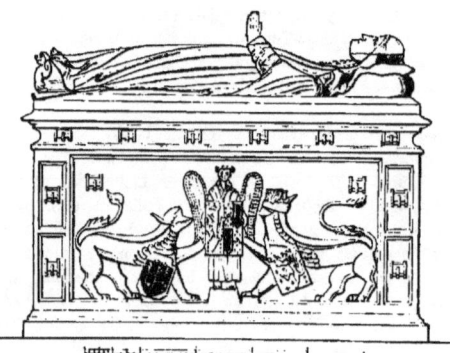

[*] See his will, at length, in *Appendix*, No. *III* [†] Le Neve's Baronets, Vol. I. Coll. Arms.
[‡] This monument, and the chapel which was built for it, is thus noticed by Aubrey, in his MSS., under "S. WRAXALL." "In the Church here in Long's Chapelle an old altar monument of freestone on wch lies a figure" "with a robe, but so cov^ed with a deske not well to be discerned. I guess it to be of a woman. In the limbe are the" "Marshall's locks as in the margin: in the middle of ye N. side is an Angel holding ye Scutcheon in the margin, sup."

Sir Thomas was son and heir of John Longe (second son to Robert), who married Margaret, sister and coheiress of Thomas Wayte, of the Temple and of Draycot, and younger daughter of Edward Wayte by Margaret Popham, who, as is stated above, in her widowhood married Robert Longe. By this intermarriage, the manor of Draycot* was acquired "*in jure uxoris,*" which was held, as Aubrey tells us, "by *petit serjeantie, viz.* by being" "marshall at the king's coronation, which was the reason the Cernes, who" "held it prior to the Waytes, gave the marshall's lock for their cog-" "nizance."† This marshall's lock was most probably adopted as a badge by Sir Thomas Longe, and on the monument in question it is profusely scattered; which circumstance may be deduced as another reason for attributing it and the chapel to his piety. He was sheriff in 1501, and executor to Richard Lord St. Amand, in 1508; he married Margery, daughter of Sir George Darell of Littlecote, Wilts. Sir Thomas was among the "𝔤𝔯𝔢𝔞𝔱𝔢 𝔠𝔬𝔪𝔭𝔞𝔦𝔤𝔫𝔢 𝔬𝔣 𝔫𝔬𝔟𝔩𝔢" "𝔪𝔢𝔫𝔫𝔢" who went, with Edward Duke of Buckingham, in 1496, to meet the King (Henry VII.) at Taunton, then in pursuit of Perkin Warbeck.‡ This circumstance, it is conjectured, was recorded by the painted glass which, in Aubrey's time, adorned the tracery-headed windows of the manor-house; not

---

* "perted with two lyons passant guardant, wch seeme to have been crowned or heaumed, and have a neckcloth wth is " "inveckted as low as his shoulders; the one hath on his shoulder the (*Shield*) of the (*Wings conjoined*); the other " "the (*Shield*) of Long. The South side was as the North, but now almost defaced. The Windows are all defaced " "of this Chappell, as also of the Church; in the E. Window of the Chancel is only sign of a Scutizon."

"In the Chapell,"

"In { "Here lieth the body of Capt. John Long, Esqr, son of John Long, Esq., Justice of the Peace and " Freestone { "Quorum, who departed this life in the City of Westminster, the 23 of Febr. 1652. A marble blank."

"In freestone, here lieth the body of Will. Long, Esq., who dyed 11 Sept. 1664."

"Here lieth Walter Long, of South Wraxhall, Gent, son of John Long, Esqr., and Justice of Peace and " "Quor., who died at East Brent, in Somerset, 11 Oct. 1669. Here lieth also the body of Barbara, his wife, who " "died 14 Oct. 1669. Here lieth the body of William Awbrey, late of Chaddenew, in the parish of Meer, in y^e " "County of Wilts, Esq., who dyed 6 Jan. 1664. Are ye RSS. of 1649 not in ye Opelle. In the Chapell are two " "handsome niches and holy water-potts."

"Over a late dore, wch opens into Long's Chapelle, R. An. Dñi 1566. L." (between the Marshall's lock and the Stag's-head).

‡ "Dant quod villa de DRAYCOT fuit de serjantia domini Regis, et *Johannes de Venoys* tenuit eam et similiter alias " "terras per serviciam inveniendi in hospicio domini Regis terciam Virgam Marescalcie, et idem Johannes dedit " "terram illam Magistro *Henrico de Cerne* per cartam suam; quod donum dominus Rex nunc confirmavit per cartam " "suam, et *Philippus de Cerne* heres ejusdem modo eam tenet."—ROTULI HUNDREDORUM, Vol. II. p. 235. Temp. Henry III.

† *Aubrey's Collections for Wilts*, Part II. p. 63. Printed by J. Davy, Queen Street, Seven Dials. London, 1821.

‡ His companions from Wiltshire were, *Morish Berkley, William Storton, John Semer, Richard Beauchamp, Roger Tokete, Edwarde Darell, Amis Paulet* and *William Saintemaur*.—THE CHRONICLE OF JOHN HARDYNG, by Richard Grafton, fol. 86. *of the Continuation in prose.* Lond. 1543.

a vestige of this elegant accompaniment of Gothic architecture now remains, save only a small portion in a window over the porch, which induced the author to visit the Ashmolean Museum at Oxford, where he transcribed Aubrey's notes, and took memoranda of the coats-of-arms (in the original, all drawn and emblazoned): they will be found in Appendix, No. IV. Sir Thomas Longe was knighted at the marriage of Prince Arthur; and his arms, as entered in Claud. C. III., are Long and Seymour quarterly.* He, the author presumes, put up the brackets of the hall-roof shewn in Plate XV., as the fetterlock appears on one of them; and, probably, added the Entrance-Gateway, as, on one of the terminations to the label over the arch (which is very flat, four-centred-pointed of late date) is the same fetterlock; on the other was a stag's head, now destroyed, but which was perfect when Aubrey wrote.†

There is a great similarity in the plan and elevation of the hall and offices to Great Chalfield (distant only three miles): so much so, that one would almost imagine South Wraxhall, which is certainly the older of the two, served as a model for that magnificent fabric, although the dimensions of the two are very different; that at Chalfield being much larger.‡

"Sir Thomas Long, Knight, lyes buried by the north wall of the chancell," "under a rich Gothique altar monument of freestone without inscription, his " "heaume and crest do yet hang up."§

The next possessor was SIR HENRY LONGE, KNIGHT, son of Sir Thomas, who was sheriff for Wilts in 1512, 1526, 1537, 1542; for Somerset in 1538; for

---

* Margery, his wife, was daughter of Sir George Darell, by *Margaret Seymour*. *MS. Pedigrees of Long*, by Beltz, in the possession of Walter Long, Esq., M.P.

† He died in 1709, at Oxford, on his way to Draycot.

‡ See Part II. EXAMPLES OF GOTHIC ARCHITECTURE, THIRD SERIES. Compare Pl. III. Great Chalfield, with Pl. II.—III. South Wraxhall.

§ *Collections for Wilts, Part II.* p. 62. "The coates of armes on this monument are as followeth :—West End ; " "I. S^t. John quartering Delamare. G. 2. lions pass. gard. O. South Side : II. Long. S. Crusuly off crosslets and a li. r." "A. III. Barkley impaling . . . . per pale O. and az. a cross moline counter changed. IV. Long impaling " "Dayrell Az. li. r. A. crowned O. East end : V. Seymour. G. two wings inverted O. About the cornice of the " "monument, thus :—West end : VI. O. on a chief G. 2 stags' heads caboosed O. VII. Cerne. Az. a horse's head " "coup. O. VIII. Sturton. S. a bend O bt. 6 fountains. IX. The Marshall's fett lock, or hand bolt. X. O. on a " "chief G. a bezant between 2 stags' heads caboosed O. XI. Long imp. a chevron quartering Seymour. A cross " "crosslet. XII. Sturton, as before. XIII. Sturton between two cross crosslets. XIV. Seymour, as before. " "XV. . . . . . On a chevron . . . . . . 3 bezants. XVI. A. on a chief G. a bezant between 2 wings " "O. XVII. A. li. r. S. collared O. langued and armed G. XVIII. Az. a bend engrail colized O. XIX. Idem " "cum XVII. XX. Long imp. quarterly . . . . . . Q. Cerne's coats, and if Wayte did not marry the " "daughter and heir of Cerne." This monument is engraved in the *Gentleman's Magazine for June* 1835, and an amended description is given of it by C. E. Long, Esq., who visited it.

Dorset in 1539; and M.P. for Wilts, 1552, 53.* He married, first, Frideswide, daughter of Sir John Hungerford, of Down Ampney, great-grandson of the Lord Treasurer; and, secondly, Eleanor, daughter of Richard Wrottesley, of Wrottesley, in Staffordshire, relict of Edmund Leversedge, of Frome Selwood, Somersetshire. Sir Henry was present at the siege of Boulogne, accompanied Henry VIII. to the Field of the Cloth of Gold, and was knighted for making a gallant charge at Theroueune, in Picardy, in the sight of Henry, when a new crest, consisting of *a lion's head, with a man's hand in its mouth*, was granted to him: his banner bears the motto,—"*Fortune soies heureux*," neither of which is to be found in the manor-house, so that with greater safety we may attribute the *pure Gothic* portion of the building to an earlier period than during his possession; since it may be fairly presumed that a crest, so nobly obtained, would have inspired vanity sufficient to "cause it to be graven in stone" on any building he may have projected. A fire-place there is indeed, but of bad detail, in the bedroom, over what is presumed to have been the ancient *parleure*, and ascended by a staircase from it, which, in one spandril, bears the initials S. H. L. for *Sir Henry Long*, and in the other, H. E., linked together by a Gordian knot, for *Henry* and *Eleanor*, his second wife. By the first marriage he had no male issue to survive him; but by the second, six sons and three daughters. The eldest son,

SIR ROBERT LONGE, KNIGHT, inherited Wraxhall and Draycot, who was sheriff for Wilts in 1575, served at the siege of Boulogne, and was Esquire of the body to King Henry VIII. He married Barbara, daughter of Sir Edward Carne, of Wenny, Glamorganshire, by whom he had issue, four sons and one daughter. Sir Robert, who probably was the first protestant member of this family, enclosed the Long's Chapel, in South Wraxhall Church, by building up a doorway to the left of the monument mentioned above, and a solid wall to the right, for the convenience, no doubt, of a family pew, by which the east and west ends were destroyed (on the east end is still to be seen one-half of an angel, with expanded wings). In after times the work of desecration was completed, for the south side was sadly mutilated before Aubrey saw it, which, he says, "was as the north, but nowe almost defaced." The sculpture seems to have been, since then, wilfully chipped off, to allow of its being more

---

* The following occurs in "Valor Ecclesiasticus (26 Hen. VIII. A.D. 1535) under *Priory of Farleigh*—
Fœd'
"HENRICI LONG milit' senⁱⁱ capit'lis dc͞i priorat' per annu' £2."

conveniently boarded up, for nothing is now discernible save the rude strokes of an untutored chisel. Over the outer door of this chapel are Sir Robert Long's initials; viz. R. An. Dñi. 1566. L. between the marshall's fetterlock and the stag's head; which evidently shews a wish on his part to be considered as the founder, for the stone on which these cognizances are sculptured has been inserted, while the jambs of the doorway are original. The same initials are also on the doorway leading from the church to the chapel. His eldest son,

SIR WALTER LONGE,* KNIGHT, next succeeded, who was M.P. for Wilts in 1592, and Sheriff in 1601. He married, first, Mary, daughter of Sir William Packington, of Westwood, in Worcestershire, Knight, by whom he had two sons and one daughter; and, secondly, Catharine, daughter of Sir John Thynne, of Longleat, Knight, by whom he had six sons and six daughters. To him we are indebted for the chimney-piece in the hall, which bears the date of An. Dñi. 1598, and the arms of *Long* impaling *Carne*—his father's coat; see Plate XIV. He also made many additions to the Manor House itself; the left wing containing, as at Chalfield, the guest chamber, was pulled down, and a stately with-drawing-room built, ornamented by a richly carved chimney-piece, and a ribbed plaster ceiling. In giving additional width to this room, it was found expedient to preserve the old roof (which still exists, as shewn in Plate XVI.), and for the support of the wall-plate to leave a pier about midway between the two end walls, thereby occasioning a curious angular projection inside the room, opposite the fire-place, ornamented with niches and dwarf columns. A view of this room is given in Plate XVII., for which the author is indebted to *Walter Long, Esq.*, M.P., the present proprietor: it did not form part of the plan of this work; but as the Gothic and the later styles (of which there are many good examples here) are so completely blended, it was deemed a pity, by those who have kindly taken an interest in the present publication, to leave this "*noble room*," as Aubrey calls it, untouched. The alteration seems, from the style of the fire-

---

* "Sir Walt. Long, of Drayent (gr. father to this Sʳ James Long), married a daughter of Sir Jo. Thynne, by " "which meanes, and their consimility of disposition, there was a very conjunct friendship between the two brothers " "(Raleighs) and him; and old John Long, who then waited on Sʳ W. Long, being one time in the Privy-Garden with " "his master, saw the Earle of Nottingham wipe the dust from Sir Walter R.'s (Raleigh's) shoes with his cloake in " "compliment. . . . . He (Sir W. Raleigh) was the first that brought tobacco into England, and into " "fashion. In our part of North Wilts,—e.g. Malmesbury hundred,—it came first into fashion by Sʳ Walter Long. " "They had, first, silver pipes. The ordinary sort made use of a walnut-shell and a strawe. I have heard my gr. " "father Lyte say, that one pipe was handed from man to man round the table."—AUBREY's *Letters and Lives of Eminent Men.* 8vo. London, 1813, Vol. II. pp. 511, 512.

place, which is much purer in detail than is usually met with, to have been made in the early part of the reign of James I. The details of the windows certainly come under the denomination of Elizabethan, as also the exterior composition of the gables; but as the niches before mentioned are proved to be coeval with the first alteration, and are of the same style as the fire-place, it may be safely attributed to that era, and only shews how gradually one fashion gave place to another. To the rear of this room, and ascended by a short flight of steps from it, is a bedroom, with a fire-place of the same style, bearing, in panels, the following inscriptions:—*Faber est quisq. fortune sue* on one side; on the other, *Aequa laus est a laudatis laudari, et ab improbo improbari;* and, in the centre, on a bracket, where sits a monkey, *Mors rapit omnia*. These steps also lead into a small closet over the north-east bay, but all communication with that over the north-west bay was cut off by the alterations: the door, however, remains some feet above the present floor of the drawing-room, behind the stone-work of the great fire-place; it is visible inside the closet, as shewn in Plate XIV. No. 3.

"The second wife," says Aubrey, "did use much artifice to render the Son"
"by the first Wife (who had not much Promethean Fire) odious to his Father."
"She would get her acquaintance to make him Drunk, and then expose him"
"in that condition to his Father; in fine, she never left off her Attempts till"
"she had got Sir Walter to disinherit him. She laid the scene for doing this"
"at *Bath*, at the Assizes, where was her brother Sir *Egrimond Thynne*, an"
"eminent Sergeant at Law, who drew the writing; and his Clerk was to sit up"
"all night to engross it. As he was Writing, he perceived a Shadow from the"
"Candle; he look'd up, and there appeared a Hand, which immediately"
"vanished; he was startled at it, but thought it might be only his fancy,"
"being Sleepy; so he Writ on; by and by, a fine white Hand interposed"
"between the Writing and the Candle (he could discern it was a Woman's"
"Hand), but vanish'd as before. I have forgot, it appeared a third Time."
"But with that the Clerk threw down his Pen, and would engross no more,"
"but goes and tells his Master of it, and absolutely Refused to do it. But"
"it was done by somebody, and Sir *Walter Long* was prevailed with to Seal"
"and Sign it. He lived not long after; and his Body did not go quiet to the"
"Grave, it being Arrested at the Church Porch by the Trustees of the first Lady."
"The Heir's Relations took his Part, and Commenced a suit against Sir *Walter*"
"(the second Son), and compel'd him to accept of a Moiety of the Estate: so"
"the eldest Son kept *South Wraxhall;* and Sir *Walter,* the second Son,"

"*Draycot-Cernes*, &c. This was about the Middle of the Reign of *James* the "First."*

JOHN LONG, ESQ., the eldest son, who was thus persecuted by his stepmother, married Anne,† daughter of Sir William Eyre, of Great Chalfield, by whom he had four sons and one daughter: the eldest,

JOHN LONG, ESQ., inherited, who married twice: by the first wife he had a daughter; and by the second, who was Catherine, daughter of John Paynter, he had a son, *Hope*, and three daughters.

HOPE LONG, ESQ., married, first, Mary, daughter of John Long, Esq., of Monkton, by whom he had a son, John, who died before his father, and one daughter; secondly, Grace, relict of —— Blanchard, Esq., of Preston, Somersetshire, by whom he had no issue. He died in 1715, when the estate passed to his uncle,

WALTER LONG, ESQ., of Bristol, whose son,

WALTER, died in 1731, æt. 84, unmarried, and bequeathed his estates to the sons of his cousin, Catherine, wife of John Long, of Monkton; her elder son,

JOHN, who was fellow of Corpus Christi College, Oxford, and rector of Meseyhampton, in Gloucestershire, died in 1748, unmarried, when the estate went to his brother,

THOMAS LONG, ESQ., of Melksham, who had married Mary, daughter of —— Abbot, Esq., of Chippenham. Next succeeded his son,

WALTER LONG, ESQ., of Wraxhall and Whaddon (well known as Mr. Walter Long, of Bath), who died, unmarried, in 1807, æt. 95, and bequeathed his estates at Wraxhall, Whaddon, &c. to trustees, remainder to

WALTER LONG, ESQ., son and heir of Richard Godolphin Long, Esq., of Rood Ashton, who is the present proprietor, and who, the author rejoices to be able to add, intends to preserve this venerable fabric from further decay. Mr. Long is maternally descended from the original proprietors of South Wraxhall, as may be seen by a reference to the pedigree, Appendix No. I. He

---

* *Aubrey's Miscellanies*, pp. 75, 76. 8vo. Lond. 1721. The following extract more fully illustrates the disposition and character of this lady:—"Sir *Walter Long's* (of *Draycot* in *Wilts*) Widow did make a solemn promise to him" "on his Death-bed, that she would not marry after his Decease. But not long after, one Sir —— *Fox*, a very" "beautiful young Gentleman, did win her Love; so that, notwithstanding her promise aforesaid, she married him:" "She married at *South Wraxhall*, where the picture of Sir *Walter* hung over the Parlour Door, as it doth now at" "*Draycot*. As Sir —— Fox led his Bride by the Hand from the Church (which is near the House) into the Parlour," "the string of the Picture broke, and the Picture fell on her Shoulder, and crack'd in the fall: (it was Painted on" "Wood, as the Fashion was in those Days): this made her Ladyship reflect on her promise, and drew some Tears from" "her Eyes."—IBID. pp. 43, 44.

† See PART II. p. 8.

is a magistrate and deputy-lieutenant, and M.P. for the Northern Division of the County of Wilts. He married, 3d August, 1819, Mary Anne, second daughter of the Right Hon. Archibald Colquhoun, of Killermont, in the county of Dumbarton, Lord Registrar of Scotland, and has issue three sons, WALTER, Richard Penruddock, and Henry William; and three daughters, Mary Anne, Catherine Flora Henrietta, and Jane Agnes.

DESCRIPTION OF THE PLATES.

PLATE I. THE FRONTISPIECE.

THIS is a *Perspective View*, from the south-west; on the right is the *Entrance Gateway*, which was, at one time, flanked by buildings;* the *Hall* and *Withdrawing-Room* occupy the centre and front the west, looking into the *Court;* on the left is a long line of *offices* and *bed-rooms*, at the further end of which is a good example of a corbelled *chimney-shaft*. The *wall* which encloses the court is shewn broken down, so as not to intercept the view. In this wall, and exactly opposite the porch of the hall, is an *old doorway*, which formerly led into the *Plaisaunce;* see

PLATE II.—III. THE GROUND PLAN.

At the bottom of the plate is the *Entrance Gateway*, flanked on the right by a room, added *temp.* Elizabeth, and formerly on the right by buildings supposed to have been *stables*. This Gateway originally extended only to the depth of 14 feet, as will be shewn hereafter: it leads into the *Court;* on entering which, to the right, is the *Porch* of the *Hall;* a *Screen*, in the style of James I., divides off a *passage*, which leads, by a *covered way*, into *another Court;* under

* In the "*Gentleman's Magazine*" for March 1838, p. 256, a woodcut is given, shewing these buildings, which seem to have been *stables*, but of later date than the gatehouse.

this covered way is the door of the *Kitchen;* to the east of which *another Kitchen* was added *temp.* Elizabeth or James I., shewn in a lighter tint. The *Parlour* was entered from the passage end of the hall; it has been subdivided by modern partitions; a staircase leads out of this up to the *Host's Chamber* (see Plates IV. and V.) At the upper end of the Hall are two *Bays;* that to the left leads into what was the *Buttery,* now a beer cellar; and that to the right by a *Staircase* up to the ancient Guest Chamber, which was enlarged and converted into a withdrawing-room :* at the foot of the staircase, to the right, is a *Dining-Room.*† A long line of *offices* occupies the upper end of this court, which has been added to at various dates. The oldest portion is shewn by the darkest tint; it seems coeval with the hall, and originally stood detached: a kind of *conservatory* was added to the east, and a communication formed with the other buildings, as the quoin still visible at *a*, and a window and door at *b b*, now stopped up, prove; a loop hole at *c*, and old quoins at *d d d d*, shew that the west wall was originally an exterior one. Various details are shewn, referred by letter to the plan.

PLATE IV.—V. THE FIRST-FLOOR PLAN.

In both plans the dark tint shews the ancient portions, the lighter tint the alterations and additions, and the light tint within dotted lines shews the situation of the original walls, which were taken down. The principal alteration from the original design was effected about the latter part of the reign of Elizabeth, or the beginning of that of James I., by removing the ancient *Guest Chamber,* marked *a a a a,* and substituting a larger and wider room, richly fitted up as a *Withdrawing-Room,* which is shewn in Plate XVII.; but the old roof, given in Plate XVI., was retained, and for the support of the wall plate, a pier was left opposite the fire-place, thereby occasioning a curious angular projection inside the room, ornamented by niches, which seem to have served as seats. There are two immense windows at opposite corners of this room, one looking over the court, into the plaisaunce, the other into the garden ; which latter is approached by a door on the landing of the stairs, from the hall. The details are referred by letter.

* Aubrey calls this "The dining-room, which is a very noble one ;" but the great distance of the kitchen from this room, induces the author to think that it was originally intended as a drawing-room.

† This Aubrey calls the Parlour ; but in other buildings of the same kind the parlour is invariably on the right, as shewn on the plate, near the kitchen, &c.

DESCRIPTION OF THE PLATES.   15

THE ENTRANCE GATEWAY.

PLATE VI. *Plan* and *Elevation*. This seems to have been built in the early part of the reign of Henry VIII., subsequent to the acquisition of the Manor of Draycot Cerne by Sir Thomas Long, as the badge borne by the possessors of that Manor, the *Marshall's-lock* or *Fetter-lock*, is still remaining on one of the terminations of the label—*viz.* that to the left; on the other was a *stag's head*, as we are told by Aubrey, and not as shewn in the plate. On the corbelling of the oriel window is a *shield*, bearing the *arms of Long*. The *angle buttresses* are peculiar, and very pleasing in effect. On entering the archway, to the right is a *Staircase* leading up to the room above; further on is a doorway, which formerly was a foot entrance into the court, corresponding with the one on the left, which entered from the road. This gateway has been added to, as the original roof extends only to the length of 14 feet, while it now measures upwards of 30 feet; on the apex of the gable has been a *finial*.

PLATE VII. *Longitudinal Section* and *First-Floor Plan*. The *original roof* is here shewn: on the plan, the darker tint shews the extent of the old walls, enclosing the *Porter's Dwelling*.

PLATE VIII. *Elevation* and *Section* of the *Oriel Window*. Above the battlements has originally been a roofing of water-tables, finished, probably, by some ornament or armorial bearing, as at Chalfield and other places; it is, at present, quite flat, as the dark tint shews. This window is provided with a stone seat and elbows, and was originally full of painted glass. The details are shewn in

PLATE IX. On the left are *Plans* at three different heights; in the centre of the plate is the *shield* at large, bearing a lion rampant on a field semé of cross crosslets, the *original arms of Long*; also the *angle jambs* and *mullions*, and the *termination of the label* over the archway, on which is carved the *marshall's-lock*; to the right is a section of the *cornice*, the *corbel-mouldings*, and the *arch-mouldings* below, together with an exterior and interior elevation of one of the *lights*, and a section of the *basement moulding:* all at large.

THE BANQUETING HALL, &c.

PLATE X. shews the *elevation* of the *Hall* to the right, and that of the *Drawing-Room* to the left. The Hall, in its masses, resembles that at Great Chalfield, and is entered, under an open archway, by a *Porch;* on the other side is a *Bay*, and the *Chimney-Shaft* occupies precisely the same situation as at Chalfield; it has been rebuilt, so that the capping is not original. The Drawing-room window is remarkable for its immense size; it was added about the time of James I. The mouldings are given in Plate IV.—V.; it extended only as far as the quoin shewn to the left of this window. At the bottom of the Plate are two of the *Gap-mouths* referred by numbers; the others are shewn in Plate XVI. On the left is a *Chimney-Shaft*, belonging to the old portion of the offices, which is seen in the Perspective View, Plate I.: it is supported on a buttress and corbels.

PLATE XI. shews the *Porch* to a larger scale, and a section through the same; in the quatrefoil of the window is the only portion of painted glass now left. The rafters of this roof are cut in one piece, like ship timbers. The *Water-Tables* of the *Buttresses*, the *Label*, and the *Jamb-Mouldings*, are given at large.

PLATE XII. gives the *Exterior* and *Interior Elevations* of the *Window of the Bay*, shewn in Plate X., with a *section* and *details* of the same. The *Mullions* are plain in their mouldings, but this window is very neatly finished inside, by a column supporting a four-centred arch.

PLATE XIII. gives an *Elevation* of one of the *Windows of the Hall*, interior and exterior, with a *Section;* these, like those of the bays, are finished inside by a column, supporting a four-centred arch, while, on the outside, their arches are two-centred. They are extremely elegant, and, though plain in their mouldings, are chaste and pleasing in effect, and, by being ornamented with tracery, make us regret the absence of it at Great Chalfield. The *Jamb* and *Mullions*, the *Label* which is peculiar in not having a bead, but coming out from the flush of the wall by a cavetto; the *Interior Arch-Mould*, the *Capital*, and *Base of the Column*, are given at large.

PLATE XIV. *Longitudinal* and *Transverse Sections* of the *Hall*, and sections of the *Bays*. The elegant open roof is shewn, which is ornamented by quatrefoils between the principal rafters, and the arched beams are supported by *brackets*, on which are *shields*, with the *armorial bearings* relating to the family of Long; one of these brackets was destroyed by increasing the thickness of the end wall to the right, in order to carry up the flue of the Drawing-room. The *Chimney-piece*, which bears the date AN. DN̄I. 1598, is interesting as a specimen of Elizabethan detail. The *Arms* on the *Shield* are those of *Long*, impaling a pelican feeding her young, for *Carne*, which shews the marriage of Sir Robert Long with Barbara, daughter of Sir Edward Carne, the parents of Sir Walter Long, by whom this was put up.

PLATE XV. gives a *Transverse Section of the Roof* to a larger scale, with details of its *timbers*, and the *brackets* supporting the arched beams of the roof, together with the *shields* at large. No. 1. bears the *Marshall's-lock*, a cognizance adopted by the Longs, as mentioned above. No. 2 bears the arms of *Popham*, which are, on a chief, two stags' heads caboshed, charged with a crescent. No. 3, which is shewn on the bracket to the right, bears *Long* impaling *Popham*. No. 4. Ten billets, 1, 3, 3, and 3, for *Cowdray*. No. 5. *Long*. No. 6. On a chevron, three torteaux between ten crosslets, for *Berkeley*. No. 7. *Long* impaling *Berkeley*. No. 8. Two wings for *Seymour*. These shields, and the mouldings on which they are placed, are carved in stone; no vestige of the emblazoning is left, but, by reference to *Appendix*, No. IV., it can be supplied: the upper part of the bracket is of oak. They seem of later date than the roof, and were probably put up by Sir Thomas Long, who built the Gatehouse.

PLATE XVI. At the top of this plate, to the right, is shewn a transverse section of the *original roof of the Guest Chamber*, still existing over the Drawing-room ceiling; and to the left, two compartments of the same longitudinally. Half of *one compartment of the Hall-roof* is shewn in plan to a larger scale, and the other *Gap-mouths* referred to Plate X. by numbers.

PLATE XVII. THE DRAWING-ROOM.

This is a *Perspective View* of the *Drawing-Room* from the door, as you enter, from off the landing of the staircase. It is in the style of the reign of James I.

The *Fire-place* on the left is much purer in its enrichments than is usually met with in this style. A male and a female figure with Ionic caps, on each side, support a rich cornice, which is surmounted by a stylobate, whereon are placed columns and entablature of the Corinthian order: between the columns, which are also enriched, are figures of *Prudence, Arithmetic, Geometry,* and *Justice.* On the pedestal supporting ARITHMETICA, is the following inscription:—

> Par impar numeris vestigo rite subactis,
> Me pete, concinne, si numerare cupis ;

and, on that supporting GEOMETRIA,—

> Mensuras rerum spatiis dimetiora equis
> Quid coelo distet Terra, locusque loco.

PRVDENTIA and JVSTISIA have no motto. In the centre is a figure of PAN. Opposite the fire-place is an angular projection, ornamented with *niches,* which seem to have served as seats. The *ceiling* is coved up to the form of the old roof shewn in Plate XVI., and is richly ribbed in plaster.

A HISTORICAL ACCOUNT
OF THE
Church of St. Peter, at Biddeston,
WILTS.

THE churches of St. Peter and St. Nicholas, at Biddeston, remarkable for their peculiar but picturesque bell-turrets, seem to be of great antiquity; and, as the presentations always mention the *church of St. Peter* before the *vicarage of St. Nicholas*, we may with safety presume that there must have been a building long anterior to the one which forms the subject of the five following plates.

The great charm of these bell-turrets being almost lost when drawn geometrically, the author has been induced to insert perspective sketches of both.

ST. PETER'S.

ST. NICHOLAS'S.

It will be seen that that of St. Nicholas is, in point of style, much older than that of St. Peter's, which latter comes under the denomination of *Perpendicular English;* while the former, from the string-course under the spire, downwards, is decidedly *Norman.* The one seems to have been copied from the other; and, most probably, the original design was executed in the old church of St. Peter's, which must have been pulled down, and has thus been perpetuated. Whether this was the primitive form of the bell-turret in Saxon times, would be a curious inquiry, and not without interest. In Pl. XXXII. of the Benedictionale of St. Æthelwold, engraved in Vol. XXIV. of the Archæologia, is the representation of a bell-turret, containing several bells; and the form of the open part, in which the bells are hung, is by no means unlike these; and at Binsey, near Oxford, is a similar one, " part of which," Ingram says, " may be older than the Norman conquest." There are two other churches in the immediate neighbourhood of Biddeston which have bell-turrets built upon the same plan; *viz.* Corston, and Leigh-de-la-mere. There is also one at Acton-turville, on the borders of Gloucestershire, between Badminton and Corsham, and one at Boxwell, in the same county.

The attention of the author was called to these churches by C. W. Loscombe, Esq., an ingenious antiquary, who considers that they were of Saxon origin: he says,—

" Finding churches, with these peculiar characteristics, so widely scattered "
" over the country, all of them exhibiting ornaments of the earliest period,"
" and differing so much in general from those we know to be Norman build- "
" ings, the inference I draw is, that they must be referred to the fashion of a "
" time, and not of a locality, and that that time must be the Saxon."

The church of St. Peter must have been at one time much larger, and what remains of the portions destroyed bear date much earlier than the present nave. Opposite to the door leading from the porch into the nave, is another door, with an early English arch and ornament; and in the north wall is a piscina, shewn in Pl. IV., of the same date: this, probably, was in a chantry chapel, belonging to some ancient owner of the manor-house, within the precincts of which the church stands. The arch is still left which led to it, but has been built up with a window inserted, the arch being still visible, as shewn in Pl. V.: there is another archway in the east wall, now filled up, which led into the chancel.

The patronage seems to have been vested in the prior of Monkton Farley, as the early presentations shew, and in " COMPUTUS PRIORATUS DE FARLEGH, *temp.*

JOH. STONE PRIORIS, A°. 17 Regis" (Henry VIII.) under "Firmae Decimarum," is the following :—

"Byddiston—X^ms... 6 0 0"
"Byddiston—Pons' eccl'.. 0 2 0"

and in the "Valor Ecclesiasticus," 26 Henry VIII., under "Prioratus de Farlegh "—

"LODOWICO nunc Priore ibm val', viz' in Spual' in Com' Wiltes' "
"Annu' Porc' Decimar' recept' in dīcs Vill' subsequen' "
"In Bydston cu' Harth* m.. 6 0 0"

and under "Procur' solut'"

"Archidec' Wiltes' Pro ecclīā de Slaughtenford, 5s. 9½d. Et Bideston, 5s. 9½d."
"Ob. 11s. 7d."*

It seems afterwards to have devolved on the lord of the manor, when the vicarage of St. Nicholas and the chapel of Slaughterford were annexed to it. It is now in the patronage of Winchester College, and is a discharged rectory, composed of the two rectories of St. Nicholas and St. Peter, in the archdeaconry of Wilts and diocess of Sarum, valued in K. B. 2*l*. 13*s*. 4*d*., ann. val. P. R. 140*l*.

PRESENTATIONS.†

	ECCLESIA, VICARIA, VEL CAPELLA.	PATRONUS.	CLERICUS.
1323	Capell. Budeston S^{ti} Petri	Prior de Farlegh	Rogerus de Sutton
1331	Capel. St. Petri de Budeston	Prior de Farlegh	Robertus Lovel de Melkesham
1347	Cap. Budesdon St. Petri	Rex	Johannes Godele, *p. r.* Roberti Lovel
1354	E. Budestone St. Pet.	Rex	Symon Cosyn
1361	E. Budesden St. Petri	Prior de Farle	Johannes de Shireburn, *p. r.* Simonis Cosyn
1391	E. Biddeston St. Petri	Prior de St Magdalena de Farley	W^{mus} Gardiner, *p. m.* Sewaldi............*u. R.*
1417	E. Budeston	Prior de Farlegh	Rogerus Priotecote, *p. m.* W^{mi} Bryd
1419	E. Biddeston	Prior *de* Farlegh	Ricardus Julian, *vice* Rogeri Prescote
1421	E. Byddyston E. Litilton Drew	Prior de Farlegh Episcopus	Ricardus Julian, *permut.* cum Johanne Whelere
1421	E. ·Byddiston	Prior de Farlegh	Johannes Leyne, *vice* Johannis Whelere

* *Dugdale's Monasticon*, Vol. V. p. 31.   † *Sir Thomas Phillipps's Institutions in Wilts.*

22   HISTORICAL ACCOUNT OF THE CHURCH OF ST. PETER, AT BIDDESTON, WILTS.

	ECCLESIA, VICARIA, VEL CAPELLA.	PATRONUS.	CLERICUS.
1434	E. Buddeston	Prior de Farley	Johannes Perus
1442	E. Byddeston St. Petri	Prior de Farlegh	Johannes Eston
1453	E. Bitteston	Episcopus, *per laps.*	Thomas Webbe
1457	E. Byttesdon	Prior de Farlegh	Henricus Harlyng, *p. r.* Thomæ Webbe
1468	E. Bydston	Prior de Farlegh	Johannes Mower, *p. r.* Ricardi Harlyng
1468	E. Bydston	Prior de Maydenbradley	W^{mus} Briggis, *p. r.* Johannis Mower
1475	E. Bidston	Episcopus, *per laps.*	Simon Elvyngton
1478	E. Budeston St. Petri	Prior de Farleygh	Henricus Palmer, *p. r.* Simonis Elvyngton
1486	E. Bidston	Prior de Farley	Christopher Notte, *p. m.* Henrici Palmer
1490	E. Byddeston	Prior de Farley	Johannes Huchenson, *p. r.* Christopheri Notte
1510	E. Bidston St. Petri	Prior *de* Farley	Henricus Goldney, *p. m.* Henrici Barocrofte
1510	E. Byddiston St. Petri	Prior *de* Farleigh	Johannes West, *p. r.* Henrici Goldney
1511	E. Bydeston St. Petri	Abbatissa de Shaston	Thomas Potercy, *p. m.* Radulfi Bery
1520	E. Budeston St. Petri	Henricus Long, *Miles et* Johannes Lacy, *per concess.* Prioris *de* Farlegh	Lodowick Bricknock, Prior de Farlegh, *p. r.* Radulfi Eyre
1592	E. Budston S. Petri	Regina	Ricardus Rydler
1605	E. Bidsdon St. Petri	Rex	W^{mus} Fawne
1620	E. Buddeston St. Petr.	Rex	Elias Tise, *p. m. U. R.*
1663	E. Biddeston S. Petr.	Thomas Mountjoy, *Generos.*	Johannes Ferris, *p. m.* Eliæ Tyse
1719	E. Biddeston S. Petri *cum* V. Biddeston S. Nich. *cum* Capellâ *de* Slaughtenford	Willielmus Mountjoy, *Gen.*	Thomas Keate, *p. m.* Thomæ Tattersall
1741	E. Biddeston St Petri V. Biddeston St Nicholas *with the Chapel* of Slaughterford	William Mountjoy, of Biddeston, *Gent.*	Thomas Needham, *p. m.* Thomas Keate
1766	E. Biddestone St Peter, *with* V. Biddeston St Nicholas *and the Chapel of* Slaughterford	Wm Mountjoy, *of* Biddeston	Charles Page, *p. m.* Cornelius Norwood
1807	E. Buddeston St. Peter, *cum* Buddeston St. Nicholas & Slattenford	Winchester College.	Charles Daubeny, *p. m.* Charles Page

DESCRIPTION OF THE PLATES.

PLATE I. shews the *South Elevation* and the *Ground Plan:* at the north-east corner is an arch filled up with a window inserted, which formerly led into a *Chantry Chapel*, as the *Piscina* still left in the north wall shews; another arch in the east wall led into the *Chancel*, now pulled down; the *Porch* is a good example, it is simple, but has some good mouldings; the *Bell-Turret* is curious, and is shewn in the following plate.

PLATE II. gives the BELL-TURRET, with *Plans*, at three different heights, referred to the *Elevation* by letter, which, with the *Section* from west to east, occupies the centre of the plate; the *corbel-mouldings* and *battlements* are shewn to a larger scale; the turret is nearly equipoised on the wall.

PLATE III. gives a *Plan, Section, Front* and *Side Elevations*, and *Details* of the PORCH, which sufficiently explain themselves.

PLATE IV. No. 1. is the *Door* leading from the Porch into the Body of the Church, which has a small *Piscina* on the right, with a Plan of the *Jamb-Mouldings* and *Piscina*, and a section of the *Label* at large. No. 2. is a *Window* of the Porch at large, with its *Jamb* and *Mullion* underneath. No. 3. *Plan, Section* and *Elevation* of the *Piscina* in the north wall of the church, which formerly belonged to a chantry chapel attached. It is of much earlier character than any other part of the church, except an arched door in the north wall, opposite the door shewn in this plate, which is also Early English; to the right are the *Water-Tables* of the *Buttress* in the South Elevation.

PLATE V. No. 1. The *Window* in the South Elevation, with plan of its *Jamb* and *Mullion*, and section of its *Label* at large: this label, like those at South Wraxhall, has no bead, but comes out from the flush of the wall by a cavetto. No. 2. The *Window*, which was inserted in the archway leading into the chantry chapel, half shews the *Exterior* and half the *Interior Elevation:* on the right a *Section* of it is given, and its label at large.

APPENDIX III.

Will of Henry Longe, Esquire, of Wraxhall; extracted from the Registry of the Prerogative Court of Canterbury.

In Dei noīe amen Primo die mensis Maij Anno dñi Millesimo ꝯꝯꝯꝯ nonagesimo Ego Henricus Long Armiger compos mentis et sane memorie condo testamentū in hunc modum Inprimis lego animā meam deo Patri omnipotenti beate Marie Virgini et oñibus Sanctis Corpus qȝ meum sepeliendum in Ecctĩa de Wroxhall coram alta cruce. Item lego ecctĩe Cath Sar vjs viijd Itm lego ecctĩe ꝑochiali De Wroxall xxs pro vestimentis Itm lego Rectori de Edyngdon iijs iiijd et cuilit Presbitero ejusdm Domus viijd et cuilit Novicio ejusdm Domũs iiijd ꝑcipiend die obitus mei ad dicend missam et exequias predicto die et ibñi orare pro me et animabus Roberti patris mei et Margarete matris mei Johanne et Margarete nuꝑ uxorum mearum Reginaldi et Johannis fratrum et pro aĩabus oīm parentum meorum et animabus oīm fideliū defunctorum Itñi lego Abbati de Stanley iijs iiijd Itñi cuilit presbitero ejusdm Domus viijd et cuilit Novicio eiusdm Domus quatuor Denar iṫm orare ut suꝑ Itñi lego Priori de Ffarley iijs iiijd et cuilit psbitero eiusdm Domus viijd et cuilit Novicio iiijd Itñi lego ecctĩe ꝑoch De North Bradley xxs pro Vestmentẛ Itñi lego paupibus Domus Sancte Margarete De Bradford vjs viijd Itñi lego Priori de Bradnestock iijs iiijd et cuilit Presbitero ejusdm Domus viijd et cuilit Novicio iiijd Itñi lego Capelle Patris mei in Monasterio de Bathe construct. vnū par Vestmentorum ꝑcy ꝯ s vel alia necessaria ad valorem ejusdm summe Itñi lego friḃus predicatoribus de Marleburgh xiijs iiijd pro vestmentẛ Itñi lego friḃȝ minoriḃȝ Sar xiijs iiijd pro vestmentẛ Itñi lego friḃus predicatoribus Sar vjs viijd pro vestmentẛ Itñi lego ecctĩe De Bradford xxs pro vestmentẛ Itñi lego Dom De Henton xls pro Vestmentẛ Itñi lego ecctĩe De Broughton xijs iiijd pro vestmentẛ Itñi lego Capelle Sancti Georgij de Semelton (Semington) xxs pro vestmentẛ Itñi lego ecctĩe de Milkesham xxs pro vestmentẛ Itñi lego ecctĩe de Hilpton xijs iiijd pro vestmentẛ Itñi lego Abbatisse de Lacocke xxs pro vestments Itñi lego ecctĩe de Chippenhm̃ xxs pro vestments Itñi lego ecctĩe de Boxe xxs pro vestmentsᵒ Itñi lego Johanne Uxori mee omĩa terras et tenementa mea que habeo in Civitate nove Sarᵖ Ac omĩa bona mea infra ciuitatem ꝑdcam et in Domo mea iṫm existenẛ habend et tenend omĩa ꝑdictᵃ terras et tenementa prefate Johanne Uxori mee at terminũ vite sue Residuū vero omĩ' bonorū meorum non legatorum Do et lego executoribus meis videlicet Johanne uxori mee Dño Ricardo Key Vicario De Boxe Johanni Goldney ut iꝑi ea disponant pro salute anime mee et aĩabus omĩ' amicorū meorum prout illis melius videbiť expediri Eciam facio et constituo magistrum Radulphum Hethcott supuisoᵣ meum tam Voluntatis terrarum et tenementorū meorũ quā testamenti qui ꝑcipiet pro labore suo xls. In testimoniū omĩ premissorum sigillum quod vtor apposui Datᵘ apud Wroxall Die et Anno supradictᵒ Itñi lego ecctĩe De Trubrigg xxs ꝑ vestmentẛ Itm lego ecctĩe - - - - - - - xxs pro vestmentẛ Itñi lego ecctĩe de Asshton xxs pro vestmentẛ.

APPENDIX IV.

Notes on South Wraxhall, from Aubrey's MSS. now in the Ashmolean Museum, Oxford.

"S. Wraxhall Howse."

"THIS is a very large well built old howse: on the gate is the Marshall's lock and the " "Stagge's head caboshed in stone. The Hall is open and high and windowes full of " "painted glasse."

"This windowe is some of a branch or beame of a stagge's horn *or*" Coats as follow: I. *Or*; three torteaux *gules* two and one, in chief a label of three points *azure*, each point charged with three plates *or*, "*Courtney*." II. *Or*; an eagle displayed *gules*, "*Rodeney*" *erased*. III. Quarterly, 1st and 4th, *azure*; a lion rampant *argent*, crowned *or*, "*Dayrell*," 2d and 3d, *argent*; two bars voided *sable* in chief, two demi-lions rampant *gules*. IV. *Gules*; three fish hauriant *argent*, "*Lucy*."

"This window is some the Marshall's lock *or*, at the bottom the salutation of the " "B. Virgin Mary." Coats: I. *Sable*; a bend *or* between six fountains *argent*, "*Sturton*." II. *Argent*; on a chief *gules*, two stags' heads *or*, "*Bradley*." III. *Or*; an eagle displayed and double-headed *gules*, beaked and legged *azure*, "*Blewet*." IV. "*Long*" impaling "*Bradley*." V. *Gules*; a chevron *ermine* between nine crosslets *argent*, "*Barkley*." VI. *Gules*; a chevron *argent* between ten crosslets *argent*, "*Barkley*." VII. Quarterly, 1st and 4th, *argent*; on a chief *gules*, two mullets *or*, "*St. John*." 2d and 3d, *gules*; two lions passant regardant *argent*. VIII. *Azure*; a bend *argent* cotized *or*, "*Fortescue*."

"On the chimney-piece, An Dñi 1598." "*Long*" impaling "*a pelican*" feeding her young, "*Kerne*."

"In the Entry that leads from the Hall to the Parlour. This window some of" "Stagges branches." Coats: I. *Gules*; a saltire *argent* charged with two annulets entwined; that to left *gules*, the other *azure*. II. Within a bordure *argent* and *azure*, Quarterly, 1st and 4th, *azure*, three fleurs de lis *or*, two and one. 2d and 3d, *gules*, three lions passant regardant *or*, "*Card. Beaufort of Winchester*." III. *Or*; on a chevron *gules* a mitre with labels *or*, within a bordure engrailed *sable*, "*Stafford. A. R. Cant*." IV. Within a bordure *azure* semée of fleurs de lis *or*; *gules*, three lions passant regardant *or*.

"This semée of Marshalls locks." Coats: I. 1st and 4th, checqué of six *or* and *azure*, a chevron *ermine*. 2d and 3d, *gules*, a fesse *or* between six crosslets *or*. II. A blank coat.

"In the Dining-roome: a very noble one in the Windowe." I. Quarterly, 1st and 4th, *azure*; on a bend *or* three "starres of five points waved" *argent*. 2d and 3d, *argent*; three demi-lions *gules*, two and one, "*Sturmy*" in pencil. II. *Or*; a chevron *argent* between nine crosslets *argent*, "*Barkley*." III. Quarterly, 1st and 4th, *azure;* three fleurs de lis *or*, two and one. 2d and 3d, *gules;* three lions passant regardant *or*, "*Ks. Arms.*" IV. "*Long.*" V. Quarterly, 1st and 4th, *argent;* three diamonds in fesse *gules*, "*Montagu.*" 2d and 3d, *or;* an eagle displayed *azure*, "*Menthurmer.*" VI. Quarterly, 1st and 4th, *azure;* on a bend *or* three stars of five points waved *argent.* 2d and 3d, *argent;* three demi-lions rampant *gules*, two and one ; impaling, quarterly, 1st and 4th, "*Long;*" 2d and 3d, *gules*, on a chevron *argent* three torteaux *gules* between six crosslets *argent.* VII. "*Long.*" VIII. Within a garter *azure*, charged with HONI SOIT QUI MAL Y PENSE *or*, quarterly, 1st and 4th, *gules*, a lion rampant *or.* 2d. *Sable*, a fret "*or.*" 3d. *Sable*, fretty *or.* IX. "*Long;*" impaling *or*, three bends *azure* within a bordure engrailed *argent.* X. *Gules;* a chevron *argent* charged with three torteaux *gules* between ten crosslets *argent,* "*Barkley of Bruton.*"

"In another chamber in the windowe the edges of this window, Long and the" "lock below" (the Marshall's lock) "as it used to be with the Saxon crowns" (it is charged in the side with an anchor *sable*). Coats: I. *Gules;* ten billets *or* 3, 3, 3, and 1, "*Cowdray of Berks*" *in pencil.* II. *Gules;* twelve billets *or* 3, 3, 3, and 3, impaling, *or;* an eagle displayed *gules* double-headed, beaked and legged *azure.* III. Quarterly, 1st and 4th, *gules;* nine billets *or* 3, 3, and 3. 2d and 3d, *argent;* on a chief *gules* two stags' heads *or* charged with a crescent *or.* "*I believe this to be inversed.*"

"In the same windowe *Bradley* without the crescent *or* as in margin," viz. *Argent* on a chief *gules;* two stags' heads *or.* "This window is full of *Marshall's locks.*"

"In another chamber window, the locks aforesaid, glasse and figures broken. In a" "chamber within that, in the windowe, beames of a stagge's head, and at the top in" "scrolles, '𝔈𝔫𝔟𝔶𝔢 𝔚𝔬𝔩𝔩 𝔏𝔶𝔢.' V. Box. p. 112, de hoc."[1]

"In the Parlour window," I. *Gules;* a chevron *argent* charged with three torteaux *gules*, between ten crosslets *argent:* impaling, party per pale *argent* and *sable* a cross flory counterchanged. II. Within a Bordure seme of skull caps ; quarterly, 1st and 4th, *gules*, a fesse *or* between six martlets *or*, "*Beauchamp*" *in pencil.* 2d. Two lions passant *argent.* 3d. *Azure*, three fish naiant *argent*, "*Roche.*"

"Over the gate is a handsome chamber and a good glasse windowe full of figures," "w^h I could not see."

---

[1] "BOX. On the S. side of the Church is a fair freestone monum. of Roman architecture born up with Ionicq" "pillars, a figure incumbent on the altar in armour. Here lyeth the body of Anthony Long, Esq. buried the 2d of" "May, 1578. Query, the Marshall lock? In a scroll the motto, ENVI WILL LYE."

NOTES TO PEDIGREES

(APPENDICES Nos. I. and II.),

ILLUSTRATING THE DESCENT OF THE WRAXALL PROPERTY.

It is seen, by Pedigree, Appendix No. I., that, on failure of male issue in the *Wraxall line*, WALTER LONG, the last male of that line, left his *Wraxall Estate* to the sons of his cousin, CATHERINE, the sister of HOPE LONG, of Wraxall: those sons were JOHN LONG, Clk. Rector of Meysey Hampton, who died s.p.; and THOMAS LONG, the father of WALTER LONG, of Bath, the *testator in favour of the present possessor.*

The said WALTER LONG, *of Bath*, in looking for his heir, found that (had he been alive) he would have been *Thomas Long, of Rowden*. Thomas Long, of Rowden, died s.p.; but his sister, ELIZABETH, had married RICHARD LONG, of *Rood Ashton*, as may be seen by Pedigree, Appendix No. II., and from HER had descended WALTER LONG, of *Rood Ashton*, the *present possessor;* and he, being *her* representative, WALTER LONG, *of Bath*, bequeathed the property to HIM.

Florentina Wrey, the mother of the present possessor, being descended from *Henry Long, of Melksham*, as is shewn by Pedigree, Appendix No. I., who married Anne, sister of HOPE LONG, of WRAXALL: she, and, consequently, her son WALTER, *the present possessor*, are, *by blood*, also descended from the LONGS of WRAXALL.

THE END.

Pedigree shewing the

WALTER LONG, ESQ. O

THE PRESENT POSSESSO[R]

2d Wife.
Maud ═══ THOMAS LONG, of I
terne. Will 1566.

JOHN LONG, of Marston, ═══ Anne
in the Parish of Potterne, Cl
junior. Died 1597. at

THOMAS LONG, of Little Cheverell, O
Esq. Sheriff for Wilts. Bur. there,
1654. Devised his lands at Mell
his eldest son, John. Will 7th Ap
pr. 1st June, 1654.

John Long, of Little Cheverell, aforesaid, Esq. eldest son and heir. Sheriff for Wilts, 1668. Died unmarried, and was buried at Little Cheverell, 27th July, 1676. Will dated 20th July, 1676, pr. 21st Nov. 1676.	RICHARD LONG, of Collingbourne—Kingston, Co. Wilts, Esq.	═══	Elizabeth, dau. of Edward Long, and sister and heir of Henry Long, of Rood Ashton, Esqrs.	Thomas Long, of Gent. Born 1 1671, æt. 54. Baptist's, Dev July, 1664, pr From
Henry Long, of Melksham, Co. Wilts, Esq. eldest son and heir. Bap. at Steeple Ashton, 20th May, 1658. Induc. after mar. 27th March, 1685, settling the manor of Collingbourne upon the issue of the same. Ob. 31st March, 1686. Bur. at South Wraxall.	═══	Anne, dau. of John Long, and sister to Hope Long, Esq. of South Wraxall (See Appendix, No. I.) Ob. 4th Oct. 1705, æt. 48. Bur. at South Wraxall.	**1st Wife.** Elizabeth, dau. of Thos. Long, of Monkton, afterwards of Rood Ashton, Esq.	═══ RICHARD LON his maternal that estate, 19th Jan. 17 Will dated 1723 ; pr. 29

Henry Long, of Melksham, Co. Wilts, Esq. ═══ Ellen, dau. of William Tronchard, of Cutteridge. Anne, bap. at South Wraxall, 6th Oct. 1685. Mar. ── Clarke, of Whaddon, Clk. RICHARD LO surviving s æt. 68. Bu 13th Jan. de bonis n

| William Long, Esq. eldest son and heir. Ob. S. P. 1773. | Henry Long, third son. Ob. S. P. 1739. | John Long, second son. Ob. 31st Oct. 1712, æt. 9 mo. Bur. at South Wraxall. | Ellen, sister and heir of William Long. Esq. mar. John Thresher, Esq. (See Appendix, No. I.) | RICHARD LONG, of Rood Ashton, Esq. eldest son and heir. Ob. 3d Sept. 1787, æt. 69. Bur. at Whaddon. | ═══ | Meliora Laul Josep Imbo Aug |

RICHARD GODOLPHIN LONG, of Rood Ashton, Esq. many years M.P. for Wilts, eldest son and heir. Born 2d Oct. 1761. Bap. at West Lavington, Co. Wilts, Nov. 12, 1761. Ob. 1835, æt. 74. ═══ Florentina, dau. of Sir Bourchier Wrey, Bart. by Ellen Thresher, his wife. Ob. 1835. Bur. at Steeple Ashton.   John Long, of Melksham Esq (second son) of M leigh. Born 1768. O 1838. Ancestor of t Monkton Farleigh.

Walter Long, of Rood Ashton and of South Wraxall, Esq. born 10th Oct. 1793. Nupt. 3d August, 1819. Magistrate and Deputy Lieutenant, and M.P. for the Northern Division of the County of Wilts. ═══ Mary Anne, second the Right Hon. Ar Colquhoun of mont, Lord Regi Scotland.

Walter Long, b. 27th Sep. 1823.   Richard Penruddock, b. 19th Dec. 1825.   Henry

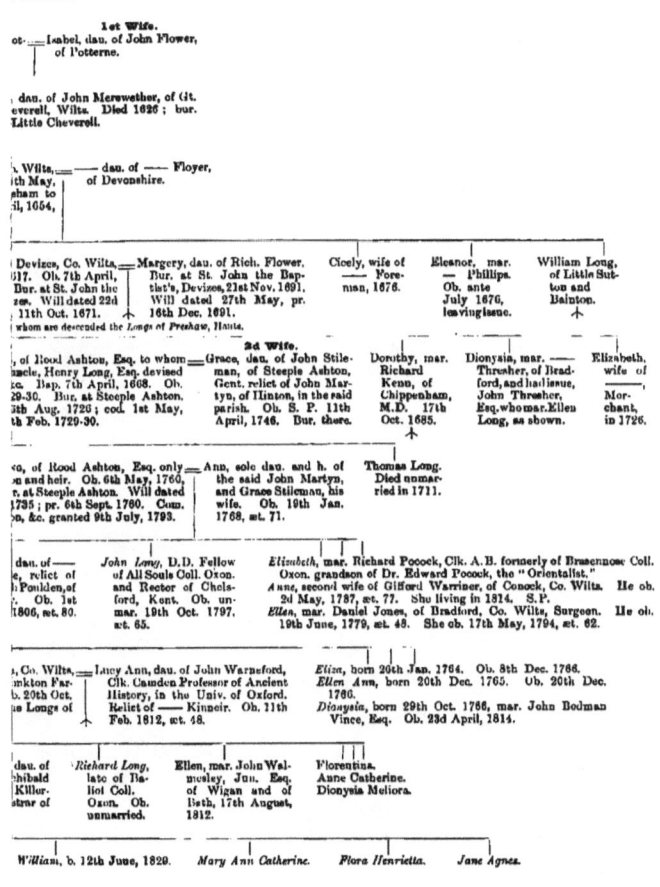

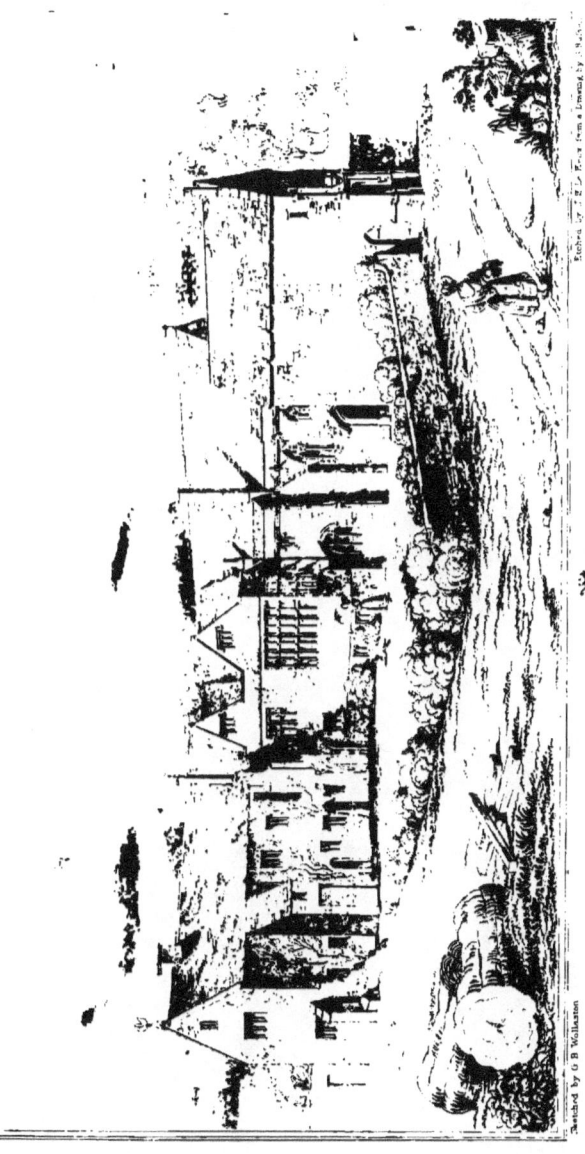

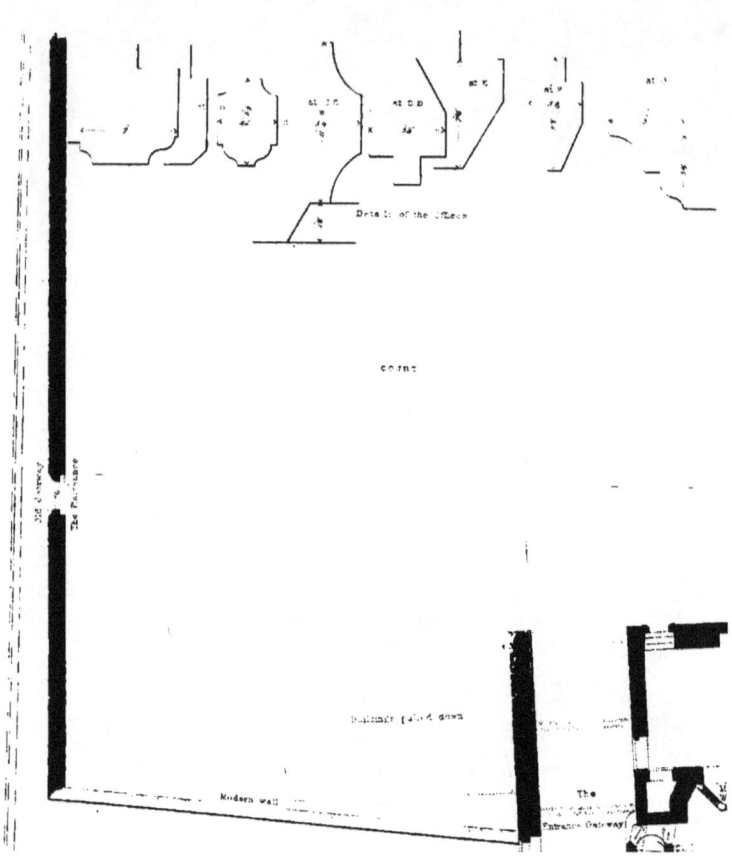

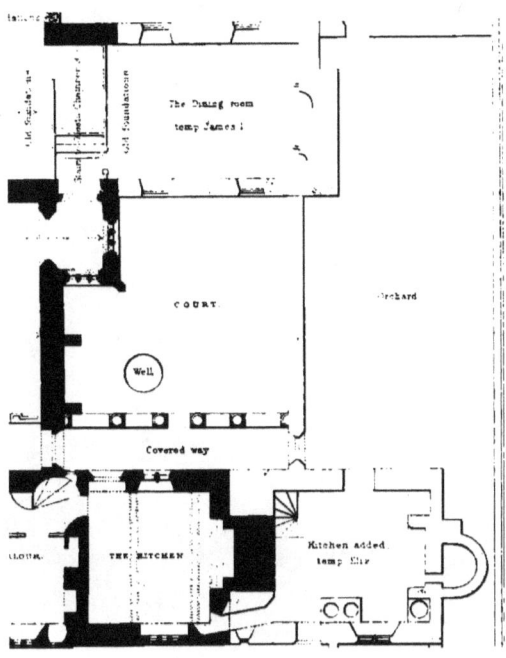

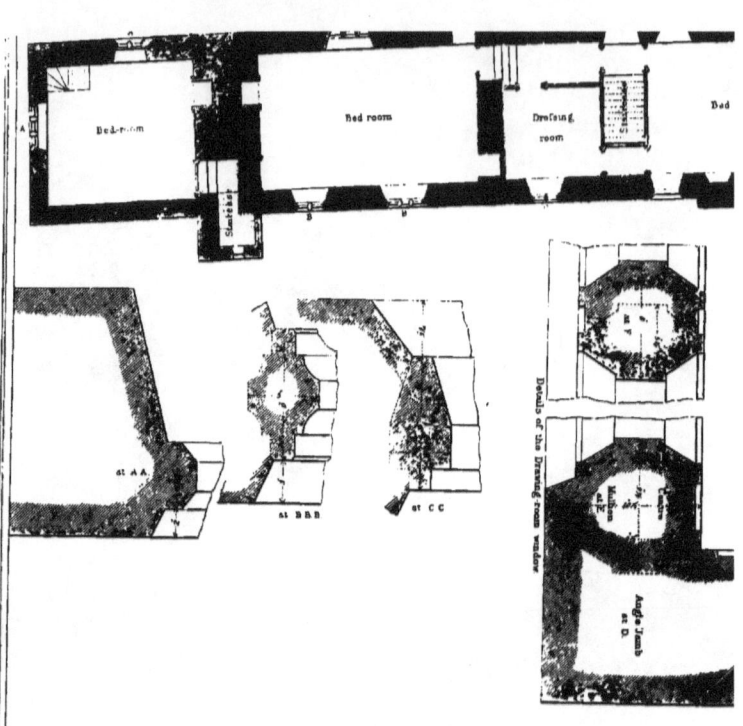
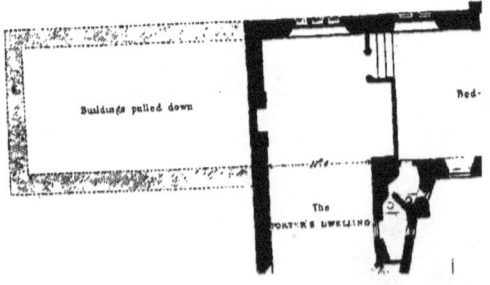

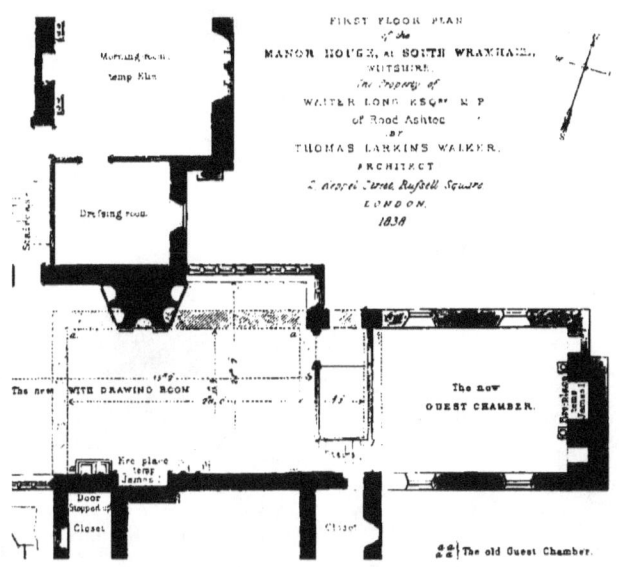

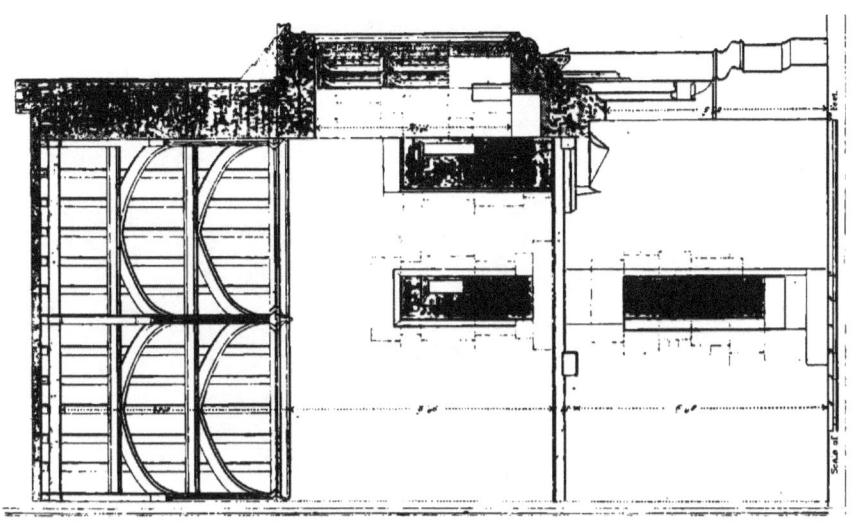

DOMESTIC ARCHITECTURE.

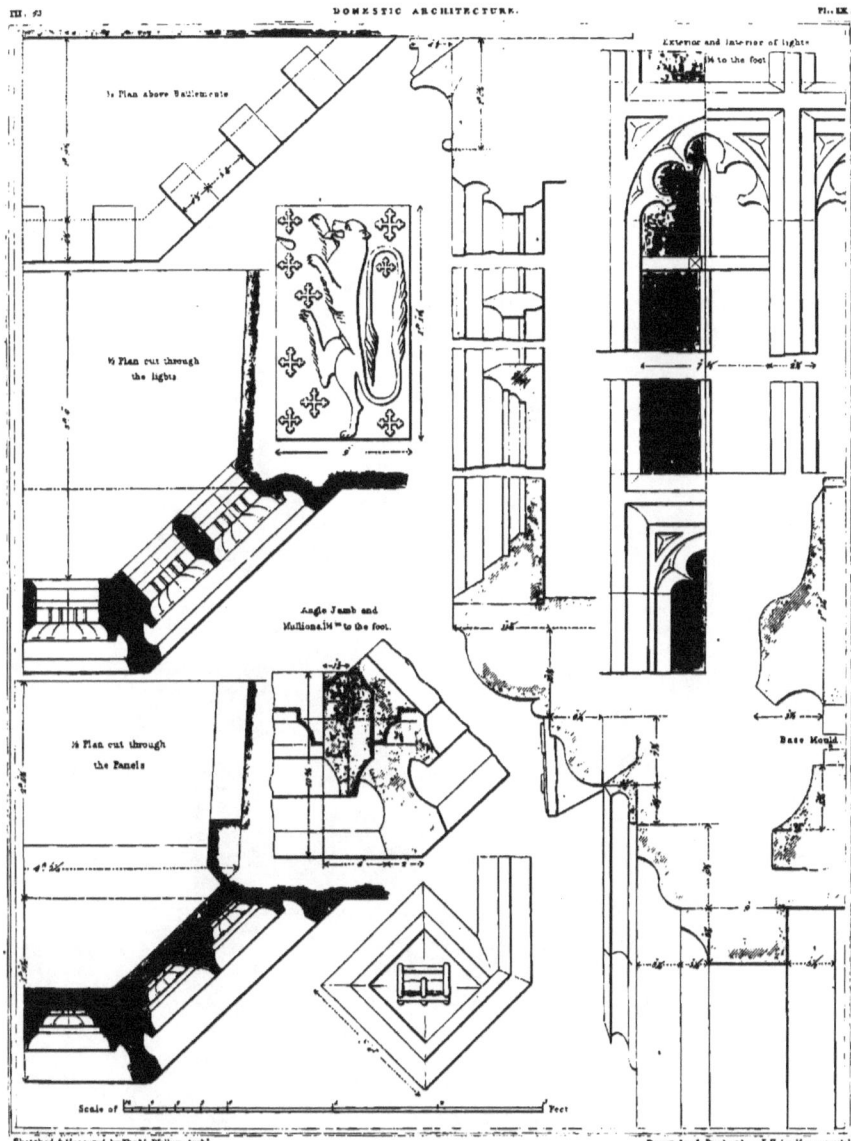

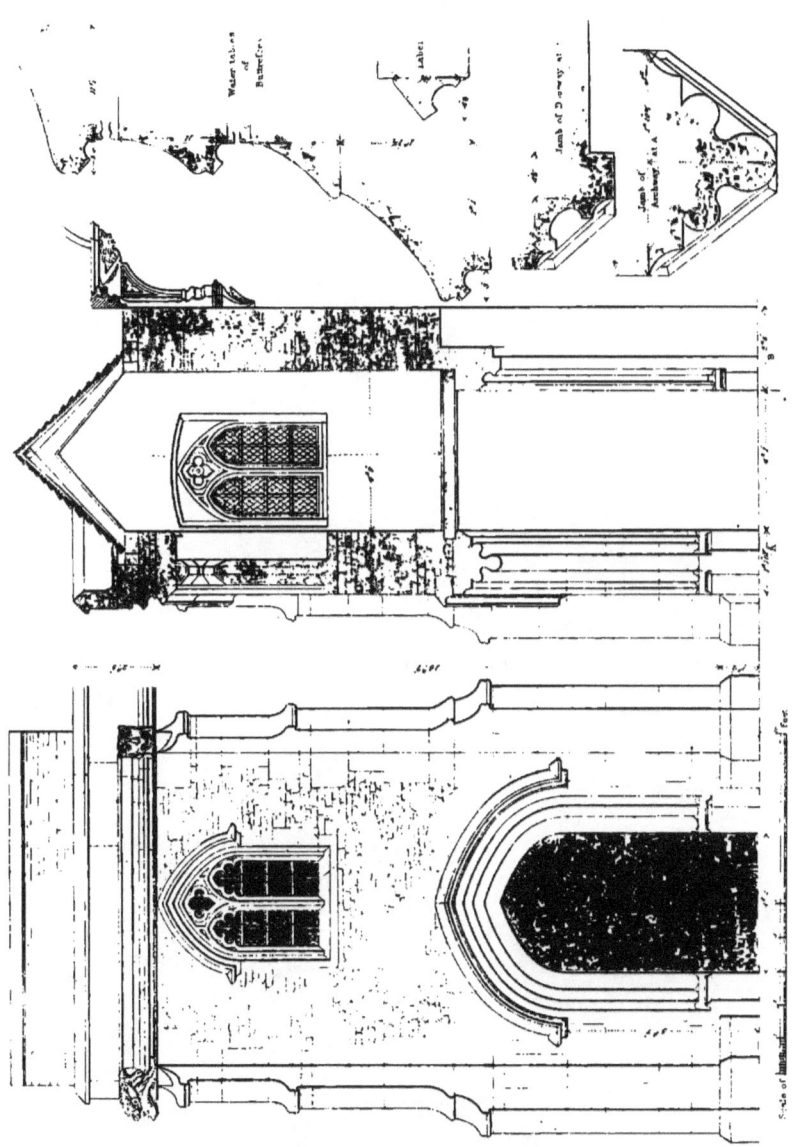

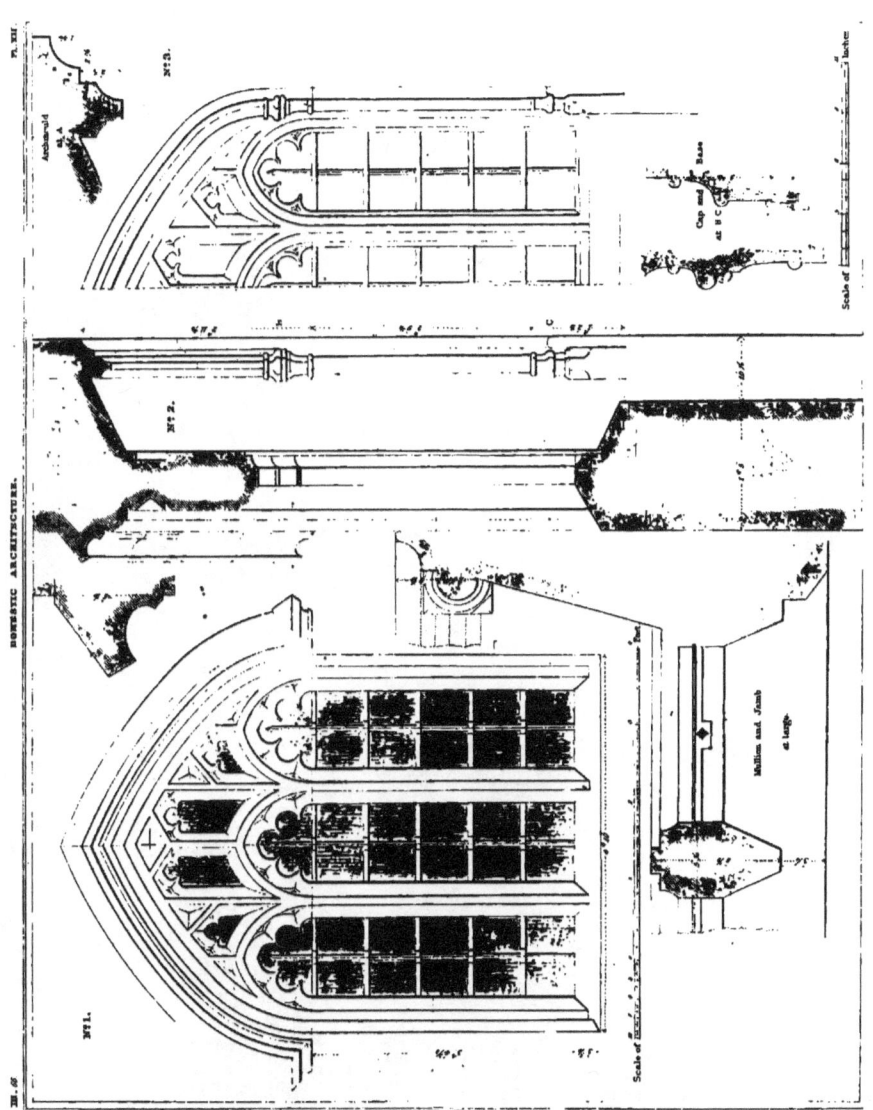

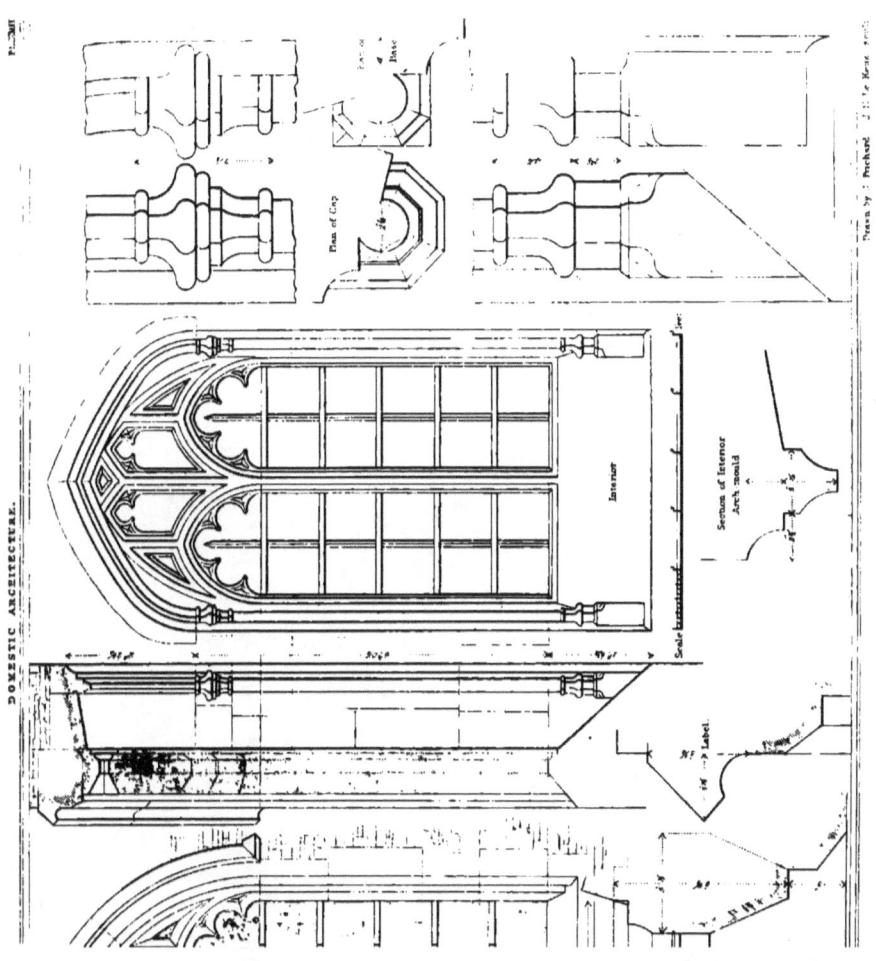

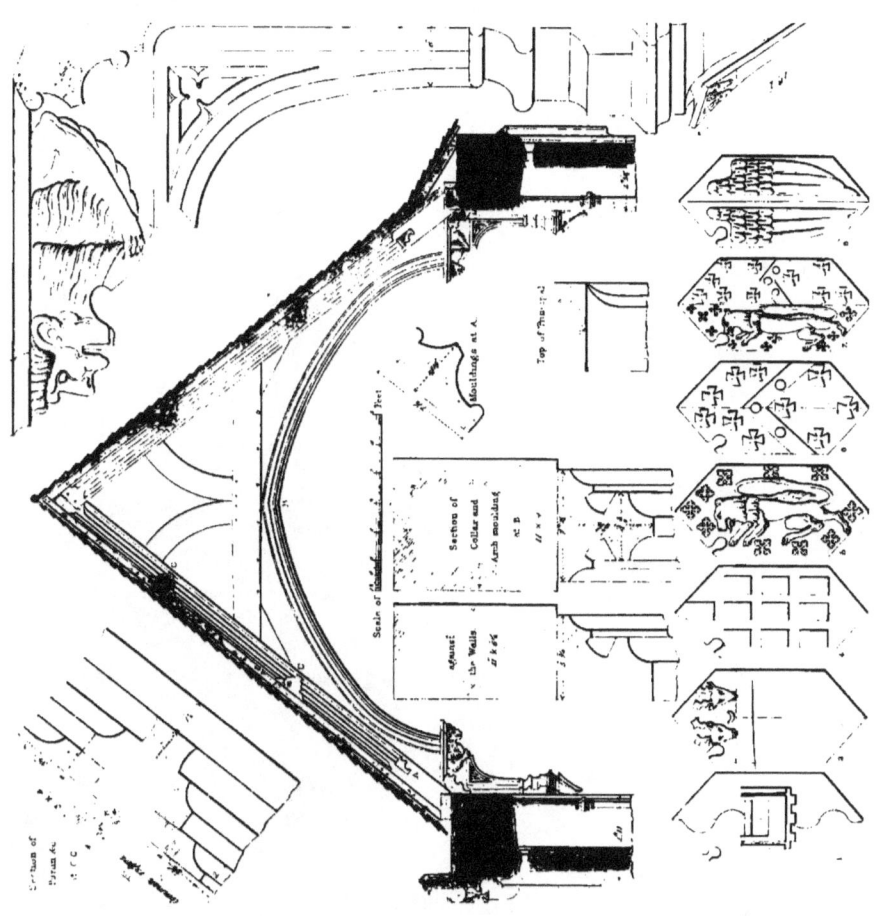

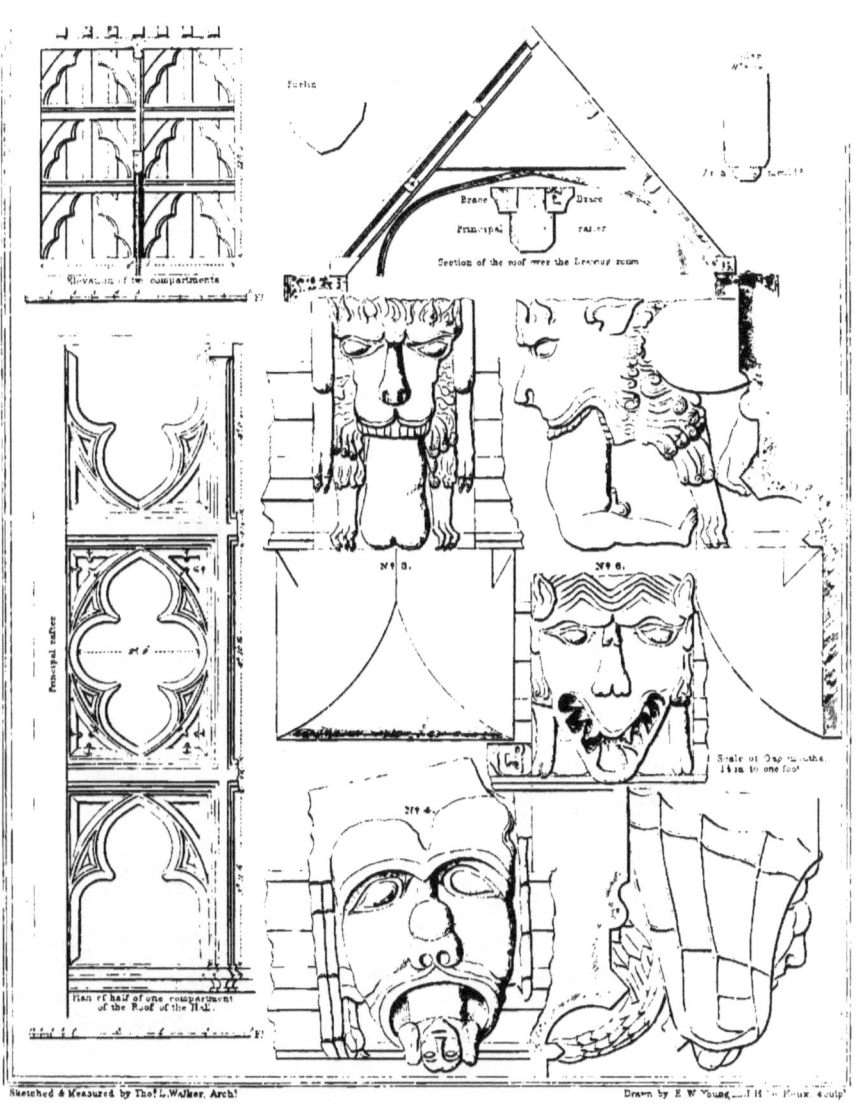

MANOR HOUSE SOUTH WRAXALL, WILTS

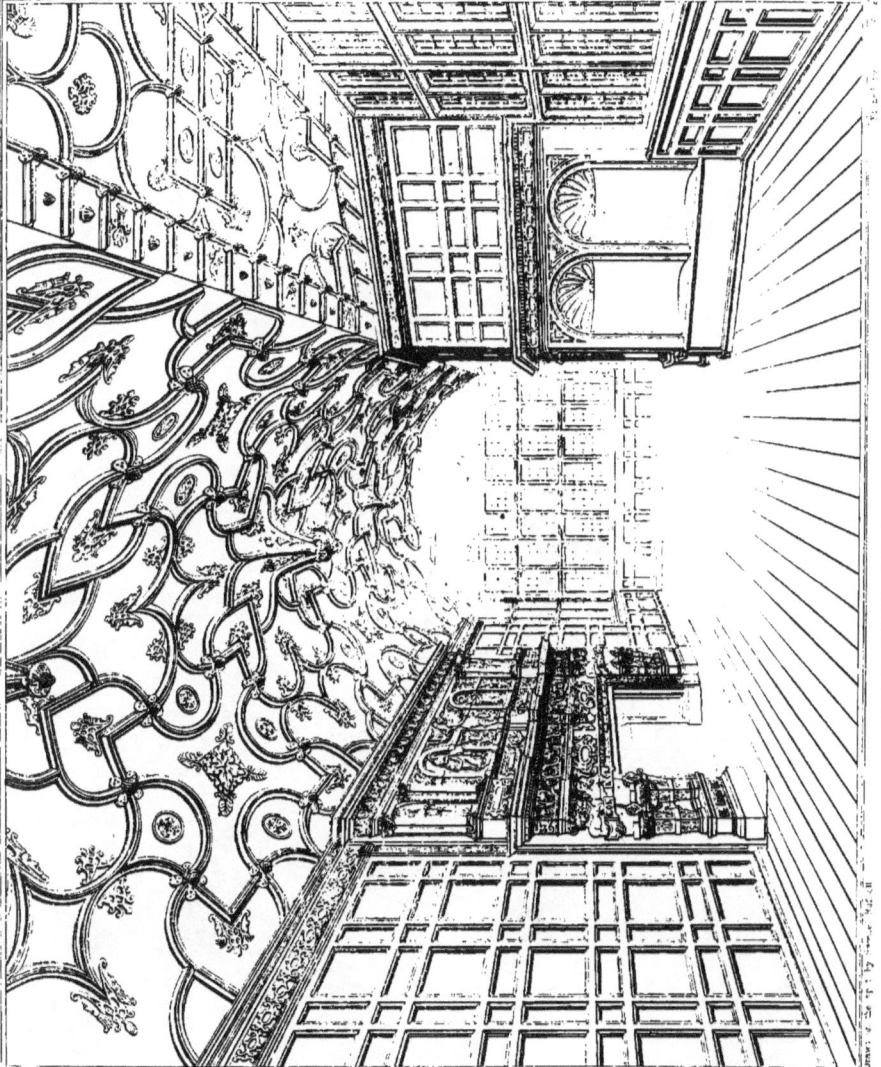

MANOR HOUSE, SOUTH WRAXHALL, WILTS.

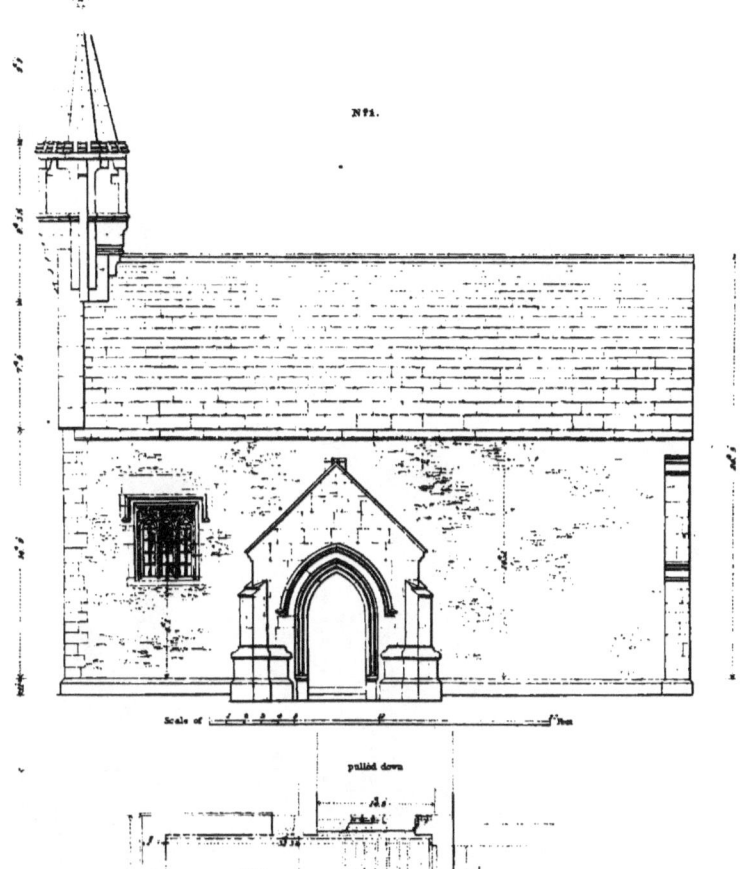

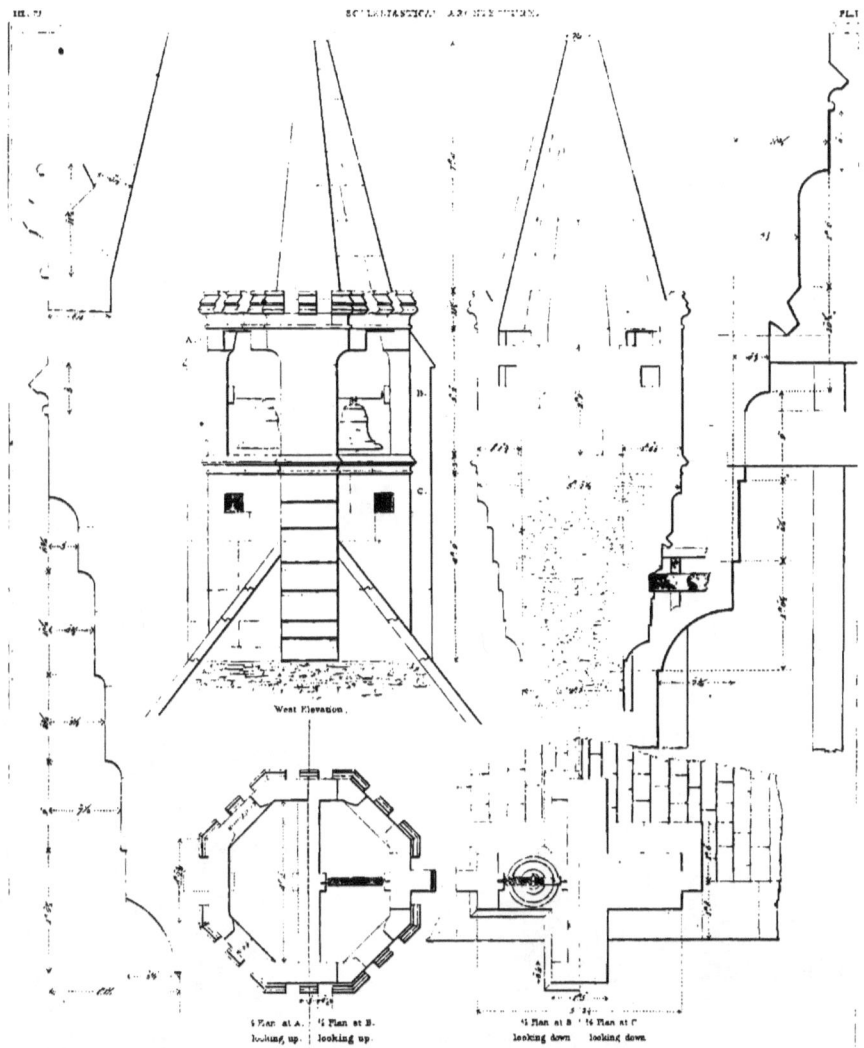

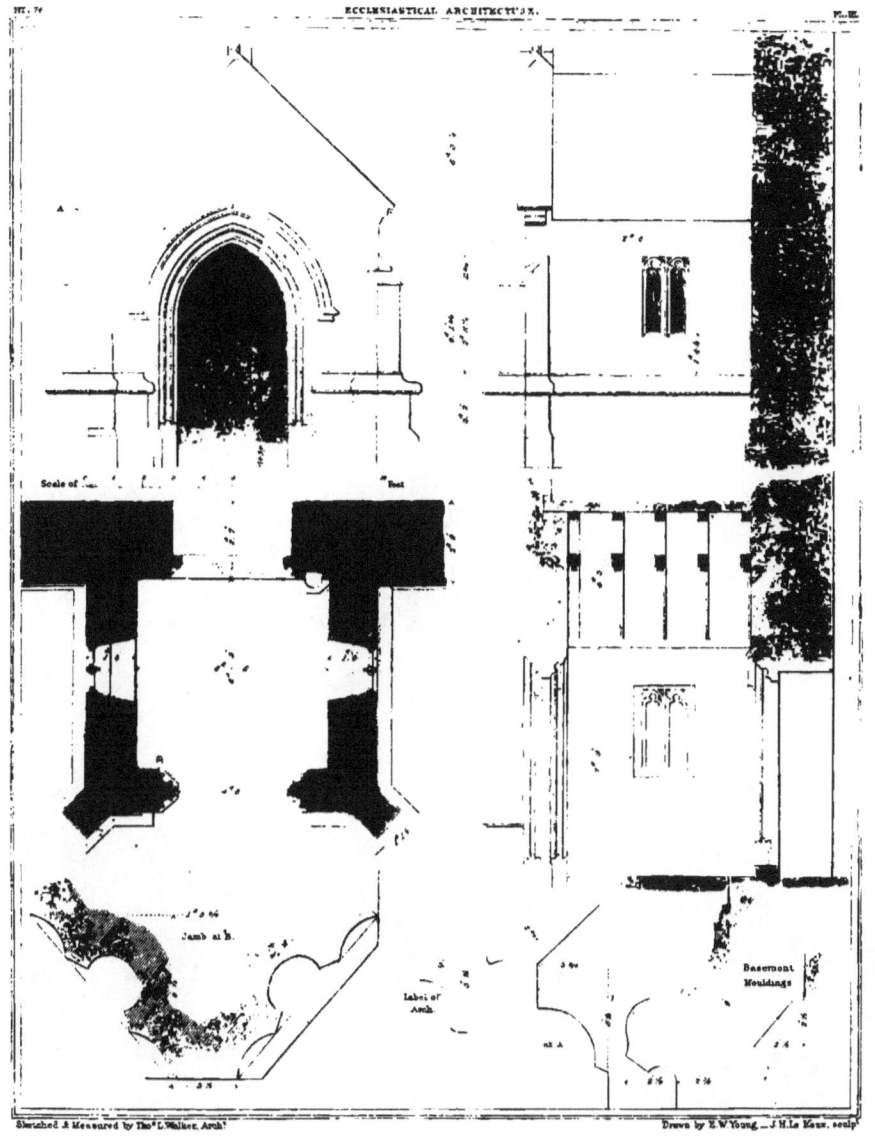

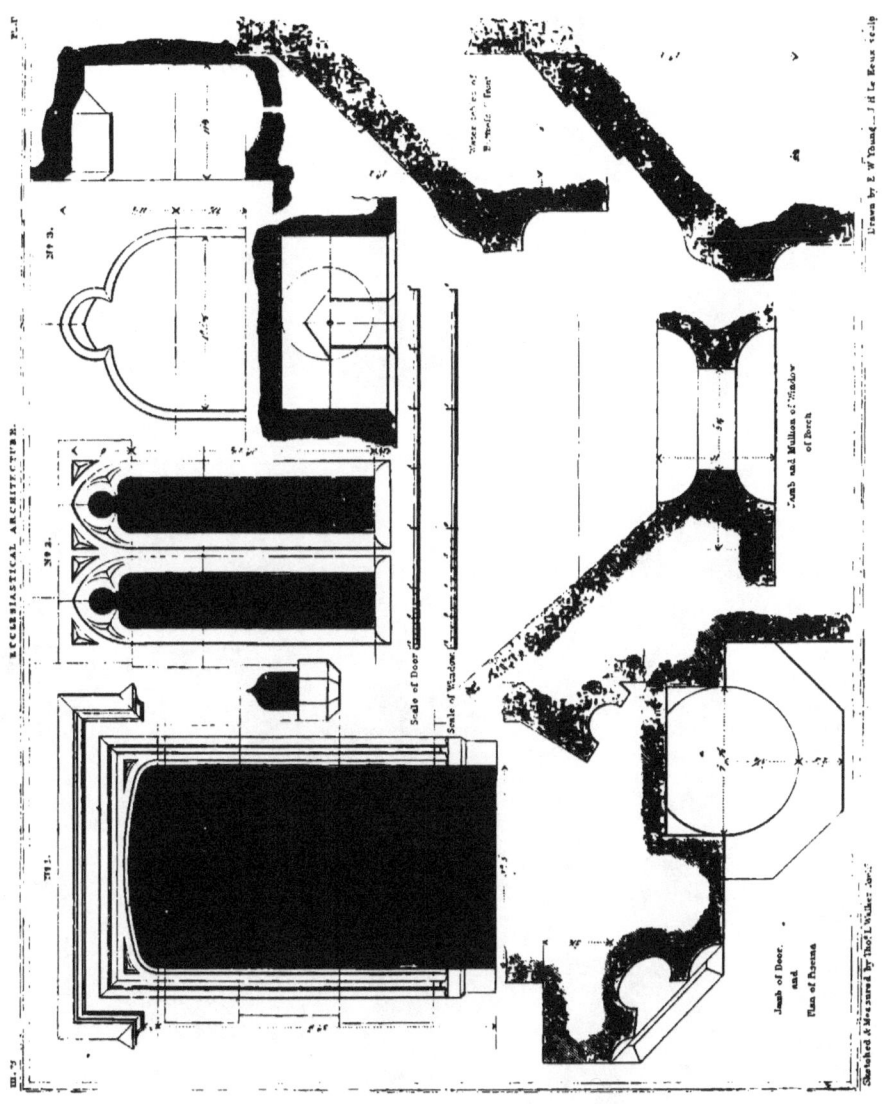

BIDDESTONE CHURCH, WILTS.

www.ingramcontent.com/pod-product-compliance
Lightning Source LLC
Chambersburg PA
CBHW021406230426
43666CB00006B/650